CLOSE
TO THE SUN

HOW AIRBUS CHALLENGED
AMERICA'S DOMINATION
OF THE SKIES

Stephen Aris

AURUM PRESS

First published in Great Britain
2002 by Aurum Press Ltd
25 Bedford Avenue, London WC1B 3AT

Design by Geoff Green
Index by Madeline Weston

A catalogue record for this book is available from the British Library.

All photographs are reproduced courtesy of Airbus Industrie except for the picture of
Boeing's Sonic Cruiser, which is reproduced by courtesy of Quadrant Picture Library.

ISBN 1 85410 830 1

1 3 5 7 9 10 8 6 4 2
2002 2004 2006 2005 2003

Typeset by M Rules
Printed in Great Britain by MPG Books Ltd, Bodmin

For Pepita

CONTENTS

ACKNOWLEDGEMENTS

HOWEVER SOLITARY THE act of writing a book may be, nobody gets to the end without the help of a very large number of people. So it is with this one. Firstly, I would like to thank my publisher and editor Piers Burnett for providing the idea, for correcting mistakes and generally improving the flow and coherence of the story. Secondly, I have, as ever, enjoyed the support and friendship of my old comrade and agent, Robert Ducas, and thirdly, without the cooperation of Barbara Kracht, the head of the Airbus press office in Toulouse, there would be no book. When approached by authors, most companies insist on some form of *quid pro quo*. Airbus didn't. Without asking for any favours in return, Barbara prepared the ground, gave me access to essential material, and introduced me to the key people. I am extremely grateful to her, David Velupillai and other members of the press office, especially Francoise Maenhaut who looked out the pictures I wanted and answered my nit-picking queries. Michel Guerard, the head of communications, and his predecessor, Bob Alizart, were both very helpful. In Hamburg I was shown round by David Voskuhl.

Like any writer of contemporary history, I owe an enormous debt to my sources. The book depends greatly on the contributions of those who were there at the beginning. Many have either died or retired many years ago. Some years ago it was decided to put the experiences of some thirty of these pioneers on record. In my view, their stories provide a vivid and surprisingly objective picture of these early years. And although I never met the people themselves, they came to life in the transcripts in such a way that I felt I had. In the notes at the end of the book, I refer to these interviews as 'Airbus archive'. Those I did meet gave generously of their time and their expertise. Among current and ex-Airbus Industrie people, I would like mention Adam Brown, Philippe Delmas, Noël Forgeard, Michel Jarry, John Leahy, Harmut Mehdorn, Jean Pierson, Manfred Porath, Gerhard Puttfarcken, Wolfgang Sommer and Jürgen Thomas. At Boeing, Randy Baseler, Lewis B. Brinson IV, Scott E. Carson, Randy Harrison, and Lawrence L. McCracken. At BAe Systems, Sir Richard Evans, Geoff Jupp, Robert McKinlay, Mike Peters, Mike Turner and Chris Voysey. At EADS, Theodor Benien, Philippe Camus and Marwan Lahoud. At Lufthansa, Carl Sigel. And at Rolls Royce, Tim Blythe, Emma Medd-Sygrove and

Robert Nuttall. Bernard Taylor, formerly of Robert Fleming and now of JPMorgan Fleming, was a much-needed guide through the last stages of the story, and Julie Green, Bernd Hoffman, Nicola McShane and Nick Sunderland smoothed passages and made useful introductions.

Apart from those in the industry, there were many others who had special knowledge and experience. Among those who gave generously with help, advice and information were Mogens Peter Carl, Les Coombs, Leandro Fernandez, Lucy Grandy, Michael Harrington, Sir Nicholas Henderson, John Hunt, Lord Keith, Peter Jay, Robert Madelin, Richard Lapthorne, Sir Austen Pearce, Don Pepper, Peter Pugh, and Carol Reed. I am especially grateful to René Lapautre, the former managing director of Air Inter and chairman of UTA, who at a late stage read the entire manuscript in draft, and put me right on a number of important questions, including the correct location of Le Train Bleu.

As always, the librarians at the various libraries I visited were unfailingly helpful. I would like to thank Brian Riddle, the librarian of the Royal Aeronautical Society, for seeking out papers and publications I would not otherwise have found. Also the staff of the British Library, Cambridge University Library, the Library of Congress, Washington, DC, the Guildhall City Library, the London Library and the Public Record Office, Kew.

I relied greatly on my friends for encouragement and support, especially when the going got tough. Leon Brittan gave me the benefit of his experience in Brussels, Tony Doggart introduced me to the merchant banking fraternity, my former colleague Nick Faith helped with the 'fly-by-wire' controversies, Joaquin and Nan del Pozo made introductions in Spain, Manfred and Gabi Scheeder looked after us in Berlin, and Berry Ritchie and Dana Rubin cheered me on and up when spirits flagged. Graham Wrathmell did a most professional job designing the cover and the picture lay-out, while my sister-in-law, Elizabeth Heesom, grappled brilliantly with hundreds of pages of transcripts in very idiomatic French and German. Above all, I thank my wife Pepita, herself a writer, for being so wise and steadfast.

INTRODUCTION

THIS BOOK TELLS a remarkable story. It starts with the vision of one man, a French engineer called Roger Béteille, and it ends at the point where the company he created was about to launch the largest commercial aircraft ever built: the Airbus A380. In itself, this would have been an impressive achievement. But what, to my mind, makes it so interesting is Béteille's success in building a multinational industrial coalition that grew to be big and powerful enough to challenge the Americans in an area where they had reigned supreme for so long.

If the French had tried to do the job themselves, they would have undoubtedly failed. So would the British and the Germans. With the unhappy experience of Concorde so fresh in their minds, it required a good deal of courage from the politicians and the industrialists of the day even to think of backing the European Airbus project. But only someone of Béteille's extraordinary technical and political skills would have been able to make it work.

When I started out on this book, although I am not in any sense a technical writer, I thought that much of the interest would be in the planning and the building of the planes themselves. But the more I got into it, the more I came to realize what an intensely political story this is. In one sense this is obvious. The sums of money involved are so huge and the numbers employed are so great that presidents and prime ministers are inevitably involved whether they like it or not. The political dimension of the Airbus story is one of the main themes of this book.

What is not quite so evident is the importance of Airbus's own internal politics. This has its origins in the nature of Airbus itself. It was a multinational consortium whose members, the French, the Germans, the British and the Spanish, all had their own agendas. This, too, is a theme that runs right through the book. It reaches its climax in the final chapter where, based on conversations with the main participants, I describe in detail the quite extraordinary manoeuvres that led to the creation of EADS, Europe's largest defence company.

I have tried to tell the Airbus story chronologically. But there are points along the way where I have been obliged to digress to put the events I am describing into their proper context. The aircraft industry is especially complicated. Not only are aircraft, for some reason, much harder to write about than cars, trains and ships, but to help readers understand what the main players are up to, I have included a certain amount of historical background which, I hope, will make a good story clearer and more understandable.

Greenwich
21 March 2002

CHAPTER ONE

THE KOLK MACHINE

THE CONCEPT FROM WHICH the first European Airbus was to spring had its origins, strangely enough, not in Europe, but in the United States. On 26 April 1966 Frank Kolk, technical director of American Airlines, wrote to Boeing, McDonnell Douglas and Lockheed, the big three of the US aircraft industry. He asked if they would be interested in making a wide-bodied, twin-engined plane that could use a small airport, carry some 250 passengers and work economically on routes of up to 1,500 miles. The notion that a twin-engined plane would be able to carry so many people over such a long distance was one that both the conservative-minded airlines and the almost equally conservative manufacturers found quite startling.

Kolk was a Texan renowned for plain speaking. 'He was a very prickly character,' says Arthur Howes, one Airbus executive who had met him on an exploratory mission to America. 'Frank had a reputation that extended throughout the aviation world and was regarded very much as an innovator. He was a very kind man when he got to know you, but he could also be rather cruel at times, and he was absolutely appalled that the Europeans were going to build the aeroplane he knew the world wanted and that the Americans didn't.'[1]

Despite these misgivings, Kolk became a good friend of the Airbus people who, quite coincidentally, had an office in the same building as American Airlines. Kolk and his staff spent a great deal of time talking to Airbus, looking at specifications and suggesting modifications that would bring the plane more closely into line with what the airlines wanted. 'He was actually very, very helpful,' says Howes. 'We had a lot of fun with Frank. You could say that Frank was one of the Americans who helped Airbus to arrive . . . without the inputs we received from Frank, the aircraft probably would not have been the success it turned out to be.'[2]

*

Kolk was concerned at the direction the aircraft business was taking. The industry was enjoying one of its periodic booms: demand was growing faster than the manufacturers could cope with and the number of passengers was increasing rapidly. It was clear that a new generation of aircraft was needed to meet these demands. Although no one realized it at the time, the industry was at one of those critical turning points that would determine not just the pattern of the future, but the fate of the leading players. However, the immediate question for the manufacturers was what sort of plane should they build?

Boeing had already staked everything on the 747 jumbo, but the other two big manufacturers of civilian aircraft, Douglas and Lockheed, were still hesitating. The year before, Douglas Aircraft had actually started work on a new jumbo, only to pull back when Boeing announced its intention to build the 747. There was much talk of a new jumbo that would be smaller than the 747 but bigger than the existing DC-8s that had served Douglas so well for so long. What kind of jumbo would it be? How many would it carry? How far would it fly? How much would it cost? It was at this point that a new word began to appear in the industry's lexicon: airbus.

One person who helped shape Kolk's ideas was Joe Sutter, the head of Boeing's 747 programme. Sutter showed him his plans for the 747. The key to the new plane was the diameter of the fuselage. The essential conundrum that Sutter and his engineers were wrestling with was how to fit upwards of 350 people, sitting six abreast, into a single metal tube without making the plane impossibly long. The obvious solution was to build a twin-decker, like a McDonald's 'Big Mac', with the passengers stacked on top of each other in what would effectively be two distinct fuselages. Pan Am's Juan Trippe thought this was a wonderful idea but Joe Sutter hated it, if for no other reason than evacuating passengers from the top deck would be, he thought, a nightmare. The breakthrough came when the engineers realized that if they built the fuselage wide enough to stack two standard cargo containers, measuring eight feet by eight, side-by-side in the cargo hold, they could seat all the passengers on a single deck above. From this idea sprang the concept of the wide-bodied jet. The plane would obviously be much wider and much heavier than anything ever built before. But by making space for both passengers and cargo within a single fuselage, the engineers satisfied one of the industry's cherished maxims: 'payload is load that pays'. As soon as he saw Sutter's widebody fuselage, Kolk saw that this was an idea that could be adapted to his own needs. The width of the fuselage and the immense power of the new high bypass fan jet engines being developed by General Electric and Pratt & Whitney would, he realized, produce a machine of great utility and economy. The cabin would be wide enough for two aisles and, most important of all, it would be powered by only two engines.

Kolk argued that what both American Airlines and America needed was an aircraft that would carry twice as many people twice as far as the Boeing 727, the industry's best-selling benchmark, at a lower cost per seat mile than any other plane on the market. If the 747 was to be the long-distance, mass transit people carrier of the 1970s, then the jumbo twin would do the same job for America's huge domestic market. Kolk's specification reflected the character of American Airlines's business in the mid-1960s. It was essentially a US domestic airline operating on short to medium haul routes across America. It was a high volume/low cost operation. And Kolk was looking for a cheap and efficient plane designed for the most densely travelled 'city pair' truck routes, like New York–Chicago and Chicago–San Francisco. Size and power were the twin concepts that drove what Kolk and his colleagues called 'the jumbo twin'. The industry quickly dubbed it 'The Kolk Machine'.

It was a great idea. The only trouble was that the industry wouldn't buy it. Over the next few months Kolk tried hard to interest the planemakers. Of the three, Lockheed's Dan Haughton was the most receptive. In January the following year, he switched the engineers who had been working on the aborted supersonic transport (SST) to the wide-body, and even dangled the prospect of a jumbo twin in front of Rolls-Royce. Boeing, absorbed as it was with the 747, was non-committal, though privately it thought that a scaled-down 747 could do the job. And Douglas was not prepared to give the idea the time of day. 'It was "pick and shovel" work to get them off the subject of a stretched DC-8,' Kolk recalled. Within nine months Douglas was in crisis, and by the following spring it had been absorbed by James Smith McDonnell's McDonnell Aircraft Company.

But what really scuppered the idea of an American jumbo twin was the hostility of the other airlines, particularly TWA. According to John Newhouse's authoritative account of this period, TWA, which had already ordered the 747, insisted that if it was to support a second jumbo, it should be capable of crossing North America non-stop. Yet it was not just the lack of range that worried the airlines. They were acutely aware that the technology of the new high bypass turbo fan engines was still in its infancy. And the idea of a plane flying for more than two hours on only two engines – no matter how powerful – scared everybody rigid. Furthermore, the Federal Aviation Authority insisted that no two-engined plane should be allowed to fly over water for more than an hour. When Kolk's boss, C.R. Smith, quietly let it be known that American Airlines had itself gone cold on the idea, Kolk's chances of success were quite gone. It was, Smith said, too early in the development of the big fan engines to risk the safety of a large aeroplane on only two. Safety came before economics, he argued. Put like that, it was hard for anyone to disagree.

With the benefit of hindsight it is easy to see that Boeing and Airbus Industrie got it right and McDonnell Douglas, as it was about to become, and Lockheed got it wrong. The decision by McDonnell Douglas and Lockheed to produce virtually identical planes, in the shape of the three-engined DC-10 and the Tristar, to cater for this new market ultimately proved disastrous. By going head-to-head in pursuit of what proved to be a much smaller tri-jet market than anyone had anticipated, McDonnell Douglas and Lockheed suffered self-inflicted wounds that ultimately proved fatal. But it could so easily have been very different. As Jean-Claud Malroux, of the French engine makers SNECMA, speculated on thirty years later, 'Can you imagine what the situation would have been if the Americans had made a four-engined 747, a tri-motored DC-10 and twin-engined Lockheed 1011?'[3] This is no hypothetical question. It nearly happened. And though it is possible that Airbus would still have been able to make an effective challenge to American hegemony, the task would have been even more difficult than it was.

*

However lukewarm the reception of Kolk's ideas may have been in his native America, some 3,000 miles away in France there was one man who was intensely interested in what Frank Kolk had to say. His name was Roger Béteille. As technical director of Sud Aviation, France's leading civil aircraft company, Béteille, who was probably the most influential and experienced aeronautical engineer in the country, had been thinking hard about a European big jet for some time.

For more than twenty years Béteille had been at or close to the centre of most of the important developments in French aeronautical life. As a test pilot he had survived a crash of the Armagnac, the first long distance French passenger plane built to rival Lockheed's Constellation; he was in charge of the flight trials of the Caravelle, France's most successful civil jet; he spent time with Hawker Siddeley at Hatfield working on Concorde; and had been in charge of the development of Sud Aviation's missile and space business. It was this that gave him practical experience of working closely with the Germans, the British, the Spanish and the Italians – something that was shortly to stand him in very good stead.

His colleagues remember him with a mixture of affection and great respect. 'He is a very complicated guy,' recalls Adam Brown, who has been with Airbus since 1973. 'Very calm, never fazed; considering he was an engineer, he was a very good businessman, and he was very good on detail. When people raised business problems, Roger would also provide the solution. I think he is probably closer to being a genius than anyone I know.'[4] Frank Borman, the astronaut who went on to become president of Eastern Airlines, agrees with this assessment. 'He is a genius,' he told John Newhouse. 'He has the broadest understanding of anyone alive of the entire range of systems in an airplane. He is a composite of qualities and capabilities that probably only three or four people in the United States combine among them.'[5]

Béteille was not one of nature's cheerleaders. He preferred to work with a small hand-picked group and struck many of his staff, who were a little frightened of him, as being rather chilly. Once, at a meeting on Christmas Eve, an office junior, feeling that he ought to strike a festive note, inquired, 'M. Béteille, might I be allowed to wish you a Happy Christmas?' 'That's quite alright,' Béteille murmured.[6]

Like many other brilliant French technocrats, including Georges Héreil, the former head of Sud Aviation and father of the Caravelle, and Henri Ziegler, the first president of Airbus Industrie, Béteille was a graduate of the École Polytechnique, the grandest and most prestigious of *Les Grandes Écoles*. Béteille went on to complete his studies at L'École Supériere de l'Aéronautique. This background gave Béteille a first-class technical education: it accounts for his mastery of technical detail and his ability to grasp the big picture. But, perhaps more importantly, it gave him an entry into the highest echelons of the French power elite. One of the most striking aspects of the careers of many *polytechniciens* is the ease and frequency with which they move between the worlds of government, the civil service and industry. The airbus may not have been a 'political plane' in the way Concorde was, but the world which Airbus Industrie was to inhabit was most certainly a political one. As we shall see, the ability of the senior Airbus people like Béteille and Ziegler to move easily and effectively in political and military circles and to mobilize political support in hours of need is part of the explanation as to why Airbus survived and why the French have succeeded so well in imposing their style and personality on the entire enterprise.

In the summer of 1966 the two French manufacturers of civilian aircraft, Sud Aviation and Breguet, both had paper aeroplanes on their drawing boards. The previous year Henri Ziegler, then boss of Breguet, reached agreement with Nord Aviation and Britain's Hawker Siddeley to develop a wide-body, twin-aisled, medium-range people carrier, known as the HBN 100. The innovative design of the fuselage, which bore a strong resemblance to that of Boeing's 747, was largely the work of Hawker's designers at Hatfield. The HBN 100 was to come in two versions: a 225-seater and 260-seater, and was to be powered either by the Rolls RB 178 or the JT 9D which Pratt & Whitney was developing for the 747. At the same time, Sud Aviation was working on something very similar called the Galion, which was, in its turn, an expanded version of a big Caravelle called, endearingly, *La Grosse Julie*. Those working on the projects say that the HBN 100 had slightly better aerodynamics than the Galion, while the Galion scored on cabin layout and other design details. But basically there was little to choose between them.

In Britain, the nationalized British Aircraft Corporation (BAC) had been lobbying hard for some months for government support for its proposed BAC 2-11, a medium range, mid-sized, twin-engined jet. The Two-Eleven was intended to be the big sister of the BAC 1-11, which had been moderately successful as a short-haul carrier. By the time BAC was nationalized, some 222 One-Elevens had been sold to sixty operators in sixty-three countries. With export sales of around £250 million, the BAC 1-11 earned more money abroad than any other British-made civil aircraft. But the plane faced fierce competition from the Douglas DC-9 and the Boeing 737, and by the mid-1960s the 1-11 was well past its sell-by date. If BAC was to maintain even a semblance of credibility as a maker of jet planes for the world market, it urgently needed a replacement for the 1-11, which was under-powered and too small for European and world markets.

In planning its move, BAC was heavily influenced by British European Airways, the government-owned, short-haul carrier. For years BEA had determined the size and shape of British-built short and medium range aircraft, just as its long-haul counterpart, BOAC, was the principal, if not the only, customer for long-range British planes like the Bristol Britannia and the Vickers VC-10. Companies like Hawker, who had a strong defence business, were less respectful, but it was more or less accepted in the British industry that if BEA didn't like it, the chances were that it would never fly. According to Charles Gardner, the 2-11 was designed specifically to woo BEA away from its preferred choice, a stretched version of the Boeing 727. The BAC plane, by contrast, would be a brand new affair with a new airframe and a new engine. It would carry 200 people over 1500 miles and would, BAC hoped, be powered by Rolls-Royce's new but as yet untried and untested engine, the RB 211. The BAC plans sounded plausible enough: the only difficulty was that the company, which was heavily committed to Concorde, had no money. All its spare cash was tied up in working capital for the fading 1-11 programme. It was for this reason that BAC asked the government for £100 million in launch aid for the plane and the engine.

*

Early in 1966 Béteille had summoned some of his British friends from the Hatfield headquarters of Britain's other major manufacturer of civil aircraft, Hawker Siddeley, builders of the Trident, the mainstay of BEA's fleet. Arthur Howes who had joined de Havilland in 1953 just after the second and disastrous Comet crash off the coast off Italy and six years before the company's take over by Hawker Siddeley, recalls, 'It was part of the first attempt to put together an Anglo-French team to work together on the idea of a large transport aircraft that we could all see a need for. And to try and see whether together we could come up with a project that was worth developing.

'I had come down first in order to prepare everything for everybody else arriving. We came down on a Caravelle with a braking parachute, which was just as well because the runway was covered in snow. It was one of those rare occasions when there was heavy snow in Toulouse. As we slid down the runway we could feel the aircraft moving from side to side. It stayed on the runway and we were met by our new French friends who were very excited. They wanted to know what it was like landing in the snow with a braking parachute. The first meeting in Toulouse actually started a little bit chaotically. But once we got together and started working we rapidly developed a good system. We had private aircraft coming everyday from Hatfield with people staying two or three days as required. I stayed here with a permanent team to act as a coordination office for everybody coming down. And we spent maybe three or four years basically working like that.'[7]

Arthur Howes and his friends even came up with a name for their unborn child. He says, 'It was very difficult to come up with a name that had a good meaning in French, English and, eventually, German. Personally I always preferred Obelix* but that was clearly something that was not as well known in England and Germany as it was in France. I remember we had a very large and high level meeting in Boulevard Montmorency (Sud Aviation's Paris headquarters) one day and the subject of why hadn't the juniors found a name for the aircraft was raised by top management. All sorts of ideas were put forward, none of which were satisfactory. And the meeting was falling into some disarray. The only thing I could think of saying at the time was, "I propose we call it the HSA 300." And everybody stared at me as if I was crazy because of course HSA stands for Hawker Siddeley Aviation. So I explained H – Hawker Siddeley, S – Sud Aviation, A – Airbus, and 300 – because that was a nice round number. Fortunately everybody saw the funny side and laughed. While they were laughing, I suddenly had an idea, and suggested why don't we call it the A300. A, because A comes before B in the alphabet, which meant that under any circumstances we would appear before Boeing in any listing of aircraft. And 300 because it was a nice round number. And just out of that joke is how the name actually derived.'[8]

Understandably, it was the French and the British, as the only two European countries with an aircraft industry to speak of, who took the initiative. But watching from the sidelines were the Germans, whose aeronautical achievements had, in the not too distant past, been every bit as brilliant as the British and the French. The pioneering work done by their wartime scientists on the aerodynamics of the swept wing were in advance of anything being done at the time in Britain or America. It was only after America had seized the papers of the German engineers after the war that their counterparts at the Massachusetts Institute of Technology and at Boeing realized how much catching up they had to do. It is fair to say that had it not been for the work of the Germans, the launch of the Boeing 707, the world's first successful commercial jetliner, would have been delayed for several years.

Eleven years after the end of the war, the German aircraft industry was still in very poor shape. Some famous names like Messerschmitt and Dornier still existed but the industry as a whole was weak and fragmented. Nonetheless, the Germans were intensely interested in the ongoing debate about the future of the industry and anxious to make a contribution. Ironically, it was the Germans who were the first to use the name Airbus in this context. It had first surfaced briefly in America in the 1930s, but it was not until the summer of 1965, when some seven German aircraft companies joined forces to form the Studiengruppe Airbus (Airbus Study Group), that the name became widely used in the industry. This development followed a

---

*   Obelix is the giant in Goscinny and Uderzo's bestselling series of *Asterix* comic books.

meeting between the Germans and the French at the Paris Air Show to discuss a mass market, medium-range jet. At first the Germans, based at the German Museum in Munich, worked independently of the British and French companies.

At this stage the Airbus project had yet to acquire its specific pan-European dimension. The French and the British at both industrial and political levels looked at it as another Concorde-type partnership – but one, they hoped, that would be without the aggravation, bureaucracy and horrifying expense. President Charles de Gaulle and his government actively disliked Airbus, which they saw as a distraction from the far more prestigious Concorde programme, while the British, increasingly uneasy about Concorde's rapidly escalating costs, took a very pragmatic line. If they could be convinced that the airbus would sell and make money, they would back it. But if not, they would pull out. But the Germans who had refused the French invitation to join Concorde looked at Airbus rather differently. They saw it both as a template for the new Europe and as a means of reviving their shattered civil aircraft industry. As Klaus von Dohnanyi, the former West German secretary of state for industry, recalls, 'We knew that there could only be one European aircraft industry; neither German, French or English. From the beginning we saw Airbus as a European project.'[9] The marked pro-European tone of German politics in the 1960s had been set by Konrad Adenauer, Germany's first post-war chancellor, who, along with Jean Monnet, Paul-Henri Spaak, and Alcide de Gasperi, had been one of the architects of European movement. Adenauer saw active membership of the European Union as a means of preventing a revival of German nationalism and of helping Germany to find a new identity. It was a view that was shared by German politicians on both the right and the left. In late 1966 the face of German politics altered when the once radical Social Democrats (SDP) joined Chancellor Kiesinger's conservative CDU/CSU alliance in the so-called 'Grand Coalition'. Among its leading members was Franz-Josef Strauss, the leader of the Bavarian CSU, who, as we shall see, was to have a seminal influence on the Airbus project.

For the moment, however, what initiative there was rested with the French and the British. The first meetings between the two governments took place in February 1966 when Fred Mulley, who had succeed Roy Jenkins as minister of aviation in Harold Wilson's Labour government, met his counterpart, Edgar Pisani, in Paris. The talks were rather low-key. Nearly all public attention was focused on Concorde, a much more glamorous project. By comparison, the European Airbus seemed dowdy and mundane: even the name was downbeat.

In May 1966, just one month after Frank Kolk had sent his famous letter to the airlines, the British and French set the process in motion by formally inviting the companies to tender for the contract to build the plane. Bidders were asked to reply by the end of the month. It was at this point that politics came into play. In July, British officials came down, predictably, on the side of the HB-100 – the Hawker Siddeley, Breguet, Nord offering – while the French, equally predictably, selected Sud

Aviation's Galion. The choice of the engine maker was equally political: the British nominated Rolls-Royce, while the French put forward SNECMA, France's leading engine company, which in partnership with the American Pratt & Whitney was currently developing the JT 9D for Boeing's 747.

While all this manoeuvring was going on, the Germans decided to assert themselves and play their European card. The first official meeting between the German group and Sud Aviation and Hawker Siddeley took place at the Farnborough Air Show, and though they were all aircraft people and engineers, there was as much talk about politics as planes. Up to this moment the Germans in Munich had been working largely on their own. There were, so the participants say, intense arguments about the kind of plane the airbus should be. Would it be better to make it a long single-decker or a shorter double-decker? Should it have two engines or four? Now, for the first time, the engineers from Munich had the welcome opportunity to compare notes with their British and French opposite numbers from Hatfield and Toulouse. 'The atmosphere,' so *Flight* reported, 'was cordial and talk centred for the first time on a *European* airbus.'[10] At this meeting it was decided that the three teams should join forces in a common effort. And three months later the three aircraft companies put in a formal request to the French, British and German governments for financial support. Meanwhile, in preparation for serious business, the German study group, which consisted of ATG Siebelwerke, Bölkow, Dornier, Flugzeug-union Sud, Hamburger Flugzeugbau, Messerschmitt, and Vereinigte Flugtechnishe Werke (VFW), reorganized to become Arbeitsgemeinschaft Airbus (Airbus AG). With this move the German aircraft companies became, in effect, a consortium inside a consortium. With the creation of Airbus AG, the Germans were putting themselves on the same footing as Sud Aviation and Hawker Siddeley but with one important difference: the role of Airbus AG was to represent the German national interest. In this the group had the blessing and full support of the politicians in Bonn.

Things were beginning to take shape. At a meeting in London in December 1966 a handpicked group of government officials, aircraft manufacturers and airline executives decided that a consortium consisting of one company in each of the three main countries involved, France, Britain and Germany, should design and build what had now officially become the European Airbus. This accord was the result of some old-fashioned horse-trading. In return for a pledge that Rolls would build the engine, the British dropped its support for the HB8-100, while the French, who had secured design leadership for Sud Aviation, agreed that SNECMA would play a junior role to Rolls-Royce in the great engine game. The big loser in all this was the HBN syndicate. 'The HB 100 was pushed to one side for political reasons,' says Henri Ziegler.[11]

It was an entirely novel approach to the business of building something as complex as a modern jet airliner, and the partners approached this daunting task in a spirit of hope born largely of ignorance. The only precedent was the Franco-British Concorde partnership, but in fact it was hardly a precedent at all. There were extremely detailed exchanges between Bristol and Toulouse but they were two separate operations: French Concordes were built in France and English Concords were made and assembled in England. The Airbus, by contrast, had no single country of origin. Made in England, France, Germany, Spain and Belgium, the first Airbus was a quintessentially European machine.

At the end of January 1967 there was a top-level ministerial meeting in Bonn between West Germany's economics minister, Karl Schiller, France's minister of transport, Edgar Pisani, and Britain's middle-ranking technology minister, John Stonehouse. The ministers accepted estimates from all three countries that development costs of the Airbus airframe would be around £130 million, including the flight testing of four prototypes and the tooling up for quantity production. The figure also included the cost of Pratt & Whitney's JT 9D, but if Rolls-Royce made the engine, then total development costs would rise to £175 million.

Dr Schiller proposed that the costs be split between the French, British and German governments, with the French and British bearing 37.5 per cent each of the airframe costs and the Germans 20 per cent. The arrangement was that the governments would give the manufacturers an unsecured, undated and interest-free loan that would only begin to be repaid after the sales of aircraft had passed the break-even point – whenever that might be. If, by some unhappy chance, this point never arrived, Schiller suggested that the industry should be asked to share between 10 and 20 per cent of the loss. What the Germans were suggesting might sound extremely generous, but such arrangements had been common in the civil airline business for many years.

Building aeroplanes had become so expensive and the returns so uncertain that European aircraft companies, without government guarantees to back them, had little or no chance of raising the millions they needed in the money markets. Either the banks would not lend at all or the money was prohibitively expensive, pushing back the break-even point on an aircraft even further into the future. If a commercial airliner reaches break-even point (the American yardstick was 600 sales) within four years of launch, it is regarded as a best-seller but in this business money is more often lost than made. When Lord Plowden did his sums in the process of compiling his report into the state of the British aircraft industry in 1964, he reckoned that of the thirty-six different transport planes produced since the war, only eight had notched up sales in excess of 100. And of the £88 million that the British government had lent the industry between 1945 and 1959 (the last date for which figures were available), it had recovered only one-third – less than £25 million. These sums, of course, were completed by overshadowed by the huge pile of taxpayers' money the British and French were spending on Concorde – by 1966 the figure for the British alone was well over £500 million – but, measured against what had gone before, at £130 million the Airbus was not exactly cheap.

In accepting the companies' estimates as to how much the Airbus might cost to develop and in coming up with a formula as to how these costs should be shared between them, the Bonn meeting of ministers made progress. Even so the most important questions remained unanswered. What did the airlines really want? How much money would the industry be willing to put up? What was the extent of government support? Which engine was right for the job? Unable to answer these questions, the ministers passed the ball back to a working party. Concerned that what *Flight* called 'the somewhat amorphous airbus project' was running out of puff, the Germans sounded the alarm.[12] The trade papers' technical writers were summoned to Munich to be told, 'This is our last chance. If the European aircraft industry and European governments do not join forces *now* to carry through the airbus project to a successful conclusion, we might as well give up all hope of ever breaking into the commercial aircraft market.'[13]

It was a message directed as much to the British as anyone. The French cabinet had approved the project in principle almost exactly a year before and the Germans had made their position very plain a number of times. But what about the British? The plain fact was that the British government was split. On the one side was the Airbus camp, led by the pro-Europeans and, *pro tem*, Tony Wedgwood Benn, heading the Ministry of Technology, or Mintech as he liked to call it, which had been set up to realize Harold Wilson's dream of an economy transformed by 'the white heat of technology'. On the other side were the BEA/BAC Two-Eleven claque, whose advocate in Cabinet was the anti-European president of the Board of Trade, Douglas Jay. These divisions were reflected in Whitehall. The Ministry of Technology and the Foreign Office were pro and the Board of Trade and the Treasury were anti. As Charles Gardner, BAC's historian, puts it: 'The fight for funds became, in effect, a fight against Airbus . . . On the side of the Two-Eleven were BEA, the Board of Trade and Rolls plus two intending customers, Laker and Autair. Against it were Wedgwood Benn and Stonehouse at the Ministry of Technology, who were insistent upon European collaborative enterprise, i.e. the big Airbus, which had no firm customers.'[14]

*

When the British cabinet met on 16 March 1967, the battle lines were quickly joined. Anthony Wedgwood Benn (as he was then called) opened the discussion with a paper arguing the pro-Airbus case. After forecasting that there should be a world market for airbuses of between 700 and 800 by 1980, he went to warn the Cabinet that 'should we not proceed with the European Airbus, the United States would acquire a monopoly in the field of large sub-sonic aircraft and this would have serious effects on the European aircraft industry and on the associated advanced technological industries.'[15] Echoing the arguments of the Plowden Report, the minister (or rather, his officials) argued that 'in view of the large launching costs for

projects of this kind, United States domination could be averted only by a collaborative European effort. The British, French and German aircraft industries had a
common interest in airframe development, but the United Kingdom had, in addition, a special interest in the development of a new engine which was proposed for
the airbus.'[16]

Having sketched in the geo-industrial case for the Airbus, Wedgwood Benn then
tried to persuade the Cabinet that it would be a paying proposition. The cost of
launching the Airbus alone, he told them, was estimated at £130 million. With
another £55 million for the Rolls engine, the total cost would rise to £185 million, of
which Britain's share would be £75 million. For the three governments to recover
their investment, it would require the sale of some 300 Airbuses. This target, he suggested, was not quite as challenging as it might appear. He offered some fancy
calculations involving foreign exchange and import savings to suggest that the real
break-even figure was closer to 150 than 300 and he added, somewhat rashly, that if
the national airlines did their bit and ordered twenty-five Airbuses apiece ('one of the
prerequisites for our participation') then 'the Airbus would . . . have a larger assured
market at the outset than any compatible project on which we have embarked in the
past'. Given BEA's hostility to the Airbus and Lufthansa's well-known reservations,
this was a very bold, if not downright misleading, assumption.

It fell to Douglas Jay, the president of the Board of Trade, to present the counter
arguments. As Jay saw it, the issue was not pan-European cooperation. It had nothing to do with the survival of the European aircraft industry or the threat of
American domination. The decision about whether or not to go ahead with the
Airbus should be determined, he argued, by whether or not it was good for British
European Airways. 'BEA would require an aircraft of the airbus type some time
after 1973–75,' he said. 'However, the immediate concern was with their requirement for an aircraft of intermediate size which would span the gap between the
aircraft now in service or on order and the airbus.

'A decision to proceed with the airbus would clearly have serious implications for
any intermediate aircraft which BEA would be allowed to order, and further consideration should be given to the latter problem before reaching a decision on
airbus.' He threatened that if BEA found itself in a situation where it had no alternative but to order what it thought was an uneconomic aircraft, it would seek
compensation from the government. And he concluded by saying, 'It now appeared
that even the best collaborative venture which could be devised on a European basis
would not be viable', and put forward four arguments stressing the negative. It
would, he argued, be difficult to pull out when once started; the market for airbus
was predominantly in the United States where the US version would be available
before the European one; there were doubts about Lufthansa; and there were worries
about the impact on other areas of public expenditure.'[17] In other words, Douglas Jay
believed that Airbus was unnecessary, unwanted and unaffordable.

The only argument Jay could find in its favour was that the development of the RB 207, an engine tailor-made for the Airbus, would both be good for Rolls and for Britain. One of the most striking aspects of the Cabinet discussion was the degree to which the fortunes of Rolls-Royce dominated the proceedings. From the way the Prime Minister summarized the discussion, it looks as if the Rolls-Royce factor was decisive. As the cabinet secretary noted, 'The Cabinet were on balance inclined to favour participation . . . At meetings of ministers of the three countries concerned we should not appear to be hampering the progress of discussions.' And the Prime Minister concluded, 'It was essential that the Rolls-Royce engine should be adopted.'[18]

Just over a month after the British government had given Airbus a distinctly cautious go-ahead, the consortium released the first details of the plane they planned to build. Called the A300, it was designed as a low-cost, mass market, twin-engined people-carrier intended to carry between 260 and 298 passengers, depending on the configuration, for up to 1,200 nautical miles. Apart from the bold idea of powering such a large aircraft with only two engines, the A300 was, in many respects, a very conventional plane. What made it remarkable was its size – the wings were far larger than any Hawker Siddeley had ever built – and its economics. 'We regarded it as a kind of Bactrian camel,' Airbus's Adam Brown told me. 'Like the camel, it had two humps – the first was the New York–Chicago route; the second was Chicago–Los Angeles. From the start, the target we had to beat was the seat-mile cost of Boeing's 727. If we could undercut that by 15 per cent, we reckoned that we would have a product that would be sellable. The 727 was the standard against which everything was measured.'[19]

The economics may have been based on the 727, but physically the A300 bore no resemblance to Boeing's small breadwinner. When the details were released, the industry was struck on how closely the design resembled a scaled-down 747. 'Perhaps the most significant feature of the A300 design,' *Flight* magazine observed, 'is the studied attempt to get maximum compatibility with the Boeing 747 in order to reduce first cost, simplify maintenance and ease problems at airports. The fuselage cross-section (shape, size and height off the ground) is similar to that of Boeing's long hauler, while systems, equipment and servicing points will in many cases be identical.'[20]

*

With the British finally off the fence, the way was open for an agreement between the three governments. The junior ministers met in Paris on 9 May to sign a document that committed them 'to proceed rapidly with a joint project definition study of the best aircraft capable of being built around two such engines [*sic*]'.

The formal go-ahead came on 25 July 1967 after yet another three-way ministerial meeting. The tone of the statement issued after the meeting was suitably weighty. The three governments had agreed, it said, 'for the purpose of strengthening European cooperation in the field of aviation technology and thereby promoting economic and technological progress in Europe, to take appropriate measures for the joint development and production of an airbus'.

On the same day, Stonehouse told the House of Commons that the British government believed that there should be an airline commitment on the part of the three national carriers – BEA, Air France and Lufthansa – to buy between them a minimum of seventy-five aircraft. Assuming a commitment of seventy-five aircraft, Stonehouse said that he foresaw sales of up to 300 aircraft by 1985 – ninety to a total value of £2,000 million, of which the British share would be £800 million. Of a total development cost of £190 million – £130 for the airframe and £60 million for the engine – Britain's share would be £50 million for the airframe and £45 million for the engine – £95 million in all. Stonehouse reported that the first flight was scheduled for February 1971; certification would be in November 1972 and he forecast that the plane would enter service in 1973. The engine in question, Stonehouse said, would be the Rolls-Royce RB 207.

As long as he stuck to his prepared script, he was confident enough. But in answering some sharp questions from Robert Carr, the Tory shadow minister, Stonehouse began to flounder. He was forced to admit that there were no safeguards against early withdrawals – 'it was up to governments to decide' – and no assurances had been received from European airlines about any sales. Carr was right to be sceptical. Everything that Stonehouse had said turned out to be either untrue or was so evasive as to be quite devoid of meaning. There was no commitment by the national airlines to buy the Airbus; there was absolutely nothing to prevent any one – or all three, for that matter – of the governments pulling out at any time; and there was not the remotest possibility that the French would ever hand over the design leadership they had fought so hard to secure.

Each of the three governments looked at the project from a slightly different angle. The French saw it as *Un Grand Projet*: one of those brilliant combinations of technological skill and political will that serve to remind the French themselves – and everybody else – just what a great nation they are. The Germans saw it both as an opportunity to rebuild what had been an important industry and as a chance for them to put the past behind them and demonstrate their credentials as full and whole-hearted members of the European Community. The British approach lacked any such metaphysical overtones. They saw it as a means of employment at a time when jobs were scarce, a support for an industry that was badly in need of any help it could get, and last, and probably least, as a card to be played in the forthcoming negotiations to join the Common Market.

The Airbus was, most people thought, a gamble worth making. Lord Plowden expressed a common view when he told the House of Lords, 'I believe that the future of this country lies in Europe. At present it is not possible for us to join the

Community. For many industries the benefits of large markets must wait. But for the aircraft industry it is in the fortunate position that since its main customers are governments, the benefits of integration could be enjoyed without political or economic union . . . The aircraft industry is an example of the choices facing the British people. We cannot do everything. We cannot go on living in a fantasy built on dreams of the past. But for all the hope and all the brave talk, there were still many practical difficulties ahead and problems to be overcome.'[21] The next eighteen months were to be, for politicians and planemakers alike, a huge test of nerve and resolve.

CHAPTER TWO

POWER GAMES

IN JULY 1967 WITHIN DAYS of the official launch, the French government invited Roger Béteille to be the director of the airbus programme. The job might have sounded impressive but the set-up at the Sud Aviation's plant in Toulouse was distinctly modest. It consisted of four people: Béteille, a couple of his most trusted engineers and a secretary. The task was daunting. There was no plane and no team to speak of. Political support for the project was tentative and heavily qualified. The experts spoke three different languages and were scattered across Europe, from Hatfield to Hamburg. 'Everybody was all over the place,' Béteille recalls. 'There were the English at Hatfield, the French at Breguet and Sud Aviation, and five lots in Germany who were beginning to regroup in Munich. And each of these had their own ideas: the Germans wanted to make a four-engined plane, the British something else.'[1]

Initially Béteille concentrated on building on the friendships he had already established with the British while working on the Comet, and with the Germans. But while there might have been an illusion of equality, everybody knew that Béteille was the boss. On accepting the French government's invitation to take charge, Béteille had insisted that there should be no dilution of his power or his responsibilities. 'When I was named as director of the airbus programme,' he says, 'I became *le patron* of every aspect of the work from the initial studies to the manufacture. My title of *directeur-général* gave me authority over everybody. If I was going to coordinate everything, I needed the powers to do the job.'[2]

Béteille's authority may have been extensive, but he was careful not to throw his weight about. He was too shy and too modest a man to even try to be a dictator. His approach was cautious and methodical. 'Let's just concentrate on the job in hand – making an aeroplane,' he told his new colleagues. His technique was not to rush into things: first study problems one by one and then take decisions later, he said. He knew how prone decision-makers and, especially, functionaries were to put off decision-making altogether when faced with a difficulty. 'If you study a problem and then take a decision a year later, it all becomes much easier,' he argued.[3]

From the beginning Béteille's job was as much political as it was aeronautical. He knew that if the airbus was to be designed and built, he needed the fullest cooperation and support from the most senior people – especially the technical directors – in Sud

Aviation, Hawker Siddeley and Airbus AG. But that was only the beginning. He also needed to gain the confidence of an entire network of ministers, under-secretaries and senior officials in France, Britain and Germany. The politicians and officials were no experts in the arcane intricacies of building a commercial jetliner, but Béteille and Henri Ziegler, who was to join him at Sud Aviation as chairman a year later, knew better than anyone that without political support *Le Grand Projet Airbus* would quickly founder. In these early months Béteillle spent most of his time exploring the options, assessing the strengths and weaknesses of the other members of the team and keeping the political channels open. Nearly all of this was done in confidence and behind closed doors. Whether deliberately or not, the general public in France, England and West Germany was kept in ignorance as to what was involved and what was going on. This shortage of information led *Flight* magazine to complain in the week the memorandum of understanding was signed in London in September 1967, 'This Ministerial game of airbus . . . had by then become one of the most completely secret non-military procurement exercises of all time. The tax-payer who will in the end foot all the bills has been told almost nothing, officially, about the problems and the decisions involved.'[4] And there were plenty of them.

Before he could tackle the problems of building the plane, Béteille needed the agreement from each of the partners as to who should do what – an all-important question that the politicians had deliberately left extremely vague. 'I wanted to use all the available talents and capacities to their utmost without worrying about the colour of the flag or what language was spoken. That was my starting point,' Béteille said. He was already clear in his own mind how the work should be divided, but he needed the approval of the others. 'It is impossible to work on a common task unless everybody agrees how the work should be divided and each one knows what to do,' he commented.[5] Accordingly, Béteille set out for Hatfield to discuss matters with Jim Thorn, Hawker's team leader, and his colleagues, Phil Smith, the head of research, and his number two, Alan Peters. In making his decision Béteille drew directly on his own experience and on what he knew about the skills and capabilities of the other members of the team. But Béteille was not just making technical judgements: the division of Airbus into three parts was, just like Caesar's Gaul, essentially a political matter.

To his British friends he proposed that Sud Aviation, under his own direct super-vision, should make the cockpit, the control systems, and the structural core of the plane where the wings are fitted to the fuselage. Impressed by their work on the Trident, which he thought was an outstanding plane of its kind, Béteille suggested that the British should make the wing, while the Germans should concentrate on making the fuselage and fitting it out. The feeling in Toulouse was that however much the Germans would have liked to play a bigger, more glamorous role, they were not ready to tackle the cockpit, with its complicated radio and navigation equipment. Final assembly would be done by the French at Toulouse. The basic idea throughout was to keep existing teams in place and working together to get the best out of everybody.

With the approval of the British in his briefcase, Béteille was in a strong position to obtain an agreement from the Germans. As they were being offered the junior role, this proved a little harder. Johann (Hans) Schäffler, who was managing director of the German end of the programme, observes, 'The Germans always had the feeling that they had somehow been left out and that they should be getting some of the more noble and better parts – something more important and technically challenging than just building fuselages.' But after some grumbling, the Germans, too, came into line. Everybody agreed with Béteille's suggestion that the work should be split on a percentage basis, with the French and British taking 33 per cent each and the Germans 25 per cent. This work-sharing formula is one of the key elements of the Airbus story, and was to be of great importance when the financial package was put together some time later.

Having enlisted the British and the Germans, Béteille then set off to pay a visit to his friends in America. 'I already had a pretty good idea of what the Europeans, Air France, British European Airways and Lufthansa were thinking,' he said. 'But to produce a commercial airliner without knowing what the Americans wanted didn't seem to be the right way of going about it.'[6] In the light of Béteille's views about the short-comings of the European aircraft industry, its products and their marketing, this is something of an understatement. As a patriotic Frenchman, Béteille was proud of his company and the success of its Caravelle. Launched in 1957, the Caravelle was sold to every European airline, with the exception of BEA, and even made a modest impact in the States. The plane raised the profile of Georges Hereil and his company Sud Est, and was a factor in its take over of Sud Ouest to become, simply, Sud Aviation. It was the first major realignment of the French civil aircraft industry since the Popular Front government had reorganized the state-owned side of the industry on regional lines in 1936.

Béteille may have been a patriot, but he was also a realist: he knew that if his airbus venture was to succeed, it was essential that the plane sold in the American as well as the European market. For far too long, he argued, Europe's plane makers had been designing and building planes for European markets and European airlines. The planes were, on the whole, well-conceived and well-made, but they lacked the carrying capacity and the power the Americans required. In addition, the European market they were serving was a fraction of the size of the American one – which put them at a huge disadvantage to Boeing, Lockheed and the other big American manufacturers whose domestic sales outnumbered their exports by a ratio of nine to one. As the Plowden report put it, 'With such a vast home market, completely assured for Government purchases and largely assured for civil aircraft, the Americans have a solid base for overseas operations. US airplane makers are not necessarily quicker off the mark to develop a new plane but once they make their mind up, they build more quickly and can deliver faster. United States salesmanship has been thorough, aggressive and ready to respond to consumer demand.'[7]

The men in charge of Britain's and France's aircraft companies were no less tough and aggressive than the Americans. But the playing field was tilted steeply against them. By the early 1960s the US had 80 per cent of world production of civil aircraft, while Britain and France, the only other players on the field of any note, had 8 and 5 per cent respectively. 'Britain's problem,' Charles Gardner remarks in his history of BAC, 'was that the domestic market was too small to provide the economies of scale needed to compete with the Americans . . . Trying to operate a high technology business, with huge research and development and tooling costs charged against a relative handful of initial production aircraft rapidly became the dominating problem of the industry in both military and civil fields.'[8]

When the era of the commercial jet dawned on 27 July 1949, with the first flight of Britain's Comet, it looked for a time as if Britain would establish a world lead. The Comet could carry thirty-six passengers, cruised at 40,000 feet and flew at 500 miles an hour, twice as fast any commercial airliner then in service. Even the Americans, who had nothing remotely like it, were impressed. When Boeing's Bill Allen first saw the Comet at the Farnborough Air Show two years later, he was startled by its sleek, futuristic appearance, and over dinner he asked his head designer, Maynard Pennell, what he thought of the British plane.[9]

'It's a very good airplane,' Pennell replied.

'Do you think we could build one as good?'

'Oh better, much better.'

What gave Boeing pause for thought was not the concept but the cost. The accountants told Bill Allen that if he wanted to build a passenger jet, the price would be $15 million – a sum equal to Boeing's total profit in the seven years since the end of the war. Nor were the airlines encouraging. They saw the jet as a rich man's plane, suitable only for those willing to pay a premium for speed and comfort. The only dissenter was Pan Am's Juan Trippe who put in an order for three Comets. For these reasons, if none other, a further three years were to pass before what was to become the Boeing 707 made its first public appearance.

To engineers and designers the Comet was a marvel. These days jet travel is so commonplace that it is difficult to appreciate just what an impression the Comet made on those early passengers half a century ago. C. Martin Sharp, the author of a somewhat dry history of de Havilland, the makers of the Comet, wrote about it as if it was some kind of out of body experience. His account is reminiscent of the astronauts' description of Earth from space:

Millions wonder what it is like to travel in the Comet at 500 miles an hour eight miles above the Earth. Paradoxically there is a sensation of being poised motionless in space. It arises mainly from four new factors. Because of the great height the scene below scarcely appears to move; because of the stability of the atmosphere the aircraft remains rock-steady; the gas turbine's complete freedom from vibration is unexpected in a vehicle of great power; and the absence of all visible signs of engines, propellers or other moving parts completes the illusion.

One arrives over distant landmarks in an incredibly short time but without the sense of having travelled. Speed does not enter into the picture. One doubts one's wristwatch.

The Earth's atmosphere below splits the light into rainbow spectra, often fantastically lovely, especially at dawn and sunset. Yet the sky above is an abyss of blue-black ink, the moon a modelled ball, almost within grasp. In a few minutes one can descend from a blaze of afternoon sunshine through all the stages of sunset and twilight, to land at nightfall at a lighted airport.[10]

With the disasters that overtook the Comet in 1953 and 1954, optimism changed to despair. De Havilland, the builders of the Comet, were, in a sense, too early. Like the Americans, they profited from German wartime research of the aerodynamics of the swept wing, but they underestimated the technical problems of building an aircraft that flew faster and higher than any previous passenger plane. The de Havilland engineers were well aware that the Comet's fuselage would have to withstand immense pressures. They built a decompression chamber at Hatfield to test parts and systems in temperatures of minus 70° centigrade and up to a simulated altitude of 70,000 feet. They then tested windows and frames every working day for three years. 'All this structural testing programme,' says C. Martin Sharp, the company historian, 'was founded on the belief that static testing with a large margin of safety would be adequate to take care of any fatigue stresses that might be present in the fuselage. De Havilland believed that by testing the structure at double the normal cabin pressure they had done enough.'[11] Tragically, they hadn't.

When the Comet's fuselage was inspected by government investigators after the disastrous two crashes within four months off the coast of Italy in 1954, new tests revealed that metal fatigue was the cause of the accidents. In the case of the first accident, which happened on 10 January 1954 when a BOAC Comet on route from Singapore to London came down in the sea near Elba with the loss of all twenty-nine passengers and crew, the tests showed that the corners of the windows in the passenger cabin had given way, causing the cabin to burst open like an overripe tomato. The force of the explosion caused the plane to veer sharply sideways and then plunge headlong into the sea. De Havilland never recovered from this disaster. All Comets then in service were then withdrawn and although work started on a new, larger Comet in the summer of 1954, by the time the Comet 4, as it was called, finally appeared in September 1958, Boeing's 707 had made its debut and the opportunity had passed. A year later, on 17 December 1959, a demoralized de Havilland lost its identity when it merged with Hawker Siddeley to form a company with 80,000 employees and assets of £87 million.

Since then, some fine planes were built, but with sales largely confined to their own domestic airlines, Britain and France never succeeded in mounting a convincing challenge in world markets. As the Plowden Report says in its dry, official language, 'British civil aircraft of the new generation of advanced jets have failed in general, in spite of their technical qualities, to realise the commercial expectations with which they were launched.'[12]

The only two European passenger jets to make money were France's Caravelle, launched in 1957, and Britain's BAC 1-11, which made its first flight in August 1963. Although there was much talk of building on the 1-11's success to create a family of aircraft, just as Boeing was doing, BAC was too weak and its market too small to support such a programme. BAC's immediate problem was that it was unable to find a suitable engine to power a stretched 1-11 when the market was ready for one. And so a rare and excellent opportunity to keep up with and even overtake the competition from Boeing and Douglas went begging.

Britain's other offerings never had a chance on world markets: they suffered from the crippling disadvantage that they were designed and built for British markets to British specifications. The big VC-10 was built to service an empire which by the mid-1960s was no longer there, while the smaller de Havilland Trident was custom-made for British European Airways. The Trident sold a total of 115, of which BEA took sixty-six; the only other major buyer being Communist China. And sales of the VC-10, which was built by Vickers for BOAC's old imperial 'hot, high and dry' routes, amounted to fifty-four of which BOAC took thirty-nine. Vickers lost £20 million making the VC-10. It was the last plane it ever built.

Aircraft manufacture is a highly capital intensive business with a very steep initial learning curve. The longer the production run, the greater the chance of lowering costs and increasing efficiency. With American production runs on average four-and-a-half times longer than the best European case, the French and the British often found that they had run out of time and customers while they were still climbing the steepest section of the curve. In his history of BAC, Charles Gardner quotes one manufacturer as saying, 'All I know about break-even numbers is that as soon as you get close, some development or redesign, or stretch, or modification needs new investment which puts the target out of sight again.'[13] Sir George Edwards, the head of BAC, was fond of saying that the problem was that the UK was always selling or trying to sell off what he called 'the thick end of the learning curve'.[14] The production runs on even quite successful aircraft tended to be so short that matching the Americans was an almost hopeless task.

*

As the newly appointed head of the European Airbus programme, Roger Béteille arrived in America in the autumn of 1967 armed with a mission and a text. His mission was to challenge American domination of the civil aircraft industry and his text was a short book written by a fellow Frenchman. A few weeks earlier the French journalist Jacques Servan-Schreiber, the editor of the Parisian weekly *L'Express*, which modelled itself on *Time* magazine, had created a great stir with the publication of his *Le Defi Americain* (*The American Challenge*). In his book Servan-Schreiber talked about 'a growing displacement of power between Europe and America'; described how American firms were moving into Europe; and argued that Europe was in the process of being overwhelmed by American economic power. It was, he maintained, the Americans who had taken advantage of the logic of the Common Market, not the Europeans. And he argued that 'if we continue to allow the major decisions on industrial innovation, on technological creativity . . . to be made in Washington, New York, Cambridge, Detroit, Seattle and Houston, there is a real danger that Europe may be confined for ever to second place'.[15]

One reason why the book made such an impact in France and England (where it was published the following year) was that it put a finger on ideas that were in the air but had not yet been clearly articulated. Many also found his conclusions persuasive. Servan-Schreiber argued that one reason why Europe was falling behind was because its nation states were too small, when compared with the Americans, to build firms or create projects large enough to compete with the IBMs, the Honeywells, the Fords, the GMs and the Boeings of the world. 'The national scale is too narrow,' he wrote, 'even when the state moves in to support certain industries. Areas like scientific research, aviation, space, and computers go far beyond the confines of a single medium-sized nation.'[16]

Servan-Schreiber ended with a peroration that mirrored Roger Béteille's own thoughts almost exactly. 'What we should try and do is achieve breakthroughs in certain fields of advanced technology. This is what French and European experts call *les grandes opérations* . . . A major operation should shake up in a thousand routine ways of doing things, bring together industrial teams whose paths would otherwise never cross, unleash a hurricane of studies, discoveries, and products from a single exciting idea.'[17] In the course of a couple of hundred pages, Servan-Schreiber never mentioned Airbus, but as a description of what Roger Béteille and his colleagues were about, this passage could not be bettered. Indeed, the main purpose of Béteille's visit to the States was to find ways of turning this prospect into reality.

One of the first people he sought out on arrival in the States was Frank Kolk, who told him that the simplest thing to do would be to hand over the technical specifications that he had circulated among the other American airlines. Béteille was already familiar with the gist of the Kolk argument, but on looking over the complete papers he was struck by the similarities between the Kolk machine and the Galion. He said, 'It was a bi-motor that closely resembled Sud Aviation's Galion.'[18] And even after the Galion had been transmuted into the Airbus there were many things about it that were derived from Frank Kolk's specifications. 'We did it not because we wanted to please Frank Kolk,' comments Béteille, 'but because it was a serious piece of work carried out in a very serious manner. In his paper Kolk did not suggest a solution, but he posed problems. It was an accumulation of detail [which] became one of the significant inputs to our work and helped us make up our minds.'[19]

The French engineer was not only in search of ideas and inspiration: he was also looking for helpers and kindred spirits. He had already recruited a handful of like-minded French and English technicians, but it was, improbably, in San Francisco that Béteille came across a man who was to play a hugely influential part in the Airbus project. Felix Kracht was a young German engineer then working for Nord Aviation but about to move to the new German airbus group as head of sales and marketing. The meeting which took place at the Mark Hopkins hotel in San Francisco, where the treaty setting up the United Nations was signed in 1945, was well-timed. It was already clear that the new venture would be a multi-national one, involving the French, British and Germans, and Béteille had already begun his search for suitable German partners. The two men spent the whole weekend exchanging ideas. And the more they talked, the more convinced Béteille became that Kracht was the man he needed to oversee and coordinate the complex task of making the A300 and fitting the pieces together. Looking back, a quarter of a century later, Felix Kracht described himself as 'the midwife' of the Airbus manufacturing system in which each partner had their own speciality. 'The essential thing,' he said, 'was to execute a given task once, and in a single place.' However, Kracht's main job in those early days was as Béteille's fireman and trouble-shooter. 'If there was some smoke, I had to find out what was making it and put it out. I developed a good nose for the slightest smell of smoke.'[20]

One reason why the system worked smoothly almost from the beginning was that the relations between the companies that were to build the Airbus were good. Hawker, as we have seen, had strong ties with a number of French companies that had already worked on a very similar plane to Béteille's, and was, unlike BAC, very Francophile. The engineers at Sud Aviation readily acknowledged Hawker's aero-dynamic expertise and knowledge of the arcane craft of wing design, while the Sud Aviation people had earned the respect of fellow engineers for their system building work on Concorde. And though the Germans had, as we have seen, had their reservations, they were pleased to be involved in what they saw as a great and exciting European adventure.

The same, however, was not true of Rolls-Royce, the UK government's chosen engine-maker. The choice of the right engine was absolutely critical to the success of the entire enterprise. With only two engines, against the three on the DC-10 and the Tristar, the A300 needed a more powerful engine than any other being built. The first thought had been that Rolls' new RB 211, which it was developing for the American market, would be able to do the job. But as the specification of the A300 became more detailed, it became clear that an engine with an even greater thrust would be necessary. With a foot in both the American and the European camps, Rolls responded with a second engine, even larger and more costly than the RB 211. It was called the RB 207.

Could the company cope with the technical and financial burdens of two such enormous projects at once? The company assured everybody that it could. Events were quickly to show just how unrealistic this rash promise was. But those around the Cabinet table (and their advisers) were so dazzled by Rolls' reputation for technological brilliance that they never sought to ask whether Rolls was taking on more than it could manage. When Wedgwood Benn was asked some years later in the wake of Rolls' collapse into bankruptcy why he took no steps to investigate its ability to do the job, he replied, 'We were dealing with Rolls-Royce here, not some bucket shop.'

In June 1967, just one month before the airbus programme was announced, the British government had agreed to put up £38 million to help with the launch costs of both the RB 207 and the RB 211. Like Rolls, the Ministry of Technology believed that Rolls' best prospects lay in America but it was concerned that if Rolls was successful in the States, it might damage the airbus. Accordingly, it advised Rolls, 'We would not wish you at present to frame any offer to America of the RB 211 in such a way that an acceptance from the aircraft manufacturer concerned could bind you in a contractual commitment. So long as the RB 207 remains on offer for the European Airbus, we should not wish its prospects or timetable to be prejudiced by the action of a third party in which we have no say.'[21] The Ministry's concern for the RB 207 is understandable: though there is no sign in the official record, perhaps it already had an inkling of just how wildly ambitious the task was that Rolls had undertaken and which the government had agreed to underwrite.

*

Unlike the others, Rolls was very definitely not a team player. From the start the partnership got off on the wrong foot. When Airbus was first mooted, SNECMA, who had worked successfully with Bristol Siddeley on the Olympus engines for Concorde, had suggested that the right engine for the job was Pratt & Whitney's JT 9D which was being developed for the 747. SNECMA and Pratt had been partners for many years, and the plan was that SNECMA and Bristol should make the JT 9D under licence for the Airbus. When news of this scheme reached Derby, Rolls reacted strongly: it argued that it was quite wrong to let an American manufacturer in on a European deal, and that to give Pratt a foothold in Europe would be to Rolls' disadvantage. In addition, Rolls argued, it would undermine its plans for its RB 207/211 range of engines. Rolls used its considerable political influence to persuade the British government to turn down the SNECMA/Bristol option and choose the all-European package consisting of Rolls, SNECMA and MTU, the German engine builders whose inclusion was wholly political.

From the beginning the French were made to feel by Rolls that they had been invited to the party just to make up the numbers. Rolls made it very clear that it felt that it was the senior partner and that SNECMA, a much smaller affair than Rolls, was only there on sufferance. Some months later, when the SNECMA people made their first, getting-to-know-you visit to the Rolls-Royce headquarters at Derby, the atmosphere were so bad, that on his return to France, Rene Raveau, the managing director of SNECMA, confided to his staff, 'The arrogance of the people at Derby is a great deal worse than that of the German officers I met during the war in France. Of the two I prefer the Germans.'[22] He was not alone. Lew Bogdan tells the story of one Frenchman asking another if he knew what the two RRs on the Rolls-Royce radiator stood for. 'No' said the first. 'It stands for aRRogance,' replied the second.[23]

Even before the first meeting, the atmosphere had been soured by Rolls-Royce's high-handed behaviour. For some time the other British engine builder, Bristol, had been working with SNECMA and Pratt & Whitney on the JT 9D engine. When, at the end of 1967, Rolls, anxious to eliminate a competitor that might conceivably be a rival on the all-important American market, launched a surprise take-over bid for Bristol, it ordered the company to stop all work on the JT 9D immediately. Bristol had no option but to obey. SNECMA was furious.

*

Although Rolls-Royce had lobbied fiercely for a pole position in the Airbus programme, it was on America rather than on Europe that the company's greatest hopes rested. Giving evidence some years later to a select committee of the House of Lords, the sharp-tongued banker and chairman of Rolls-Royce, Sir Kenneth Keith, whose third wife was American, was to give a characteristically crisp summary of Rolls' attitude. 'Much of our collaboration within Europe has been in a one-way direction, with Rolls on the giving end.'[24] This was a distinctly unfriendly coded reference to SNECMA, the French engine company, and Rolls' partner on the airbus project.

In fact Rolls-Royce, encouraged by the British government, soon took a decisive step that was ultimately to lead to the company's bankruptcy. In March 1968 it signed a deal with Lockheed which committed the latter to the exclusive use of Rolls' RB 211 in the Tristar. This may have secured Rolls 11 per cent of the US market, but by the early 1970s the shine was beginning to fade. By the time Lockheed stopped making the Tristar, it had sold only 244 – well short of the 1,000 that had been hoped for. And it was the failure of the Tristar that led Lockheed to abandon the airliner business once and for all in 1983. Airbus, by contrast, had taken firm orders or options for more than 500 of the A300 and the smaller A310.

With the benefit of hindsight it is easy to be too critical. At the time, putting all one's money into an untested and uncertain European venture in preference to a joint venture with the Americans might have seemed reckless and foolhardy. Viewed from Derby, the drab town in the Midlands where Rolls-Royce had its headquarters, the big prize was the contract to build the engines for the Lockheed Tristar or the McDonnell Douglas DC-10 (preferably both). What is less excusable is the contempt with which Rolls-Royce treated its European partners and its arrogant assumption that, in the face of all the evidence, it could satisfy both the Americans and the Europeans. It was a mistake for which the company was to pay extremely dearly.

In expressing a preference for doing business with the Americans rather than the Europeans, Rolls was illustrating a theme that, as we shall see, runs right through the British end of the Airbus story. John Newhouse puts it well when he says, 'This illustrious company mirrored Britain's deep and continuing uncertainty as to whether its larger political and commercial interests lay in Europe or the United States. And the conflict that developed between Rolls-Royce's proprietory interest in the Airbus and its yearning for a solid American connection was to blacken its future, do serious injury to Lockheed and create difficulties for several airlines, not to mention the political leadership of Britain and the United States.'[25]

Rolls-Royce, led by Sir Denning Pearson, who joined as a young designer in the early 1930s to become one of the chief architects of Rolls' aero engine business, was a company that, on the surface at least, exuded immense self-confidence. As Europe's leading engine manufacturer, Rolls-Royce suffered from hubris. The company had an awesome reputation for quality and technical brilliance, but in truth it was nothing like as solid as it seemed.

Surveying the market in the mid-1960s, Derby found that of the five engines currently in production, only the Spey, the civilian version of which powered the BAC 1-11, would be contributing significantly to turnover beyond 1970. The future was alarming, to say the least. The forecast showed that sales would run down from £59 million in 1969 to a mere £3.5 million in 1975. Rolls concluded from this that there was an urgent need to develop and sell a big, high-powered engine to replace the Conway, used in the VC-10 and some of BOAC's 707s. As the DTI inspectors observed in their report after Rolls had collapsed in 1971, 'It seemed obvious to the company that failure to obtain a share of the market for large transport engines would result in the relegation from its proud position in the major league of aero-engine manufacturers.'[26]

When discussing new developments, writers and industry historians tend to focus most of their attention on the planes themselves – their range, their speed, their carrying capacity and so on. The engines that drive them are often taken rather for granted. But this is to ignore a vital element. Not only is the cost of the engine package a significant percentage of the cost of the plane itself, but the performance of the engine – its thrust and the rate at which it burns fuel – is a key component in the performance and thus the saleability of the plane itself. This is true of nearly every plane, but it was particularly true of the 747 and, more than a decade later, of the Airbus A300.

For all its innovation, the 747 would not have been possible without the dramatic developments taking place in jet engine technology; specifically the high bypass engine. The main feature of the new engine was the huge size of its fan. The bigger the fan, the greater the volume of air being sucked into the engine. The fan had a 'push-me-pull-you' action: it not only pushed the plane along by increasing the thrust of the exhaust gases, but by acting as a huge propeller it also pulled the plane through the air. The giant fan was one element of the new engine; the other was the so-called bypass design. This feature was so-called because the air being drawn into the engine was in two separate streams: one flowed fast through the hot core and the other, denser, cooler and more slow moving, passed between the core engine and the outer cowling. The outer air stream added greatly to the engine's thrust. General Electric was the first to develop this new family of high bypass engines which, it claimed, could deliver twice the power of any existing engine at a third of the cost. But GE was quickly followed by Pratt & Whitney and Rolls-Royce.

The race between the engine companies to develop a really large commercial jet engine was triggered, as so often in the American aerospace business, by military rather than civilian imperatives. Just as Boeing's 707 was a direct development from Boeing's work on the B-47 and B-52 bombers (Boeing's first attempt at a commercial jet was a scaled-down version of the B-52), so the next big step in engine technology was in response to the US Air Force's request for a massive transport plane. The growing involvement in the Vietnam war meant that the Air Force needed a plane that could carry troops, tanks, armoured personnel carriers and jeeps over very long distances and be able to land and unload quickly on primitive airstrips. The answer was the C-5A Galaxy, a 700,000-lb, four-engined colossus which became the workhorse of the Vietnam war.

The big three – Boeing, Lockheed and Douglas – fought fiercely for the contract. Boeing was bitterly disappointed when Lockheed snatched the prize with a $1.9 billion bid from Lockheed. When the news came through that Boeing had lost, Thornton Wilson, who was later to become president of the company and was universally known as 'T', addressed the workforce over the tannoy. As the machinists were then on strike, few people were around to hear him. But for those that did, the message was plain enough: 'I regret to report that Boeing has lost the C-5A contract to Lockheed,' he announced. 'It is an understatement to say we are disappointed: however, we are not disappointed in our people. What we learned will be applied to our other business efforts.'[27] This an oblique reference to talks that had been going on between Bill Allen, Boeing's president, and Pan Am's Juan Trippe. One of the most powerful and adventurous men in the airline business, Trippe had been urging the case for a very large, sub-sonic commercial aircraft for some time. In the summer of 1965, just before the C-5A discussion, the two men, accompanied by their wives, went on a fishing expedition in the seas off Alaska. Mostly it was fishing talk. But from time to time the conversation turned to the big plane. Nothing final was agreed. But Trippe had succeeded in planting his idea. And when, a month or so later, Trippe heard that Boeing had lost the C-5A contract, he was straight on the phone to Allen to ask if he would develop a civilian equivalent of the C-5A. If Allen would build it, Pan Am would buy it, he said.

It was a tempting offer. But it was also a hugely risky one. The building of the 747 would take Boeing into largely unknown territory: the jumbo was the first wide-bodied commercial jet; it had a faster wing than any manufacturer had yet risked; it had a unique body profile with a flight deck as high as a four-storey house; it had a sixteen-wheel landing gear; and it all depended on an engine design that was speculative.

Among the first people Allen talked to was Pratt & Whitney, to ask if it was willing and able to develop the engines that would power the 747. Just as the plane itself broke entirely new ground, so the engines it needed would have to be just as revolutionary. Like Boeing, Pratt & Whitney had lost out in the battle for the C-5A and was anxious to recover lost ground. Boldly it agreed to commit a billion dollars to developing a huge bypass engine, much larger and more radical in design than any that had been built to date. The main innovation was that the ratio of cold to hot air passing through the engine was increased to an extent that Pratt had previously thought to be impractical. Pratt may have been the market leader by a large margin, but even so, it was not prepared to give either Rolls-Royce or GE the smallest chance to steal its business.

On 22 December 1965, after receiving reassuring noises from Pratt, Juan Trippe and Boeing's Bill Allen signed a statement of intent which declared that Boeing would build and Pan Am would buy what would be the world's largest and most expensive civil airliner. It was the beginning of the most heroic venture ever made in the civil aviation business. It would take four years and $2 billion to complete, and it brought Boeing to the very edge of bankruptcy. In giving the 747 the go-ahead, Bill Allen was quite literally 'betting the company'.

Rolls-Royce's first bid for this market was the RB 178, a two-shaft bypass engine with a thrust of 25,000 lbs. The company offered this engine to Boeing for the 747 but was turned down in favour of Pratt & Whitney's JT 9D. The RB 178 was, in effect, the forerunner of the RB 211, an engine in which Rolls had invested all of its hopes and more of its money than it could, strictly speaking, afford. Rolls may not have been the first off the line in the great engine race, but by the late 1960s it had made some important innovations.

On paper at least, the RB 211 was ahead of the game. It promised to be cheaper, lighter and more economical than its American rivals. It had three drive shafts instead of the more conventional two and the Rolls-Royce salesmen laid great stress on the fact that the blades of the big fan were made of a composite material called Hyfil, consisting of a thin outer layer of steel with a core of carbon fibre. The main advantage of Hyfil was that it was much lighter than the more usual titanium. The weight of the engines is a critical factor, and every pound that can be saved on the engines can be translated into big savings in operating costs. Thus the selling of Hyfil was an integral part of the selling of the RB 211. But the questions remained: firstly, could Rolls bring it off, and secondly, was Hyfil strong enough to do the job?

From the beginning Boeing had its doubts. In the winter of 1965/66 a team from Boeing made several trips to Derby and concluded that Rolls-Royce was unable to fulfil the claims it was making. In his book *Widebody*, which tells the story of the 747, Clive Irving relates how Joe Sutter, Boeing's chief designer on the 747, travelled to New York to meet the Rolls sales team at their headquarters in a suite at the Ritz Towers on Park Avenue. Sutter took one look at Hyfil and muttered 'oatmeal'.[28] But Adrian Lombard, Rolls' chief engineer, was undeterred. When Sutter asked Lombard how well the blades would withstand a bird strike, the indignant Lombard disappeared in to his bedroom to remerge with a Hyfil blade. Brandishing it like a samurai sword, he demolished a coffee table with a single stroke.

It was Sutter who was proved right. When the first prototypes were flight tested on a VC-10, the engineers discovered that hailstones and even raindrops pitted the surface. There was also the much greater problem of bird strikes. Accordingly, it set up a test rig in a field and for forty hours it was bombarded with dead chickens, scattering flesh, blood and bones all over the field. But the ultimate test was still to come. To replicate the twin hazards of birds and ice in a single test, Rolls fired frozen chickens at the rig: this time Hyfil disintegrated. That was the last that was heard of Hyfil. But replacing Hyfil with solid titanium was costly and added at least 300 lbs to the weight of the engine. While the engineers at Derby wrestled with these problems, the Rolls sales team in New York continued to talk the engine up.

By the autumn of 1967 the debate in America over the configuration of the new widebodies had been resolved with Lockheed's announcement that it was ready to take orders for its L-1011. Two months later the newly-merged McDonnell Douglas followed suit by announcing that it, too, would build a three-engined, wide-bodied airbus: the DC-10. The odd man out was Boeing, which had turned its back on this segment of the market in favour of the 747. Boeing's Joe Sutter never liked the three-engined idea. 'Too much plane for the job,' he muttered.[29]

That's not how Rolls-Royce saw it. It may have failed to convince the sceptical Joe Sutter, but the men from Derby believed that the Tristar and the DC-10 programmes offered the prospect of rich pickings. Lockheed, which needed a new engine for its three-engined 1011, soon to be known as the Tristar, was much more enthusiastic than Boeing about the RB 211. The American firm hoped that by equipping the

Tristar with a Rolls-Royce engine it could steal a march on Boeing in European markets, especially when Britain was so close, or so it thought, to joining the Common Market.

But where did that leave Airbus? In promising to develop a brand-new engine for both the European Airbus *and* the American widebodies, Rolls was placing an each-way bet. It wanted it both ways, as did the British government who was being asked to finance a programme which, at an estimated £110 million, was nor far short of Airbus itself. Rolls knew very well that it could never hope to meet the costs from its own resources. But neither the British government nor Rolls itself had the slightest idea of the risks the company was taking in committing itself to such an ambitious programme. 'We have seen no evidence,' reported the DTI inspectors called in to inspect the wreckage when Rolls went bankrupt in 1971, 'to suggest that during this period the main board sought to evaluate the possible financial risks inherent in the proposed RB 207/211 project by relating them to the net worth of the group.'[30]

Given the difficulties it was having with the RB 211, Rolls must have known from the start that the chances of delivering the larger and more powerful Airbus engine on time and within budget were less than zero. But officially it remained bullish about the RB 207 and its prospects. In May that year it put out a statement saying that the design was well advanced and that the company was planning to run the first development engine within eighteen months. 'The RB 207 is specifically designed to achieve a fuel consumption 25 per cent lower than the engines now in service with the lowest possible weight and cost,' the company boasted. 'These aims have been met by the adoption of a three-shaft layout for the engine . . . The use of a three-shaft layout for the RB 207 represents a considerable technical development and possibly the most important since Rolls introduced the first turbofan into airline service in 1960.'[31]

However reassuring this might have been to the British government and its Airbus partners, it was more an expression of hope than a statement of fact. According to the DTI inspectors, 'The experience the company had had of such engines at this time was confined to the limited running of the RB 178 demonstrator (stopped in the late summer of 1966 through lack of funds after the project had run into technical problems and was £218,000 over budget) and to the development of the three shaft-concept incorporated in the Trent engine which had not yet run. The thrust offered was considerably in excess of anything previously achieved by Rolls-Royce.'[32]

In late March 1968 the efforts of Rolls-Royce's chief salesman David Huddie and his sales team in New York were blessed with success when, to huge relief and delight all round, Lockheed, on the same day that Eastern Airlines and TWA ordered ninety-four 1011s, placed an order with Rolls for 150 sets of the RB 211-22. It looked as if the Rolls gamble had paid off. The government was delighted. And David Huddie earned a knighthood. 'This order is of particular importance,' Tony Wedgwood

Benn told the House of Commons on 1 April. 'It constitutes a foothold in the American civil aircraft market far bigger than anything which we have achieved before. It is of special value to the British economy, and is, above all, an outstanding encouragement for the skills and technology of British industry.'

Despite the euphoria, the UK government, mindful of its European obligations, struck a note of caution. As the minister pointed out, 'The House is aware that the Rolls RB 207 engine, which is of the same advanced technology design, has been adopted for the European Airbus. This aircraft will be complementary to, rather than a rival to, the American aircraft. It will be of shorter range, more economical, and hence should be better suited to many airline routes, particularly in Europe. The securing of the RB 211 order by Rolls-Royce does not lessen in any way our determination in association with our French and German partners to do all we can to ensure that this aircraft meets the airline requirements and can thus be a commercial success.'

The French, however, were not convinced. In fact they were becoming a trifle paranoid. They suspected that behind the scenes the British government had been using its influence to persuade Lockheed to buy British and that its commitment to Airbus was, at best, half-hearted.

*

In May, just a couple of weeks after Rolls had won the Tristar order, Roger Béteille set out for Derby to discover if he could find out what Rolls-Royce's real intentions were. The trip was eventful. France was in uproar. The students had occupied the universities and the workers were staging sit-ins or were on strike. Sud Aviation's plant at Toulouse was at the centre of the uprising and its workforce was amongst the most militant. The only way Béteille could reach Rolls-Royce in England was by private jet. But as the plane was taxiing out for take-off, the tower radioed to say that it had no authority to clear the plane: only the strike committee could do that. Béteille, a qualified pilot, was at the controls. 'I radioed the tower and said, "The strike committee is on the plane and we have permission to take off" – which I did'.[33]

Even before his arrival at Derby, Béteille was highly suspicious about Rolls-Royce's intentions. He had not yet actually been jilted, but he strongly suspected that he was about to be. It did not take long for him to conclude that the RB 207 was dead. It was clear that Rolls had taken the decision to devote all its efforts to the Lockheed Tristar engine and that it was, so the French believed, using the money it had obtained from the British government to finance the Airbus engine for work on the RB 211. At the same time, the Rolls team that had been assembled to work on the Airbus engine was melting away.

What made matters even worse was that when Béteille came to talk money with Rolls, it became clear that it was proposing to sell the Americans three Tristar engines for the same price as two Airbus ones. In other words, the economic advantage of the Airbus having two engines as opposed to the Tristar's three would be wiped out completely. As the engines account for something like a quarter of the purchase price of an aircraft, this was a knock-out blow. The reluctance of Rolls-Royce to press on with the RB 207 threw Béteille's plans into chaos: his plane was still on the drawing board and now he had no engine – not even a paper one. As Hawker Siddeley's Arnold Hall warned Henri Ziegler, 'We are in serious danger of building the world's biggest glider.'[34]

Rolls' failure to produce the RB 207 nearly killed Airbus before the project was properly under way. It was not only Airbus that suffered: the strain of trying to develop two enormous engine programmes simultaneously was to drive Rolls-Royce into bankruptcy within three years. The debacle also caused a breach between Rolls-Royce and the Airbus consortium that was to last for twenty years. The damage to the British engine-maker's business was immense. It was not until the launch of the A330/340 in 1987 that a Rolls engine made its first appearance on an Airbus.

Béteille returned to Paris an extremely angry man. Without an engine his plans for the A300 were looking distinctly unpractical. The plane needed to be smaller and less expensive. The difficulty was that if he told his British and German partners about his new plans, the news would leak out and the politicians, already restless about the increasing costs and delays, would pull the plug. Béteille therefore decided that the only thing to do was to set up, in great secrecy, a team of some half a dozen of his most trusted people at Sud Aviation to redesign the A300. Béteille called them 'the pirates'. His idea, he says, was to present the governments and the partners with a *fait accompli* before anybody could find out what he was doing and tell him not to. But events were moving faster than he had anticipated. Just as France was preparing to shut down for the summer holidays, he received a very unwelcome piece of news from an unexpected quarter.

CHAPTER THREE

THINGS FALL APART

O N 2 6 J U L Y 1 9 6 8, A Y E A R to the day after the French, British and German governments had given their blessing to the airbus project, Henri Ziegler, received a call from a senior government official at the Defence Ministry. Ziegler was about to take over as president of Sud Aviation. The Concorde programme was in trouble and the French government thought Ziegler was just the man to sort it out. Ziegler himself was not so sure. 'Concorde's a remarkable technical achievement but don't you know I'm against it?' he said. 'It doesn't amount to anything (*il ne sert à rien*) and it's not going to sell. The programme that interests me is Airbus.'[1] The caller told him to forget Airbus and concentrate on Concorde. It was the first clear indication that Airbus had fallen out of favour with the government.

That the French government should have called on Ziegler to help with Concorde was not surprising. As a war hero, resistance fighter and chief of staff of General de Gaulle's Free French forces in London during the war, Ziegler was part of Gaullist France in a way that Roger Béteille, a fellow graduate of that forcing house of engineering talent, the *École Polytechnique*, could never be. If Béteille's talents were those of an operator and a problem solver, Ziegler's were those of a trouble-shooter and fixer. He moved smoothly and effectively between the worlds of high politics and big business. His twin passions were mountaineering and the aircraft business.

Ziegler began his post-war career by creating his own trouble when as an official at the War Ministry he argued the case for a unified, European aerospace industry and criticized French efforts to go it alone. 'A country like France simply hasn't got the means to compete with the Americans,' he says.[2] On being asked to leave government service, Ziegler went into private industry, flirted for a while with the idea of a full-time political career, was a close associate of Prime Minister Jacques Chaban-Dalmas and eventually was coopted by the government to become head of Air France, the state airline.

Three days after the first warning, Ziegler received a call from the Minister of Transport himself, Jean Chamant. 'Listen, Henri,' the minister said, 'given the state of our finances, it is out of the question for us to support three prestige aircraft programmes, Concorde, the Mercure and Airbus.* There is no way we can abandon Concorde. The General is adamant on that point. So what can we do? There's the Mercure question. Well, Marcel Dassault knows what he's doing and makes good aeroplanes. What's more, it's a machine that has great commercial potential.' When Ziegler protested that Dassault had no experience of making civil aircraft, the minister said, 'We have talked to the other departments involved and have come to the conclusion that the time has come to stop the Airbus programme. You have eight days to present your arguments for carrying on.'[3]

Ziegler was not a man to be pushed into a corner in this way. Instead, he seized the initiative. Five days after this ultimatum, Ziegler had a face-to-face meeting with Chamant. There were no officials present – the two men were alone. Ziegler went straight to the point. 'To stop Airbus is to condemn 30,000 workers, most of them French, to unemployment,' he said bluntly. 'Do you want to take the responsibility for that?' he enquired.[4] As the project was still in the design stage, this threat was more rhetorical than real, but the tactic was effective: the government backed away and Ziegler was given a six-month stay of execution. When, at the beginning of the following year, the news came through that the government had changed its mind and had accepted Ziegler's reconstruction plan, Ziegler himself was climbing in the Himalayas. The message was thought so important that a sherpa was sent up the mountain to tell him.

The main reason why the French government had developed a severe case of cold feet was that the costs of the project had begun to rise rather alarmingly. From a total of £190 million at the outset, by mid-1968 the cost of developing the airframe and engine had risen to an estimated £280 million. The following month the figure was up by a further £10 million, bringing the cost of overall package to £290 million. It was the development of the airframe rather than the engine that was causing the damage.

In a little over a year the cost of the airframe had swelled by nearly £100 million, from £130 million to £220 million, while that of the engine had risen from a notional £60 million to an equally notional £70 million. These figures were not of Concorde-like dimensions but, bruised by the experience of the cost overruns on the supersonic project, both the French and the British were ultra-sensitive on this point. There were some French and many British senior politicians who did not share the enthusiasm of the engineers and technocrats for large aircraft projects. As Britain's Denis Healey caustically remarked some years later, 'The civil aviation

---

* Le Mercure was a pet project of Marcel Dassault, the defence contractor whose company was best known for the Mystere and Mirage fighter planes. Based on an expanded version of the Caravelle, the Mercure, a short haul 150-seater, represented Dassault's bid to break into the civil aviation business. Ziegler ridiculed Dassault's intervention. 'It's a daft project. Dassault makes great military planes but knows nothing about the civil transport business,' he said.

projects are always justified on the grounds that unless you waste this money now you won't be able to waste any more money in the future, and they are all to be regarded with the deepest possible suspicion.'[5]

If the French government was wobbling, so too was the British. In July, John Stonehouse told the House of Commons that the government was 'hopeful' that the airbus would be built but said it was a commercial project not a political one. In other words, the Airbus was no Concorde. Pointedly, he reminded MPs that the government had only given its approval on condition that airlines showed an interest and that orders from British Airways, Air France and Lufthansa were forthcoming. The Wilson government had never been very keen on the Airbus project from the outset. The main argument in favour was that it would provide much-needed work for Rolls-Royce, but with Rolls' American prospects looking brighter, the British government was seeking a way to wriggle out of its commitment to the European project.

Tony Wedgwood Benn had, it seems, already changed sides. His enthusiasm of some eighteen months earlier when he had argued the case for Airbus in cabinet had completely vanished. Tony Benn, the modernizing, pan-European technocrat of 1967, had become Tony Benn, the Francophobe, little Englander of 1969. Some years later in a reply to a question from an interviewer about Airbus, he said, 'I cannot see one factor in its favour. We have proved unable to cancel Concorde, but I am determined we shall have no more costly and pointless projects like this, where we are not even masters in our own house. My advisers tell me it will not sell . . . We have to take the broad view, to consider what kind of country we want to live in, how we can best spend our money. We have no intention in spending it on Airbuses.'[6]

Other influential members of the Wilson government, notably Roy Jenkins, the former aircraft minister, and Richard Crossman, were of the same opinion. In his diary entry for 22 July, Richard Crossman noted that the cabinet discussed 'the joint plan for a European airbus which is being built to beat the American airbus. Again there seemed to be a repetition of past mistakes. The price was escalating once again, particularly of the airframe . . . The Chancellor wanted to cut the project now and it was fairly obvious that he was mainly concerned that if we postpone the decision on this we shall find it more difficult to cancel Concorde in December. But I've got a feeling the French won't allow us to cancel Concorde anyway and we must be content to cancel the airbus by itself.'[7]

While the politicians conspired to end the project, the men in charge plotted how best to continue. On his return from his encounter with Jean Chamant, Ziegler learned of the existence of Béteille's 'pirate team' and of his new plan to buy what he called 'a take-away engine' off the shelf. From the beginning Béteille had known just how risky developing a brand new, prototype design, powered by a brand new, prototype engine, would be. He had followed attentively the difficulties Pratt & Whitney was having in developing its JT 9D for the 747, and he realized that he would, in effect, be betting the airbus company before there was even a company to wager. What made the venture even more risky was that it now looked as if the American airbuses, the McDonnell Douglas DC-10 and the Lockheed 1011, might well kill off the A300 even before it was born. Why should American airlines buy what they saw as an inferior European model when they could buy American – especially as the planes were being offered with discounts of $1 million and more? As M. Bruté de Rémur, a senior adviser to the French minister of transport, observed, 'As we saw it, the simultaneous launching of the two tri-engined planes was a major threat to the Airbus programme.'[8] Plainly, if Béteille wanted to retain the support of his own government, let alone anyone else, he needed to do some hard thinking about exactly what sort of plane the A300 should be.

Béteille's immediate concern was that Ziegler should endorse his new plan and agree, after the holidays were over, that the British and German partners would be told of the change of plan and asked for their support. The two men decided they would draw up an extremely detailed dossier describing all aspects of the project which Ziegler would show to the British and German partners in September and enlist their support.

It was not until the end of the year, however, that the consortium was ready to show its hand publicly. On 11 December 1968 at a press conference in London, Sud Aviation and Hawker Siddeley unveiled a new version of the A300 called, rather unimaginatively, the A300B. The announcement was triggered, so Sir Harry Broadhurst, the chairman of Hawker Siddeley, said, by Rolls-Royce's announcement that it was to drop its plans for the RB 207, which would be replaced, the company claimed, by a higher thrust version of the RB 211-28 that would be upgraded to 47,500 lbs with a promise of 51,000 lbs in two years' time. The plan was that the new, improved RB 211 would do double-duty for the Airbus and a stretched version of the Tristar.

There was in all this a strong element of window-dressing. The 'new' RB 211 was every bit as speculative as the now-abandoned RB 207. Rolls-Royce was having a hard enough time bringing the standard version of the RB 211 up to specification, let alone building an upgrade. And Lockheed's ambitions to stretch a plane which it had not even launched looked equally premature. But blind optimism has always been a salient feature of the aircraft business.

However, the real news was not Rolls-Royce and its engines, but the fact that Béteille and his team had decided to downgrade their plans and make a smaller and cheaper plane than the original A300 design. The diameter of the fuselage was reduced from 21ft (6.4m) to 18ft 6in. (5.6m) and its length cut back from 176ft 11in. (53.92m) to 158ft 6in. (48.3m). The plane was lighter by 25 tonnes and the number of passengers came down from 300 to 250. The new plane should, perhaps, have been called the A250, but it had been called the A300 long enough for the name to stick. The irony was that by cutting the number of seats, the new A300B was actually closer to the famous Kolk machine than the old one. There were some changes, but the basic concept of a medium-range, wide-bodied, jumbo twin that could serve all European markets and cross the United States with only one hop remained intact. The general perception of the politicians and the public was that the European Airbus was in head-to-head competition with the American airbuses, the DC-10 and L1011, but the A300B was, as events were to prove, a very different aeroplane. It was lighter, smaller and, above all, cheaper to operate.

Sir Harry disclosed that the consortium had redone its sums and had concluded that if the A300 was to be competitive, the cost of each aircraft had to be cut from $13.65 million to around $11 million. The simplest way of doing this would be to reduce the size of the plane. This would have the effect of driving up the seat mile costs of the new A300B to something very close to those of the larger American airbuses over distances of under 1,200 miles, significantly reducing the launch and basic running costs.

When measuring the efficiency and competitiveness of their planes, all commercial aircraft companies almost always use two yardsticks: the first is a calculation of the running costs of the plane in terms of fuel consumption, maintenance, speed of turn round, etc; the second is the seat mile cost, which is the sum total of the operating costs divided by the number of passengers carried. As these figures are affected by a large number of variables – the size of the plane, its range, the number of passengers and so forth – these calculations can become both extremely complex and open to manipulation. And as they are the basic tools in any aircraft manufacturer's sales kit, they should be treated with some care. The ultimate test of any aircraft is not what its manufacturer claims its seat mile cost to be – the figures can be so twisted to prove that an absolute turkey is the best in its class – but whether or not it succeeds in the market place.

Sir Harry provided new figures that purported to show that the team had cut the cost of the airbus by some £50 million: the airframe now accounted for £170 million and the engine for £70 million. The only problem was that while the first figure was more or less firmly based; the second, relating to the development of the engine, was outside the consortium's control. Moreover, there was still no word from the politicians as to when work on the Airbus would actually begin. Keeping costs under control was one problem, keeping the politicians in line was quite another. When asked when there would be a decision about the future of airbus, Sir Harry replied, 'This is the problem of the whole consortium: carrying three governments along with you. It is a question of how fast they can react.'[9]

In fact the response of the British government to the new-look plane was very quick and, for the consortium, very discouraging. On 12 December, the day after the consortium had announced the A300B, Tony Wedgwood Benn told the House of Commons that 'the withdrawal of the A300 design presents the three governments with a new situation which they will have to consider . . . I must make it absolutely clear that I cannot in any way commit the government to give financial support to any new proposals which may be brought forward by the consortium.' The British government was signalling that the rug was about to be pulled.

The crunch came just three months later. On 17 March 1969 the British cabinet met to decide whether or not to continue backing Airbus. As he had eighteen months previously, Benn led off the discussion. And though his language was more moderate than it had been in private, from the outset it was clear that the minister and his officials had switched sides. After telling the cabinet that the French and the Germans were in favour of the new slimmed-down airbus and were waiting for a British response, the minister declared, 'I believe there is a strong case for taking a major share in a civil aircraft project of this size, but do not believe that an adequate case has yet been made out for Government support of the A300B.' He continued, 'For their own reasons, the French and the Germans have rushed the decision before airlines have had an opportunity to decide about the new aircraft, and before a real attempt had been made to improve the terms on which the consortium are [sic] seeking Government assistance.'[10]

The minister then described to the Cabinet what, as he saw it, the alternatives were – none of which seemed very attractive. There was, for example, the BAC 311 option. This was yet another paper aircraft BAC had put up as a direct competitor to the airbus. But as, the minister explained, it was too expensive for Britain to go it alone and as the French and Germans had already said that they would have nothing to do with it, the only hope was that the Americans might come to the rescue. The minister pointed out that Lockheed was currently talking to BAC but it was unlikely that anything would emerge much before the end of April at the earliest. The second alternative was the 'stretched' Rolls-Royce RB 211 option, which both the Airbus consortium and BAC had said they would like. But there were problems here too. 'A . . . real difficulty,' Tony Benn told the cabinet, 'is the fact that Lockheed have not yet made their mind up about the 'stretched' version of the RB 211, and that no arrangements for financing its developments have yet been made. I am still examining a request from Rolls-Royce for 50 per cent launching aid, amounting to some £20 million on present estimates.' The third option was to give the A300B the thumbs down and hope that the BAC 3-11 deal with Lockheed would come good. 'The decision will be a crucial one both for our European technology policy and for the aircraft industry,' the minister announced piously. 'There can be no question of supporting either aircraft until we are reasonably assured that it will command a good market and measure up to our normal economic criteria for Government-aided projects. The case for one project or another must stand up in comparison with other claims for Government support.'[11]

Although Concorde was not mentioned during the British cabinet's discussion about the fate of the A300, it cast a long shadow over the debate. On the very same day that Tony Benn submitted his A300 paper, the attorney general wrote a memo to the cabinet about the conditions under which the British could withdraw from Concorde. The government thought that it had been agreed that if the costs went over £600 million and fewer than four airlines decided to buy the plane, then Britain was free to withdraw. But as the attorney general pointed out, even if these conditions had been met, the French would still have to agree. And if they didn't, he said, and Britain withdrew unilaterally, it was his opinion that France could successfully sue the British government in the International Court. The effect of this unwelcome piece of news was to make the Wilson government more determined than ever not to make the same mistake with Airbus.

Just over a week later the cabinet met again to agree that 'the A300B project had little to recommend it to the United Kingdom'. It thought that the airbus, in the form now proposed by the French and German governments, was 'an unattractive project in which we should not participate', and preferred the prospects, however uncertain, offered by the BAC/Lockheed partnership. Not content with abandoning an agreement it had formally entered into with the French and German governments less than eighteen months previously, the Wilson government agreed to keep its decision secret for the time being. The cabinet minutes record that, 'We should if possible avoid having to give a firm refusal to participate in the A300B while the BAC 311 was being defined and arrangements for its development were being discussed with Lockheed. If the Minister of Technology accepted the invitation of the French and German governments to discuss the A300B with them, his aim would be to play for time by probing the possibilities of improving the Consortium's terms for Government support for the project, and of a German offset contribution.'[12]

In other words, the government had decided to betray its European partners and then, rather than admit what it had done, it had agreed to dissemble. That there were doubts about the viability of the Airbus was understandable; even the people most closely involved had those. Nonetheless, the behaviour of the British government was small-minded and shabby. The case for a BAC/Lockheed 311 was infinitely more shaky than that for the Airbus. Yet the government preferred to accept BAC's flimsy arguments that rested on little more than the vague and unlikely prospect that Lockheed, which was fully engaged in a life and death struggle with McDonnell Douglas, would have the inclination and resources to support BAC's tattered reputation as a civil aircraft manufacturer. If nothing else, the BAC 311 would be a competitor to its own Tristar. Once again, given a choice between Europe and the United States, the British had preferred the Americans and Little England.

On 9 April, Benn travelled to Bristol to witness the inaugural flight of Concorde 002. In his diary he wrote, 'Having heard last night at Stansgate that Concorde 002 was to fly for the first time today I got up at 5, drove to London and caught a plane to Bristol. We landed at Filton and it was an extraordinary atmosphere. There was this beautiful bird being pulled on the tarmac, the most advanced aircraft project anywhere in the world, and it was just like a sort of village cricket match . . . Brian

Trubshaw, the test pilot, dressed in his yellow flying suit, kept going backwards and forwards muttering, "It's the paperwork that's holding us up, it's those chaps doing the paperwork." As he left to get into his car everyone shouted, "Good old Trubby, good old Trubby." I thoroughly enjoyed it as a matter of fact, but I wondered whether the occasion reflected a degree of amateurism in modern technology that wasn't quite right.'

The next day the minister was back in London for some less agreeable aircraft business of which there is no mention in the diary. At a meeting with the French Minister of Transport, Jean Chamant, Benn told him that the British government was no longer interested in the airbus programme and did not intend to participate further. He offered no explanation, no apologies and only one very small consolation: the British government did not intend to participate in the BAC 311 programme either. According to the French, Benn told them during the morning that the airbus was finished; by the beginning of the afternoon he had drawn up the communiqué. On this rather sour note, the British government departed the scene, leaving the French and the Germans to sort things out as best they could.

*

As it had been clear for some time that the British enthusiasm for the Airbus was cooling fast, this news did not come as a total surprise. Earlier that year Karl Schiller, the German economics minister, had sent one of his most senior officials, Klaus von Dohnanyi, permanent secretary at the West German ministry of trade, to Paris to tell the French that if Britain pulled out, West Germany was prepared to fill the gap. 'If the British are unwilling to support the European Airbus,' the envoy said, 'the Federal Republic is ready to contribute up to 50 per cent of the programme on condition that the French do the same'. It was, by any standards, a generous offer: the Germans were proposing, without conditions and without any further ado, that they should double their contribution to the Airbus programme from DM500 million to a DM1,000 million overnight. As the proposition had not yet been approved by the Bundestag, the German parliament, it was not only an extremely generous gesture, it was also, from a political point of view, an extremely bold one.

That the Germans were prepared to step in at such short notice to rescue the Airbus programme owes much to the persuasive powers of one of West Germany's most flamboyant and best-known politicians, Franz-Josef Strauss. The British, in particular, were rather suspicious of him and his independent-minded Bavarian Christian Social Union (CSU) that provided the platform for his spectacular leap into national politics. Son of a village butcher and married to a brewer's daughter, to outsiders he seemed to be the quintessential beer-drinking Bavarian: large, loud and over-bearing. In his case, however, appearances were deceptive. Behind his large frame there was a brilliant academic intellect: at school he had excelled in Greek,

Latin and history. After helping the Allies with their post-war de-Nazification programme, he rapidly climbed up the political ladder, rising from small-time local
politics to become Minister of Defence under Konrad Adenauer in the 1950s. Yet his
style was over-bearing and high-handed. And he was prone to over-reacting to criticism to the point where liberal Germans questioned his democratic credentials. In
1962 he fell from grace when the editor of *Der Speigel*, Rudolph Augstein, was
arrested after publishing an article critical of Strauss's defence policy. For a while it
looked as if Strauss's political career was over, but in 1966 the CSU joined forces with
the socialist SPD to form the so-called 'Grand Coalition' under the mild-mannered
Dr Kiesinger, who appointed Strauss as Minister of Finance to work alongside the
SPD's Dr Karl Schiller, the Minister of Economics.

They made an incongruous pair: the bespectacled Karl Schiller was as dry and as
fastidious as Strauss was noisy and exuberant. But the two men had more in
common than might have appeared on the surface. Both saw in Airbus not only the
opportunity for Germany to rebuild her aircraft industry that had still not recovered
from the war, but they also regarded it as an exemplar of the new Europe. To Strauss,
in particular, the project epitomized the sort of Europe he hoped to see. He liked the
idea that European countries and people should pool their resources and their skills
in this way, and he was delighted that somebody was meeting the American challenge. His Europeanism was formed partly by a hatred of nationalism and partly by
a strong belief in European identity. 'It's not natural for 300 million Europeans to be
dependent on either 190 million Americans or 200 million Russians,' he told the
British author and journalist Anthony Sampson in 1968.[13]

The negotiations between the French and the Germans lasted about a month.
Despite the goodwill and the very obvious desire to succeed on both sides, the discussions were far from easy. The understanding was that there should be complete
equality between the two partners. But the basic problem was that the 50:50 split the
Germans were asking for did not correspond to the industrial facts of life, where the
French civil aircraft industry was much more sophisticated and developed than
West Germany's. Consequently, there was a good deal of haggling between the two
governments and their officials about the shape of the deal, how it should be
financed, and what work should stay in France and what should be shifted to
Germany.

Over-hanging these discussions was one over-riding question: what to do about
Hawker Siddeley and its wing? Hawker itself was mortified by the British government's decision to pull out. Its relations with Sud Aviation were excellent: as a
company it was as Francophile as BAC was Francophobe. The moment it became
clear that Britain was pulling out, Hawker Siddeley signalled that it was keen, if
possible, to stay in. 'We are ready to finance 40 per cent of the development of the
wing from our own resources,' said Hawker's managing director, Arnold Hall. It
believed it could find the £35 million it needed to develop the machinery to build a

state-of-the-art wing for the Airbus, but there was no way it could find a further £35 million to pay for the necessary brains and and know-how.

The Germans knew that unless somebody was prepared to help the company bridge the gap, Hawker Siddeley would have no alternative but to withdraw and the Airbus would have to find a new wing. And nobody wanted that – especially the Germans. This is why Franz-Josef Strauss twisted his government's arm to produce the bulk of the money that Hawker Siddeley needed. At the height of the crisis Strauss sent a telex to the consortium saying that 'I am here on [such and such a date], then I have to travel. So if you want the one billion Deutschmark then confirm that now . . . or else I'm gone and you'll have to wait until my return.' The consortium did not wait to be asked a second time. And it was so grateful for his assistance that when Airbus Industrie was formed in December 1970, Franz-Josef was appointed its first president.

As a result of the German intervention, Hawker Siddeley signed a new fixed-price contract to design and manufacture four sets of wings – two for the prototype aircraft and two for testing – plus the money for tooling up to make four sets a month. Although, strictly speaking, Hawker had lost its partner status, it remained very much at the heart of the project, attending all meetings and taking part in the whole range of activities. Initially the making of the Airbus was largely a Franco-German affair, but before long, men from Hatfield were arriving to help out with sales, marketing and other non-technical jobs. Adam Brown, one of Airbus Industrie's longest-serving executives whose job was to outwit and bamboozle Boeing's salesmen, arrived in 1973.

In the immediate aftermath of the British withdrawal, the Airbus partners took a hard look at the programme to examine the size of the hole left by the British and what could be done to fill it. 'We started by removing everything we could from the wing assembly,' says Schäffler. 'Firstly the moveable parts like flaps, rudders and so on. Some went to Germany, some to Holland, which got involved later. And then there was the whole question of the construction of systems in the wing which had been moved over to Germany for the A300.'[14] The British decision to pull out was to cost British companies and British suppliers millions of pounds in business. Bill Gunston, an aviation writer, maintains it caused immense damage to Britain's already weakened civil aviation business.

'It resulted,' he says, 'in a large and sustained flow of the very best British engineering and sales talent to the A300B management centres, initially in Paris and Munich and later at Toulouse. It resulted in the British aircraft industry progressively losing contact with the world's major airlines to the point where, until the launch of the smaller BAe 146, there was no contact in the field of civil airlines between any British planemaker and any major operator. It resulted in a massive expansion of the French and German equipment accessory industry, in almost every case duplicating products which could have been obtained from Britain.'[15]

However much Britain may have lost by her decision to leave Airbus, the fact that it kept the basic wing structure was crucial. If there is one single element that is critical to the performance an aircraft, it is the wing. The plane hangs on the wings, rather than vice versa, and this is as true of the Airbus as it was of the *Kitty Hawk*. The Germans readily acknowledged that no one in Europe could build aircraft wings like the British. And in Britain there was no one better than Hawker Siddeley. 'The English had conducted a very rigorous wing development programme over the years,' says Jean Roeder. 'This led to the most modern wings in the world. The English had profound knowledge of all wing problems: they had mastered the subject.'[16] While the Germans specialized in fabrication, the British preferred to machine or cast the pieces from solid metal. For the A300B, Hawker built special benches 60ft long and 12ft wide and installed numerically controlled milling machinery to cut the metal with great speed, precision and economy. It was a trick others found hard to match.

At the same time, Hawker's engineers at Hatfield had developed a new design that gave the wing much greater lift than the traditional type. According to Bill Gunston, what they did was 'to reshape the wing profile with a blunter leading edge, flatter top, greater depth (with bulged underside) and down-turned rear portion. Such a wing behaves in a way dramatically different from the traditional type. As the air encounters the wing, it is still speeded up as it rushes over the leading edge but the acceleration is barely half as great as before. Instead of having a violent peak in speed, the air speeds up only modestly; but it then retains this increased speed right back across the wing . . . As a result, instead of generating intense lift across a narrow strip near the leading edge, the new wing generates powerful lift over virtually the entire area.'[17] It was this extra lift that Hawker's engineers had succeeded in conjuring out of their wing that was, so Toulouse believed, the key to the Airbus performance.

'One thing became very quickly evident: that the considerable English share of the wing could not be shifted. There was, firstly, simply a lack of expertise,' says Schäffler. 'Furthermore, there was a lack of industrial capacity: the large machines needed simply didn't exist in France and Germany. That meant that we simply would have had to begin a completely new programme of investment, and we would certainly have lost time had we not kept the English with us.'[18]

There were some who did not share this view and looked back to an earlier era in Germany's aeronautical history. As heads were scratched about the airbus wing, two of Germany's most famous aircraft engineers, Willi Messerschmitt and Ludwig Bölkow, mounted a campaign to persuade the powers that be that they could build a lighter and simpler wing than the British.

As Schäffler tells it, the two old men, both well over seventy, built a model they trailed about after them. It was all rather embarrassing. 'We tried to prevent a situation that could have been damaging for the two men, because basically one should not make famous people look ridiculous in any way. We were confronted with a situation where people, especially the politicians, said, "Is there anything in it? Could it be that you are making aircraft that are really much more expensive and less competitive than they need be? Or are these two old gentlemen wrong?"' The question of 'the German wing' was debated at great length by all sorts of people in all sorts of places. The key question was: how vulnerable was the German wing to metal fatigue? The memory of the Comet disasters was still fresh, and people questioned whether a wing designed by the man behind the Messerschmitt 109 would stand the strain of commercial service with constant take-offs and landings. The question was raised, if a trifle pithily, during a visit to England. 'Dr Messerschmitt,' the questioner remarked, 'I believe the fatigue life of the BF 109 was about fifty hours – provided it didn't meet a Spitfire!'[19]

*

The delays caused by the political prevarication so typical of our story meant that the Europeans had lost their early lead in the airbus race to the Americans. But the news from America was not all bad. As the battle between the American engine makers for the contracts to power the American airbuses intensified, new prospects began to open up. One of the most promising was the CF6, a civil version of a state-of-the-art, high bypass engine that General Electric had developed for the military and which was now being offered to McDonnell Douglas as the power plant for a projected long-range version of the DC-10. Here, so Béteille thought, might be the engine he was looking for to replace the RB 207. What's more, if the A300 could be made a little smaller, then it would not need quite such a powerful, custom-built engine. Maybe he could buy off-the-shelf. The gap in power between the engines being developed for the long-range versions of the American tri-jets and the one Béteille needed for his airbus was beginning to close. In theory, at least, any one of the big three engine makers, including Rolls-Royce, would be in a position to help.

Béteille's difficulty, however, was that the decision was not up to him. Who supplied the engine for Airbus was, at bottom, a matter for the politicians, not the engineers. It was the governments who would have to find the money and it was the politicians who would have to answer to their taxpayers whose money it was. What would the reaction be to a European airbus powered by an American engine? Obviously, the British would be against it: they would reject any proposal that did not involve Rolls-Royce; the Germans, too, were Rolls supporters at this stage, though more for political reasons than commercial ones. The Germans were strong supporters of British membership of the Common Market, and they initially thought that a Rolls engine for Airbus would strengthen Britain's own commitment to Europe. The French, on the other hand, thought that an American-powered

Airbus might improve its chances of American sales, although they would insist that SNECMA should participate in some form or other.

When SNECMA was asked if it would like to help Airbus out, the SNECMA people were rather taken aback. It was, they thought, a bit rich to ask them to drop a long-established business connection with such an important company as Pratt & Whitney to gamble everything on something as uncertain as the Airbus. 'It could be another Caravelle,' they said. They also found it a bit shocking. The company which built engines for France's fighter aircraft had a strong military tradition. Its engineers had old-fashioned ideas about loyalty and would, so senior management believed, react badly to the idea that they should, as they saw it, betray Pratt by going over to GE whom they regarded as the enemy. Of course, Béteille could have made a direct approach to GE, but the politics were such that he needed to present this, as far as he could, as a European deal.

Shortly before the British pulled out, the three governments met in Paris to decide whether they should approve the purchase of an American engine. That the French, who never wanted Rolls-Royce anyway, would come done on the side of the Americans was never in doubt. The Germans, who initially favoured Rolls-Royce, switched sides, leaving the British in the minority.

But this did not automatically mean that Rolls-Royce was out of the race. The British company was on the list because that's what British European Airways wanted. But what dished its chances was Rolls-Royce's insistence that Airbus take second place to Lockheed. Likewise, Pratt & Whitney's JT 9D was found wanting. GE won the battle, partly because its engine was lighter, less thirsty and cheaper than the competition; partly because it had a existing track record in service with the military; and partly because it succeeded in convincing the French government that it could work happily with SNECMA.

The GE CF6-50A, which produced 49,000 lbs of thrust, was every bit as powerful as anything Rolls-Royce and Pratt & Whitney could offer. But what made it even more attractive was that Ziegler had done a deal with James Smith McDonnell of McDonnell Douglas, who allowed him to use the nacelles (the pod which houses the engine) that had been designed for the GE-powered DC-10 in return for a contribution to the cost of development. As the design of the nacelle is one of the trickier problems in aircraft manufacture, it was a decision that saved Airbus much time and money. That 'Mr Mac' was willing to help a European rival at this stage is an indication of just how little the Americans thought of the Airbus operation.

In Henri Ziegler's view the contribution that GE made to Airbus at this critical juncture is hard to overestimate. 'It is to me incomprehensible,' he says, 'that the only engine manufacturer who believed in the Airbus adventure from the outset was . . . a US manufacturer, managed, it is true, by an exceptional man, a former Wehrmacht officer. Without the support of this engine manufacturer, the A300 would not have sold on the market and would not, little by little, have eliminated the three-engined aircraft . . . on which the main engine manufacturer had placed its stakes. GE may have helped Airbus, but both the American company and its new French partner benefited substantially. Its engine . . . went on to be a bestseller and the relationship led within a few years to the formation of a joint GE/SNECMA operation called CFM International.'[20]

CHAPTER FOUR

AIRBUS MECCANO

THE AGREEMENT SIGNED by Karl Schiller for the Federal Republic and by Jean Chamant for France in a mock-up of the A300B at the Paris Air Show at Le Bourget on 29 May 1969 was a defining moment in the history of Airbus. It represented a pact between the European governments and the aerospace industry: the governments agreed to provide the money and the political support, while the member firms of the Airbus consortium undertook to produce a commercial product that would appeal to a world market.

The Le Bourget agreement reflected the change in the balance of power in Airbus. With the departure of the British, the Germans moved from being the junior partner in what had been an essentially Anglo-French venture, to being one of the two major players. At a cost of DM500 million, the Federal Republic doubled its contribution to put itself on an equal footing with the French. The two governments agreed to split the development costs for the airframe 50:50; but when the Hawker Siddeley money is taken into account, the German share of the project rose to just over 60 per cent. According to Hans Schäffler, head of Deutsche Airbus at the time, the Hawker Siddeley money was a gift from the German government. He said, 'The critical question after the British withdrawal was how was the programme going to be financed? There was . . . a tremendous readiness here on the part of the government to make things possible . . . To raise the German contribution from five hundred million deutschmarks to a thousand million in such a short time from inside the government was a huge achievement by the politicians – with Strauss and Schiller at the forefront.'[1]

Under the agreement the money was to be handed out to the main contractors, Sud Aviation and Deutsche Airbus, in annual instalments over a period of five or six years to cover the cost of research and development, for building the prototype airframes and for flight and ground testing. In addition, the governments agreed to underwrite commercial loans raised by the consortium to cover the initial production costs such as tooling, materials and work in progress. In all, the bill was close to £1,000 million.

There were two categories of loan: the first was to meet the costs of bringing the plane into production; the second was for research and development. According to sources quoted by *Flight* magazine in the autumn of 1971, the total bill for bringing the A300B up to full production by 1975 was around £700 million. Of this, the Germans were expected to pay £354 million, the French £274 million, while the remainder came from the Dutch governments and others.* The bill for research and development of the A300B was £209 million, of which £179 million came from the French and West German governments. The Dutch government and Hawker Siddeley put in £13 million apiece, but Hawker's contribution was underwritten by the government of the Federal Republic.

Apart from the cash the Germans put in to keep Hawker Siddeley, the government money was not intended as an outright gift. It was what the Germans called a *zahlbare rückwenden* or repayable loan. It was given on the understanding that once the project had reached break-even, the loan would be repaid in instalments over twenty or even thirty years, the income coming from a percentage levy on sales. If, on the other hand, the plane never reached break-even, the money was not repayable and therefore could be regarded as a gift or subsidy.

It was a far more generous arrangement than anything the banks would have offered. The loans were super soft. The government money was interest-free and there was no set schedule for repayment or even a target date for break-even. The German government was especially lenient. According to Hartmut Mehdorn, head of Deutsche Airbus and a member of the supervisory board for over twenty years, when times were hard, loans were rolled over and repayments were either postponed or cancelled completely. Initially Airbus said that it needed to sell 350 A300Bs to break even, and confidently forecast that it would comfortably pass that point within four years. But this estimate proved to be wildly optimistic.

With the British officially out of the picture (Hawker Siddeley was now simply a private contractor), Béteille and Ziegler could press ahead with renewed confidence and vigour. 'For us,' says Jean Roeder, the chief engineer of Deutsche Airbus, 'the signature of the Franco-German agreement in Paris in 1969 was really the building decision for the Airbus.'[2] Six months later, on 1 January 1970, the French rationalized their side of the operation by merging three aerospace companies, Sud Aviation, Nord Aviation and SEREB, to form Aerospatiale, which became France's largest aerospace company and its fifteenth biggest industrial group. Though officially a merger, it was, in fact, a Sud Aviation take-over.

From the outset Béteille and Ziegler, both outspoken critics of Concorde, insisted that it should be the executives of the individual companies, not the politicians, who would run the Airbus show. Both sides were keen not to repeat the Concorde mistakes. The Concorde project had become a byword for bureaucracy

---

*   The disparity between the French and German government contributions is accounted for by the fact that the Deutsche Airbus would have to rely on sub-contractors to a much greater extent than Sud Aviation.

and political interference. Concorde was a 'political' plane that owed its origin to a decision taken by the politicians, not the industry. Both sides were bound by an agreement that had the force of an international treaty which, as we have seen, neither side could bow out of without the express permission of the other. Technically, the plane makers Sud Aviation and BAC were working as sub-contractors to the French and British governments. The plane makers could not take a single decision without approval from their political masters in London and Paris. There was little or no coordination between the two sides and everything was duplicated, there being one committee for the British end of the operation and another for the French. Furthermore, the British measured in inches, while the French did it in millimetres. The French wanted a short-haul plane flying overland; the British wanted a trans-oceanic long-haul. And nobody bothered to take into account what the market actually wanted. As Matthew Lynn remarks, '[Concorde] was inspired in a mood of great optimism, but like many other products of European industry, it fundamentally missed its mark. It was a luxury product introduced into a mass market; but the people who had designed and built it had not understood the economics of the airline business: pack in as many as possible on big, cheap-to-run planes . . .'[3]

Famously, the British called it 'Concord', while the French insisted on 'Concorde'. But however it was spelt, the programme belied its name. As costs rose and committees proliferated, Franco-British relations deteriorated to the point where the British, at least, were making anti-French jokes at official functions. The American author Wayne Biddle tells the story of a British speaker whose comment about French brains was, 'Good as new and never been used.'[4] For their part, the French ruled that no document in English had any force until it was translated into French.

But there was also a positive side to Concorde, which was, so insiders say, of great benefit to Airbus. At working level there was a great deal of mutual respect between the French and British engineers. Some of those who were to play decisive roles in the Airbus story, like Jean Pierson, spent many fruitful months in Weybridge working alongside the BAC people on Concorde, and the same is true, in the reverse direction, of the British. Before becoming the British 'Mr Airbus', BAC's Bob McKinlay, who was later one of the two British representatives on the Airbus supervisory board, was in the charge of the British Concorde operation at Filton. Even more important, for companies like Sud Aviation the experience of working on such a high-tech project as Concorde was immensely valuable when it came to building the Airbus. As Jean Pierson, who was in charge of Concorde production at Toulouse before taking over as managing director of Airbus Industrie in 1985, told me, 'A lot of the Airbus technology was started with Concorde. When Aerospatiale came to design the Airbus, they used the design office of Concorde. It was the same with the systems. The Aerospatiale design of

the Airbus cockpit owed a great deal to its experience with Concorde, and the
same is true of suppliers like Dowty.'[5]

*

In the wake of the Le Bourget agreement morale was high. After all the delays it
looked, at long last, as if the politics were over and the plane-making could begin.
Nonetheless, it took another eighteen months of sometimes quite difficult talks
between the French and the Germans before they could decide what kind of corporate animal Airbus should be. There were a number of alternatives. Should it be a
fully-fledged independent limited company with private shareholders and investors
like Boeing or McDonnell Douglas? Should it be a wholly owned government enterprise with the taxpayer not only picking up the tab but taking the risk as well? Or
should it be a mixed enterprise, half private and half public?

As a private company, Airbus stood no chance. What bank or institution in its
right mind would be willing to fund a brand new, multinational start-up company
whose only assets were the promise of government funds; whose income was nil;
whose appetite for development capital would be gargantuan; and whose mission
was to make an aeroplane which might or might not sell in sufficient quantities to
produce, if it was very lucky, a profit in ten years' time? Furthermore, to ask the par-
ticipating companies, such as state-owned but cash-strapped Sud Aviation which
had not paid a dividend for ten years, or Hawker Siddeley, to find the money to buy
shares in the new enterprise was plainly a non-starter. If Airbus as a private enterprise was impractical, so too was the concept of it as a state-owned enterprise.
Ideology apart, the memory of Concorde was too fresh in politicians' minds for that
idea to be a runner.

What was needed was an organizational structure that would give the Airbus
business the commercial muscle and flexibility it needed, while at the same time
minimizing the risk for the shareholder/partners. The trick was to create the impression that the partners had put their own money on the line, but to eliminate the risk
by getting the governments to underwrite the operation. The Germans argued the
case for limited liability. Airbus Industrie, they said, should be a limited company
with a capital of no more than £11.4 million, the idea being that if everything went
wrong, this was the maximum the shareholders would lose. But the French were
unimpressed. Their idea was bigger, bolder and much more ingenious.

Two years earlier the French government had decided to create a new kind of corporate entity called a *groupement d'intérêt économique* (GIE). Designed to help the
wine industry and other small enterprises, the GIE was a mechanism to make it
easier for small businessmen to set up cooperatives. Instead of going to the trouble
and expense of forming partnerships or companies themselves, the businesses
would become part of a GIE whose function was 'to enable its members to avail

themselves of all means to develop and improve their own economic activity or increase the results of such activity'. How this was to be done was deliberately left extremely vague. It was up to the members of the GIE themselves to decide exactly what they wanted the GIE to do and how it was going to do it. The only rules were that the GIE was to be a non-profit making body that paid no taxes and could negotiate and enter into binding contracts with third parties. It was subject to outside audit, but the full accounts were confidential to the partners.

The way it worked in the wine industry was that the individual vineyards joined to form a cooperative, which made and marketed the wine from the grapes supplied by the growers. The cultivation of the grapes was the work of the individual vineyards. Each member of the cooperative, or GIE, had two income streams. As a supplier to the GIE, each vineyard was paid for its contribution, and as a shareholder in the GIE, it received dividends in proportion to its stake in the business. At the same time, there was no reason why vineyards could not continue to maintain their identity as independent businesses. The GIE system was nothing if not flexible.

The more the founding fathers of Airbus thought about it, the more suitable the GIE formula seemed to be for their own business. Aerospatiale and Deutsche Airbus may have been somewhat larger than the average French vineyard, but the founders reasoned that if the GIE idea could work for the wine industry, it might be equally good for Airbus, whose whole rationale, after all, was based on partnership and the pooling of resources to a common end. As Adam Brown explained, 'The partnership arrangement gave us a lot of flexibility. It meant that new partners could be added. But it also helped to answer the conundrum: how do you sell a multi-million pound product with no capacity? The GIE was a tool to enable members to make profits.'[6]

Airbus Industrie formally came into existence on 18 December 1970. From the outset it was agreed that each industrial partner should have an equity share in the GIE which corresponded to its government's share in the project. Thus when Airbus Industrie came into being, France's Aerospatiale and Germany's Deutsche Airbus were each given a 46.7 per cent stake in the consortium. The balance was held by the Dutch firm VFW-Fokker, which came in after the British had left. Nine months later these three partners were joined by a fourth, Spain's Construcciones Aeronauticas SA (CASA), which had been awarded the contract to build the horizontal part of the tail. Founded in 1923 to build planes for the Spanish Air Force, CASA had enjoyed mixed fortunes. During the 1950s and the 1960s it had a rough ride and produced mixed results. It had invested unsuccessfully in the automotive and railway business and had done some maintenance work for the US Air Force. It had also worked with Dassault, making fuselage sections for the Mercure. But in the early 1970s the technocrats who took charge of Spain's economy in the last years of General Franco's regime shook up the company's management. As part of a nationwide drive to open up Spain to foreign investment, younger, more outward-looking managers were recruited and the company became more involved in cooperative ventures with foreign companies.

It was against this background that Spain's largest aerospace company became Airbus's smallest partner. The move, part of a wider campaign to draw Franco's Spain more fully into the European mainstream, was largely political. But there were industrial advantages. A great deal of money was spent on the highly-automated tail-making plant, which soon acquired a reputation as one of the most efficient and profitable of all the seventeen Airbus plants in Europe. In 2000 I was told by a senior, recently retired CASA official that Airbus work that year had accounted for 60 per cent of its turnover and 66 per cent of its profits of 15,000 million pesetas.

But with only a 4.2 per cent share in the consortium, the Spanish, with a single representative on the supervisory board, lacked the clout to have much influence on internal Airbus politics. CASA people still talk of the time when the company's president arrived in Munich for a supervisory board meeting at the appointed hour, only to find no one there. Half an hour later the French and Germans showed up, having used the time to agree on their position.

*

The management company, Airbus Industrie, was to all intents and purposes a shell: it had no share capital, paid no taxes and owned virtually nothing apart from its head office buildings overlooking the Blagnac airfield just outside Toulouse. It published no accounts. And its sole liabilities were the staff wages and the cost of equipping the offices. Everything else about the making and manufacture of the Airbus was the responsibility of the partners and their sub-contractors, the most important of which was Hawker Siddeley, the makers of the wing. The fact that Airbus Industrie was a corporate pygmy did not, of course, disguise the fact that it was Toulouse that set the pace.

Headed by a small management team whose boss has been a Frenchman with a German as a second-in-command ever since its inception, Airbus Industrie was from the very beginning responsible for the design, development, flight testing, sales and marketing of the aircraft. It handled all PR, media relations and publicity.

The Airbus Industrie publicity machine quickly established a reputation as a very skilful, if not ruthless, operation, devoted to harassing and harrying the opposition, particularly Boeing, at every opportunity. Insiders say that because it was so far behind the Americans, it took the deliberate decision to present itself as a class act. Everything had to be of the best. The buildings were glossy and the wine used for the christening of new aircraft was *premier cru*. The best chef in Toulouse was hired to prepare the food in the executive dining rooms. Airbus *chic* was in marked contrast to the more laid-back, informal atmosphere at Boeing where the engineers, and even the executives, went to work wearing crew-cuts, plaid shirts and blue jeans.

Many years later Ziegler was to admit that the Airbus style was perhaps too aggressive. But he made no apologies. In 1996, looking back more than a quarter of a century, he remarked in a comment that suffers a little in translation but whose meaning is clear enough: 'Molested more often than our turn between the compassionate smiles of dubious operators and not always backed up by our own founders, we became aggressive simply by our instinct of survival. We have several times been criticized for this aggressiveness, sometimes excessive as it is difficult to modulate. But I think that especially at the start we would not have survived without it.'[7]

For over thirty years AI was to be the spider at the centre of the Airbus web. But it was far from all-powerful. The executive team at Toulouse may have called the shots, but the *administrateur gérant*, as the managing director of the GIE was called, was answerable to a supervisory board. With the formal creation of Airbus Industrie on 18 December 1970, Franz-Josef Strauss was appointed president and chairman of the supervisory board – thus setting a tradition whereby the Airbus president is a German and the managing director is French. As Henri Ziegler said many years later, 'I knew it was essential to have the industrial partners as members of a legally-established corporation, with a board, a chairman and president. Otherwise nobody was responsible.'[8]

The supervisory board was an unwieldy beast that proved hard to manage. It was at its largest during the early 1980s, shortly after the British had rejoined, when its numbers grew to seventeen, of which Aerospatiale and Deutsche Airbus provided six members apiece, the British four and the Spanish one. As the former president of American Airlines, George Warde knew all about life in the boardroom. But even he was taken aback by what he found when he joined Airbus as head of product support. 'When I came to a board meeting for the first time, I was somewhat overwhelmed. It was in Germany somewhere. And I thought I was in the United Nations because we had individual booths, with interpreters that were interpreting German, French, English and Dutch. I was also overwhelmed to see the room full of people. I counted at one point in time forty-six people in this board meeting. It reminded me of this joke about how does one govern a country like France which has 352 different kinds of cheese? Well, it turns out that each member had only one vote and the rest of the people were advisors: there were spare part advisors, engineering advisors, support advisors, sales advisors and what have you. So that you always had a support in Airbus . . . fair game to be shot at by whoever decides to shoot.'[9]

The British, in particular, found this cumbersome system very irksome. 'In the early days the board was extremely large, with up to forty-five people in the room,' says Bob McKinlay, one of the four representatives of British Aerospace. 'It wasn't very effective, though it got better later after Jean Pierson had taken over.'[10] But whatever its imperfections, the supervisory board was the one mechanism that gave the partners a formal say in the running of the business.

Headed by a president and made up of the representatives of the industrial partners, the board met three or four times a year. Its job was to decide broad lines of policy, to approve the accounts and to authorize the launch of new programmes. But most important of all, the supervisory board was the forum in which the partners bargained amongst themselves about how the work on any one programme should be shared out. The loyalties of the partners were divided. As shareholders, they had every interest that Airbus Industrie bought cheap and sold dear. But as suppliers, their aim was to sell expensive and to buy cheaply, and they held the view that the more money they could make out of their Airbus business, the better. As shareholders, the position was quite the reverse. As members of the supervisory board, which oversaw the contractual arrangements between Airbus Industrie and its suppliers, they were, for the most part, negotiating with themselves. It was all very awkward.

Since Airbus Industrie did not haggle with its members over individual prices for individual items, but only argued about how the work should be divided, one might reasonably conclude that the suppliers were in an unusually strong position. If, after Britan's re-entry in 1978, Airbus Industrie had been, for example, unhappy about the cost of the English wing, its only sanction would have been to give the work to the Germans. But as a move of this kind would have undoubtedly caused the British government to withdraw its funding, this was hardly a practical proposition.

On occasion, by all accounts, the meetings of the supervisory board to decide the work-share took on the air of an oriental bazaar. Because nobody told the truth during these sessions, it was known in Airbus Industrie as 'the liars' club'. The debate was sometimes heated and almost always prolonged. In 2001, for example, ten years after the first flight of the A340, the details of the share-out between the partners for their work on the plane had still not been agreed.

The concept of work-share was an integral part of the Airbus system. Although each company in the consortium had its own legal and corporate identity, each was allocated its own share of work. On the A300B the French did the nose, the flight deck, the control systems, the lower part of the fuselage's centre section that housed the landing gear and the final assembly; the Germans did both ends of the fuselage and the upper part of the centre section; the British built the all-important wing box that contained the fuel tanks; the Dutch did the moving parts of the wing, such as the flaps, spoilers etc; and the Spanish made the tail.

It is this novel work-sharing arrangement, conceived and executed by Roger Béteille, which is at the heart of the Airbus idea. That the making of something as complex as an airliner should be broken down into its discrete parts was, of course, nothing new. On the 747 programme Boeing subcontracted 65 per cent of the work to some 20,000 different companies in fifty states and several foreign countries. Only the wings and front half of the fuselage, including the flight deck, were made at Everett plant, the world's largest factory building; it is so large that, as every visitor to Seattle is told, it has its own micro-climate where, in certain conditions, clouds form under the roof. But while Boeing relied heavily on sub-contractors, Béteille took the idea a great deal further.

What made the Airbus system so revolutionary was the idea that the main parts of the aircraft – the fuselage, the cockpit, the wings and the tailplane – should be made quite independently of each other in different places, in different countries hundreds of miles apart. The concept was that each section would be as complete as possible with all equipment, controls and cabling already fitted. And it would only be at the very last moment that the pieces of what Béteille called 'Airbus Meccano' would be brought together for final assembly.

Just as Airbus evolved a new way of making planes, so it invented a new way of paying its partners/suppliers. It was a system that most outsiders – and even some insiders – found hard to understand. Payment was determined not by Airbus Industrie setting a price for the component parts, but by talking through with the partners what the overall cost of the programme might be, negotiating with them what part each should play, and allocating to each player an agreed percentage. As the money from sales flowed in, each partner was then paid according to the formula. That, at least, was the theory.

As Bob McKinlay explained:

Airbus doesn't negotiate a price with individual partners. It negotiates with all the partners. And all it does is that it negotiates on the sub-division of the manufacturing costs between partners. Essentially it negotiates percentages. It then tries to negotiate the 100 per cent – trying to set the 100 per cent at a level where Airbus Industrie is capable of making a profit. When you negotiate a price for a component – be it a wing or a fuselage – no money changes hands. It is only a value statement which is then added up and the bottom line is the sum of the production costs, the sum of the profit and loss at the aircraft's selling level.

Airbus doesn't have a mechanism where it pays for wings and then sorts out the profits of the business. It actually works out what is called a key account. It predicts for a year what the situation is going to be taking into account transfer prices; it takes into account the sales that are known in that year for each product; and then it constructs a key for each partner. And then when for every amount of money that comes in from an airline, you get that percentage. So money is flowing in all the time. If Airbus Industrie were short of money, it would flow out as cash. In the very early days when we were partners, we did actually have to provide them with cash. That stopped fairly early on when they became cash positive.

You always know what money is coming in from the year's production. And then the accounts do an analysis which shows whether you have made a profit or not. For British Aerospace things began to change in around 1990, but it is a very complex situation because we were still negotiating prices for the A320 – long after the aircraft was delivered.[11]

However closely locked together the companies might be in Airbus, the one thing they did not share with each other was any information about how much money they were making, or losing, from their share of the operation. Once their share of the project had been established, it was up to the company to extract as much profit as it could by any method it thought appropriate. If it discovered new ways of cutting costs or raising productivity, it was under no obligation to pass these savings on either to Airbus Industrie or its other partners. Beneath the surface, the national companies constantly schemed and manoeuvred to increase their share of the work at the expense of the others. The Germans were envious of the British near-monopoly of the wing work, and the British were resentful of the French stranglehold on the design leadership. For their part, the French resisted any serious challenge to the primacy of Toulouse. But as we shall see later, positions were absolutely not fixed. Exactly who did what was to be the stuff of Airbus politics for the next quarter of a century. The Airbus operation was, above all, a consortium of state-owned and private companies. It was not, by any stretch of the imagination, a cooperative.

The other feature of the GIE system was that its finances were completely impenetrable. As the partners insisted in playing their cards so close to their chests, the Airbus Industrie management itself used to complain that it had no clear idea how much money the business as a whole was making or losing. It simply had to take what it was told by the partners on trust. Bob McKinlay informed me, 'The problem is that with a GIE you know what the joint programme is like but you don't know the individual parts. The standard answer that you look at the partners' results to see how Airbus is doing was for the benefit of the Americans; to remind them that it was a GIE and it is not necessary for a GIE to make a profit. You can actually find in the literature that a GIE is not intended to make a profit. The financial responsibility and the profits lie with the partners. But to some extent that was an answer to turn away wrath. You can't get much detail from partners' individual accounts.'[12]

Those outside the Airbus family are more critical. 'The whole process has been utterly untransparent,' says Keith Hayward. 'Under this system it is quite possible for Airbus to make a thumping great loss on the component, while the contractor makes an equally large profit on his private account. Airbus Industrie publishes no accounts and the contractors conceal what they make or lose on Airbus operations within their own balance sheets.'[13]

The GIE was not set up with the deliberate intention of concealing what the Airbus partners were up to, but that is how the Americans came to regard it. They were to be particularly critical of what they regarded as the lack of transparency and financial accountability, and were deeply suspicious of an organization that paid no taxes and published no accounts. They came to regard Airbus Industrie as some sort of government-sponsored Trojan horse whose mission was to defeat the forces of honest American private enterprise in a thoroughly underhand and unAmerican manner. But this is to anticipate: some years were to pass before these questions became a burning issue.

*

At first sight Airbus Industrie looks like just another multi-national company with its head in France and the various parts of its body scattered all over Europe. But what was so original about the Airbus idea was the virtually total separation of the production and management of the enterprise. If the president of Boeing wanted to see how things were going on the shop floor, he only had to step outside the executive suite a few blocks away.† If his counterpart at Airbus wanted to do the same thing, he would need to take the company plane to England or Germany. However closely Aerospatiale and Hawker Siddeley might work together on the Airbus, each company was responsible for its own contribution, and each had complete control over its own affairs with its own board and its shareholders. As it so happened, the French company was state-owned and the British was private, but each was an autonomous entity. The set-up in Germany was a little more complicated: it was, in effect, a consortium within a consortium. There, the five companies who worked together on Airbus were members of the Deutsche Airbus group which acted as paymaster and negotiated on their behalf with Airbus Industrie. But apart from regular planning meetings with Airbus Industrie, the only formal contact the executives of the partner companies had with the Airbus management were the quarterly meetings of the Airbus supervisory board.

Given the political need to share out the work between the member countries and member firms, an arrangement of this kind, however improbable it might seem, was inevitable. As Béteille himself admits, '"Airbus Meccano" was the direct consequence of the division of labour.' Yet the system would only function properly if all the firms involved were organized and trained to work in precise harmony. Every individual piece of the jigsaw had to be designed and manufactured to fit exactly. There was, says Béteille, no margin for error. 'On a fuselage with a diameter of 5 metres 64 centimetres, the tolerance was of the order of one-tenth of a millimetre – that's to say, more precise than a Swiss watch.'

---

† Since Boeing has now moved its head office to Chicago, this is no longer true.

The only way such results could be achieved was by scrupulous coordination and constant checking. It was no good for Hawker Siddeley to devote its best efforts to produce the wing if it didn't fit exactly onto the fuselage section built by French engineers in Toulouse 800 miles away. Before finishing the wing, Hawker Siddeley inserted specially-made plugs whose dimensions were identical to those of the French-built section of the fuselage into which the wing was to be fitted. Once the final corrections and adjustments had been made, the final settings were locked, wired and sealed with lead seals that remained in position until the wing was delivered safely to Toulouse. Airbus people say that solving these technical difficulties was the least of their worries. 'We never had big problems with making these interfaces,' says Jean Roeder, the chief engineer for Deutsche Airbus. 'The plans for separating the sections had been very carefully defined. And a great amount of time had been spent developing the parts so that they would fit together.'[14]

From the beginning Airbus argued that however Heath Robinson-like this system might appear, it was at least as good, if not better, than the more conventional Boeing approach. As Hans Schäffler puts it, 'The shed for the final assembly is usually an enormously costly building which means a huge investment for all the built-in parts for the tests and checks and so forth. It really is nonsense to do all those things in a final assembly shed, just because it's there when you could easily do them more cheaply elsewhere.'[15] Schäffler argues that what he describes as 'this pushing away' of the subsystems and the related subcontractors in the production factory had an extremely positive effect on the cost-effectiveness of the aeroplane. 'These days,' he says, 'all that happens in Toulouse is that a few fuselage seams are welded, the whole thing is stuck and screwed together, and air, electricity, and hydraulics are added. It really is an evident improvement on what was the norm before Airbus.' According to Schäffler, the A300 was the world's first 'plug-and-play' plane. 'The whole basic concept has already been made. The systems will be built in beforehand. The plugs will be attached. The screws are in place. And basically the whole thing can just be put together. Mechanics are in retreat and electronics in advance.'

However starry-eyed the vision, at the beginning there were a vast number of humdrum but nonetheless important problems to be sorted out. Should the measurements be metric or imperial? How should the drawings be labelled and what would the working language be? It was quickly agreed that as Airbus was trying to build a plane for world markets, it would speak English and use the same measurements as the Americans. Béteille thought it would be hard enough trying to sell to American airlines without the added complications of translating everything from centimetres into inches. 'If you have to convince them that they have to buy new sets of tools and re-train their mechanics, your chances are going to be nil,' he argued.[16] Even so, it proved harder than Airbus imagined to iron out national differences, which extended even to the way in which joints were riveted and screws were screwed.

In the early days Airbus people say you could look at a particular join and tell just by looking at it which were French rivets and which were German screws. One production chief became so frustrated by this lack of common standards that he asked his wife, an artist, to knit him a pullover on which the different screws and screw heads were depicted. He would then point to the different pictures on his pullover and say, 'It's got to be like this and it's not got to be like that.' One man recalls a controller of Air France – the first customer – as saying, 'You can blindfold me. Lead me into the aeroplane. Turn me round ten times until I don't know where I am. And then let me touch parts of the plane and I will tell who built it.'[17]

The real problem posed by 'Airbus Meccano' was not the creation of common rules and standards, but the logistics of an operation whose main factories were hundreds of miles apart. It is, for example, 800 miles from Chester to Toulouse and 900 miles from Toulouse to Hamburg and that's how the crow flies; the distance by sea is much longer. The first plan was to build the really large components such as the wings and fuselage in plants which had direct access to the sea. It was no accident that the German contributions were built in the port cities of Hamburg and Bremen, while the English did their work in a factory with good motorway links to Liverpool. The main drawback to this sensible plan was that Toulouse, the main centre of operations, is about 100 miles from the sea. 'It is not exactly the ideal place in which to assemble the parts of a very big aeroplane,' a British Aerospace man said to me dryly. On arrival at Bordeaux, the next stage was to send the English wings and German fuselage sections up the River Garonne for about 50 miles, and then across country by transporter to Toulouse. Because of the disruption to traffic caused by loads weighing many tonnes and over 100 feet long, the journeys had to be mostly at night. And to clear the way through the small towns and villages of the French countryside, telegraph poles had to be taken down and electricity supplies cut off. As Bernard Lathière recalls, 'The convoy from Bordeaux to Toulouse was huge, with three teams of police; one at the front who protected the people who broke down walls or cut down trees, another which protected the convoy itself, and the last one which protected the people trying to replant the trees and mend the walls.'[18] It was all very dramatic and exciting. But level heads in Toulouse soon realized that if this routine was to be repeated on a regular weekly basis, then they would soon have a revolution in south-west France on their hands. It just wasn't practical.

It was Felix Kracht, the production manager, who came up with the idea that saved the day. Through his American contacts he came to hear of the exploits of a former Boeing pilot called Jack Conway, who with his small moustache and black silk scarf cut a dashing, Erroll Flynn-like figure. He had been asked by NASA to build something that would carry parts of its Saturn rocket from California to Florida. In the Mojave desert where old aircraft were sent to die, Conway found what he was looking for: pieces of a Boeing 377 Stratocruiser and its military version, a C97, which he cobbled together to make a plane 34 metres long and 7 metres in diameter. Conway called the first version that flew in September 1962 the Pregnant Guppy, which three years later became the Super Guppy. The moment he saw it, Kracht realized that here was the answer to Airbus's logistical problems. The plane's nose swung away to allow whole wing and fuselage sections to be loaded and flown back and forth across Europe with the minimum of fuss. It was not exactly cheap, but the convenience and saving in time compared to the previous method more than compensated for the expense. As the battle with Boeing warmed up in the late 1970s, Seattle's publicists would pour scorn on these arrangements. Airbus hit back by superimposing a map of Europe on one of North America which attempted to demonstrate that Boeing's network of sub-contractors for the 747 was more widely-spread than Airbus's and that no site was more than two hours as the Super Guppy flies from any other. What's more, the Airbus PR section said, the people that loaded the parts were the same people who had made them, and those that unloaded them were the ones who put them together: so they took care. And as nobody took pot shots from the side of track while the goods were in transit, which is what happened in America, there was no need for a repair shop at the other end. At air shows the attention the Super Guppy invariably attracted provided Airbus with useful publicity.

Quite apart from the logistical and technical problems, there were real cultural differences among the members of the Airbus team. And though the French and Germans had worked together on the Transall military transport aircraft, the Airbus was another thing entirely. Just as the stakes were much higher, so were the pressures. The Germans took some time to get used to the French way of working and vice versa. Oddly, the Germans found the French a trifle rigid and formal: 'If you compare a French and a German business, the structure is very different,' says Hans Schäffler. 'A French business has a much stronger hierarchy and it is much more affected by decisions from the top. In France, an issue goes up to board which says, "It's like this and like that" and then there's no more discussion'. In France someone has to be there to say what to do, and the others have to do it. End of discussion, or else nothing happens . . . I still remember one time in Toulouse, a German was having a meeting, so he takes out his piece of paper and writes down an agenda, goes to the meeting and thinks he will start with point 1, then point 2, 3, 4 and 5. The first thing I learnt was that it won't work. Basically at the end of a meeting nothing is decided. It's more about putting a paper on the table so that everybody has a feeling we're going to talk about that today. But skip trying to keep to a particular order, but let the discussions take their course, join in and be sure that by the end that everything has been talked about. And if necessary, if the talks were insufficient, stick to the French principle: anything which wasn't decided properly, write into the minutes. This will be distributed and if no one protests, then we've attained what we wanted anyway.'[19]

At the beginning the atmosphere in Toulouse was more than a little tense. Some people were homesick, others were protective of their professional reputations, and nobody had much experience of working together so intensely and so closely. It took some time, Schäffler says, for preconceptions and prejudices about each other to evaporate. 'The Germans always believed the French only drink red wine and do nothing twice over. And as for the Germans . . . they are just mindless workers who will do anything if you just shove a piece of paper in their hand and tell them what to do.' But as the French and Germans became more used to working together and as increasing numbers of Germans came to live and work in France and *vice versa*, the feeling that they were all engaged on a common programme began to develop. The Germans no longer automatically looked to the German side of the operation for leadership and problem-solving, and the same was true of the French.

From time to time there were outbreaks of the 'not invented here' syndrome. Everybody was very conscious that this was an experiment conducted by Frenchmen in France. The French team was playing at home. For everybody else it was an away game. 'The French saw themselves a bit like godparents to the Germans and always felt they had to keep an eye on them or else they would come to a sticky end,' recalls Schäffler. 'Things were made worse by the language problem. Because there were translators at almost every meeting, things could get very difficult and drawn out. Because the subject was technical, the translators got bogged down and, unable to communicate on their own, people suffered a loss of confidence. Helping to over-come these problems was one of Felix Kracht's greatest achievements. He could not only translate literally, but he could convey the essence of what was being said and basically bring people together.' Kracht was apparently brilliant at defusing con-frontation and creating consensus. 'Management by Translation', he called it. Béteille preferred 'Management by Persuasion'. But whatever it was called, it amounted to the same thing.

Despite these difficulties, the progress of the A300 from definition to its first flight was, so the engineers say, remarkably smooth. From the start Béteille went to great lengths to ensure that the airlines, led by Air France, Lufthansa, AirInter (the French domestic airline) and BEA, were involved as consultants in the planning and development. The team listened carefully to what they had to say but, mindful of the fact that they were building a plane to sell in world markets, they did not take everything they were told for gospel. The views of BEA were treated with particular caution, as the British airline was well known for what was described as its 'special wishes', which had to be catered for on every project.

Although Air France and Lufthansa could, as the national airlines of the two main sponsor countries, hardly avoid ordering the plane, they both indicated that they were not prepared to be pushed about. Air France said flatly that the 250-seat A300B was too small for its needs. The response was to stretch the fuselage enough to add another three rows of seats, taking capacity to 270. The B1 became the B2, and on 3 September 1970 Air France duly signed a letter of intent to buy six. It was the consortium's very first order. Lufthansa delayed for what seemed an age before ordering three, and there were also orders from AirInter.

There were great hopes for Spain. As the price for its share in the consortium, the Spanish government had agreed that the state airline, Iberia, would buy no fewer than thirty A300Bs. But nobody, it seems, had told Iberia. When in January 1972 CASA came to place its order, it was for no more than four airbuses with an option on a further eight. It was still a long way short of the seventy-five orders from Air France, Lufthansa and BEA that the politicians had talked about, but at least it was a start. On 28 October 1972 the A300B prototype flew for the first time. And when the plane made its commercial debut with an Air France flight from Paris to London on 23 May 1974, it was five years almost to the day since the French and the Germans had signed the agreement at Le Bourget. Six and half years had passed since the Lancaster House ceremony in London that had launched the project. But now, after all the talk, the planning, the double-dealing and the double-crosses, something tangible had been accomplished.

CHAPTER FIVE

SLEEPLESS IN SEATTLE

W HEN THE EUROPEAN AIRBUS was first mooted, the Americans first ignored it, then patronized it and eventually mocked it. The idea of the Europeans, who had never yet built a civil airliner that could compete on world markets, matching Boeing, Lockheed and McDonnell Douglas at their own game was regarded as laughable. 'When we started off,' Adam Brown told me, 'this industry was completely dominated by the Americans. First they said, "the plane will never fly"; then they said, "it will never get certificated"; then they said, "it will never sell"; and finally they said that with the makers thousands of miles away, "it will never get the support".'[1]

Jean Roeder remembers all too clearly his first encounter with a big-time American plane maker. In the autumn of 1976, when things looked as if they couldn't get any worse for the Europeans, Roeder was sent to the McDonnell Douglas headquarters at St Louis to talk to the Americans about joining forces to build a 200-seat passenger jet. While keen to cooperate, Douglas had clearly decided it would do no harm to put the Europeans in their place. On arrival the Airbus team was presented with a large sheet of paper bearing the logos of all McDonnell Douglas's airline customers. 'When we counted them,' Roeder recalls, 'we saw that Douglas had sixty or seventy. We thought, "how many did we have?" And so we sat there quite miserably.'[2]

For Airbus salesmen in the States the going was extremely hard. In the early 1970s Arthur Howes, an ex-Hawker Siddeley engineer, was sent to the Sud Aviation's New York office at 633 Third Avenue to start the Airbus sales effort in North America. He quickly discovered that the reputation of European aircraft in North America was not high. He recalls one airline president telling him, 'The trouble with you people is that you build excellent Grand Prix racing cars but what we actually want is a Ford pick-up truck that you turn the key in the morning, the engine starts, and the thing continues to operate all day without any problems. And if it has a problem, it can still go on functioning satisfactorily until we can repair the problem overnight. With your Grand Prix cars that, of course, is not possible: they need maintaining all the time.'[3]

On its very first appearance on the North American continent, Airbus came uncomfortably close to confirming this unhappy reputation. In September 1973

Béteille and Ziegler decided the moment had come to show the Americans what the A300 could do. The plan was to fly from Toulouse to Dakar in West Africa and then across the Atlantic to San Paolo in Brazil before flying on to West Palm Beach in Florida to touch down in North America for the first time. The plane was heavily loaded. Not only was it necessary to take all the spare parts, but as Airbus was anxious to make a good impression, there was, as one old hand remembers, 'a tremendous supply of very expensive glassware and champagne'.

Everything went smoothly until the plane arrived in Florida, where it was discovered that there was some foreign matter in one of the engines, probably the result of a bird strike in Africa. And although there was some damage, the engine was unaffected and temperatures and oil pressures were normal. The next day, on arrival at Mexico City, there was another inspection before the plane took off that afternoon for Chicago. Almost immediately after take-off the warning lights indicated that the oil pressure in one of the two engines was dangerously low. It seems that the ground crew had not fastened the covering properly, thus causing an oil leak. The pilots shut down the engine and requested permission to land. Even on two engines, Mexico City requires some care. It is over 7,000 feet high and the afternoon is very hot. At the very last minute, with the aircraft already lined up for the runway, the tower told the pilot to switch runways. The plane was by this time so low that in making the manoeuvre it brushed the trees on the edge of the airport. The people in the front of the plane said that as they were at 400 feet at the time, there was no reason for anxiety: the people in the cabin said that if that's the case, Mexico City has got 400-foot trees. There was one point of agreement. However alarming the incident might have been, it proved how well the plane could fly on only one engine.

Nonetheless, the autumn of 1973 was a bad time to be trying to sell new aircraft, let alone one from what the Americans regarded as a rag-bag of European manufacturers with different languages, different cultures, different systems of measurement and with no commercial track record to speak of. The Americans admired the technology of Britain's Trident and had even bought France's Caravelle but were rightly scornful of the Europeans' capacity to sell or even market their planes to anyone other than themselves. The prospects for the Airbus in North America were not helped by the fact that the appearance of the A300 in American skies coincided, almost exactly, with the decision of Pan Am and other American airlines to reject Concorde.

These factors all played a part in the muted reception for Airbus in the States. But it was the events that flowed from the renewed outbreak of war in the Middle East in October 1973 that changed the picture completely. Less than a month after the A300's debut in the United States, Egypt and Syria invaded Israel. In response to American support for Israel, the member states of OPEC, the Arab oil-producing cartel led by Saudi Arabia and Iran, imposed a series of production cut-backs and price hikes. Coupled with an embargo on oil exports to North America, these moves quadrupled the price of oil. The effect on the economies of Western countries was devastating. Overnight, assumptions about the growth and prosperity of key industries were overturned as economists came to terms with a world where fuel was no longer cheap. No industry was hit harder than the aircraft business. The resulting recession discouraged passengers and led airlines either to cancel existing orders or to postpone new ones. At the same time, the increase in the price of fuel completely altered the economics of air travel. The cost of fuel had, of course, always been an important factor. But with an increase of this magnitude, airline bosses who had ordered the fuel-hungry DC-10s and Tristars began to look at their fleets with a fresh eye.

Of the three major American civil aircraft makers, Boeing was probably the best-placed to withstand the oil-price shock. But even so, Seattle was not in the best of health. While McDonnell Douglas and Lockheed were embarking on their costly, if not foolhardy, airbus adventures, Boeing was only just beginning to recover from the crisis brought on by its extraordinarily bold, not to say reckless, decision to launch the 747. By building their wide-bodied tri-jets, Lockheed and Douglas were aiming to satisfy a market that they believed was already there; on the other hand Boeing, much more daring, had been trying to create an entirely new market – one that could only be defined by the airplane itself. Ultimately, Boeing, with a characteristic combination of determination and ruthlessness, succeeded – but the venture very nearly killed the company. Even for an industry that likes to play what it describes as 'a sporty game', this was one for the record books.

Quite early on, Boeing knew that the 747 would probably cost more than the company could afford. After a board meeting on October 1965, Bill Allen turned to John Yeasting, the vice-president of the commercial airplane division, to tell him, 'I woke up this morning in a cold sweat. That 747 of yours! Here I have been going all over the country saying how impossible it would be to undertake the supersonic transport without government support. This 747 will cost us at least half what the SST development will cost.'[4] Yeasting did not disagree. He thought the 747 was a terrifying project. But what no one knew at the time was that it would cost nearly four times as much as Boeing had invested in its entire commercial airplane family.

Few people, apart from Pan Am's Juan Trippe, wanted the 747 – at least not at first. Even Boeing did not have a great deal of faith in it: it never believed it would become the company's cash cow over the next three decades and thought of it as a stop-gap before the age of supersonic travel dawned. Large as it was, the jumbo seemed rather boring by comparison. In 1967, as work on the 747 was reaching a crescendo, Bill Allen, in a flush of enthusiasm, predicted that work on building the SST prototypes would generate 9,000 jobs. There seemed every reason to be confident. On the other side of the Atlantic, Concorde was about to make its first appearance, and the space race in which Boeing, as the makers of NASA's Lunar Orbiter, was heavily involved, was in full swing. It was only after the US Senate voted on 23 March 1971 to cut off all further funding for the SST project that Boeing was forced to realize just what an important part the 747 had to play in the company's future.

The 747's first appearance on the world stage was on 15 January 1970, when Pat Nixon, the president's wife, christened *Clipper Young America* at Washington's Dulles Airport for the 747's first commercial flight. Unhappily, not everything went smoothly. While still on the tarmac one of the engines overheated and the passengers were forced to disembark. Six hours later, at around 1.30 in the morning, they set off again in another plane, the *Clipper Constitution*, to a new destination. Instead of going to Paris, the flight had been diverted to London, where after an uneventful flight the 324 passengers, refreshed by quantities of champagne and strawberries, duly arrived.

A new era in jet transport had begun. In less than twenty years air travel had changed from being something reserved for a privileged minority to an aggressively promoted mass market commodity. With the 747 came cheap long-distance flights, package tours, identi-kit hotel chains, global car hire and all the other features of mass travel. In big cities throughout the world, airports grew to such a size that they became small cities in their own right, with their own shops, restaurants, medical services and places of worship. While airports were, for the great majority, places of transit, some individuals took up permanent residence.

Anthony Sampson captures the spirit of the age when he writes, 'The jets and the jumbos brought new standards of reliability, punctuality and safety; but they also abolished almost any sense of travelling . . . The headsets, the in-flight movies and the constant meals were designed to obliterate the experience of travelling, and the definition of a good trip was one which had been hardly noticed . . . The jumbos could accommodate a train-load, but they could never conjure up the association of a long-distance train.'[5] With the jumbos came not only size, but conformity. It became harder and harder for airlines to stand out from the crowd. To the average passenger one jumbo was very much like the other, and although there was room for individuality in first and even business class, the jumbo ushered in the era of mass transit. While Concorde looked backwards to an age when air travel was the privilege of a pampered few, the jumbo looked forward to the day when boarding a plane would, for most people, become as routine as buying a bus ticket. As a statement of equality, the jumbo, promoted as the people's plane, was very much a product of the 1960s.

Not only did the jumbo change the face of air travel for ever, but it was something more than an aeroplane. It became a popular icon and gave an old word an entirely new meaning. The jumbo defined air travel in the last quarter of the twentieth century and set the stage for the twenty-first. The superjumbo tag that commentators have given to the A380 behemoth makes Airbus Industrie executives grit their teeth, but it is an indication of the extent to which the 747 has become part of popular imagination and culture. Its hump-backed outline is as much part of the century's iconography as the Coca-Cola bottle. Its appearance in the skies over the big cities of America and Europe caused excitement and astonishment.

*

To say that the 747 had a difficult birth is to put it mildly: there were problems every step of the way. It was difficult to build, it was difficult to fly and trying to find engines sufficiently powerful proved to be a nightmare. Nor did Pan Am's changes of mind about the kind of aeroplane it wanted help matters.

Changes in Pan Am's specification led to a significant increase in weight, which in turn meant that the chosen Pratt & Whitney engine, the JT 9D, did not have sufficient power for the heavier plane. Originally, Boeing and Pan Am had agreed on a plane with a take-off weight of 270 tonnes with the JT 9D producing 41,000 lbs of thrust. But as Boeing struggled to meet Pan Am's changing specifications, the plane became 40 tonnes heavier. As the 747 passed the 310 tonne mark, Boeing called on Pratt & Whitney for an engine with 43,500 lbs of thrust. Faced with a delay that could have cost the company anything between $250 million and $400 million, Boeing refused to slow down and twisted Pratt & Whitney's arm to squeeze more power out of the existing design. Even so, things fell behind schedule. As the launch date approached, 747s were rolling off the production line at Everett with cement blocks hanging from the wings where the engines should have been. As Mal Stamper, then director of the 747 programme, said, 'We were rolling out gliders instead of airplanes. We had our guarantees to our customers to worry about. Pan Am was holding our feet to the fire. And Pratt & Whitney didn't fix it fast enough. That makes you sore.'[6]

There was, inevitably, a price to pay for all this. Pan Am threatened to withhold $5 million from the purchase price of each 747 – a total of some $18 million – until Boeing had sorted out the problems. (They eventually settled for $2 million with Pratt & Whitney paying all but $500,000). '[Pan Am] is locked in a shrinking box, with the top, the bottom and the sides all closing in at once,' said Najeeb Halaby, who had taken over from Juan Trippe a couple of years after his retirement.[7] But if these troubles cost Pan Am dearly, Boeing's predicament was even worse.

There was no shortage of orders. Once Pan Am had taken the lead, other airlines were quick to follow. By 1969, the year in which the jumbo took to the air, Boeing had orders for no fewer than 196 jumbos from thirty-one different airlines across the world. The pace was so hectic that planes were being built at the giant Everett plant in Seattle even before the roof had been put on, and Boeing was gearing up to produce seven 747s a month – a truly heroic figure. But so were the losses. In 1969 Boeing reported an operating loss of $14.3 million, the first in twenty-two years.

Over the next two years the crisis worsened. Penalty payments to the airlines for late delivery and the cost of financing a large inventory of unfinished 747s had a disastrous effect on the company's cash flow. The problems were compounded by the recession triggered by the Nixon administration's decision to cool an overheated economy by imposing a wage and price freeze. In the US, aircraft sales dried up to the point that there was not a single order for the 747 from a domestic airline between 1969 – the year the 747 was launched – and 1971. Boeing came 'within a gnat's whisker', as Tex Boullioun, head of the commercial aircraft group, put it, of going bust. The company was forced to go to the market to raise a loan from the bankers of $1.2 billion – at the time the largest amount of money ever raised by a US corporation.

With the bankers holding a gun to Boeing's head, the company's new president, Thornton Arnold Wilson, a plain-speaking, sometimes profane aeronautical engineer from small-town Missouri, known to everybody as 'T', set in train the most savage cutback Seattle had ever seen. In the autumn of 1969 the situation was so bad that Boeing, desperate for cash, was forced to cut the operating budget of the commercial aircraft division by $100 million. It was middle and senior management who bore the brunt. As Wilson remarked at the time, 'The logic is simple. If I don't do it, the board will bring in some ice water guy from outside who will. I decided I might as well be the ice water guy.'[8] Over the next eighteen months the 1700 staff of the corporate HQ were reduced to 200. Eleven vice-presidents left. The cutbacks, which lasted some three years from 1969 to 1971 and cost over 86,000 employees their jobs, became known as the 'Boeing Bust'. To save money, factories were closed down (plant capacity was cut by 4 million square feet in one year alone), routine maintenance work on buildings was halted and even the flower beds were neglected. As unemployment in Seattle rose to a record 17 per cent, some wag put up a big sign on the side of the road leading to the airport which read, 'Will the last person leaving Seattle, please turn out the lights.'

For a time Boeing thought of pulling out of the civil aircraft business altogether. Among the alternatives considered were: light rail transport and driverless trains, commercial hydrofoils, waste water purification, desalination plants and even property development. But there was never much enthusiasm for these ideas; the plans were quietly shelved as Boeing people reminded themselves that its business was building aeroplanes. In 1972 the commercial aircraft group was reorganized to become the commercial aircraft company, and its boss, Tex Boullioun, was told that his top priority was to concentrate on overseas sales – an instruction that was to bring Boeing into direct conflict with Airbus for the first time.

*

In deciding to put all its chips on a single spin of the wheel, Boeing had hoped to repeat the coup it had pulled off in the early 1950s when it started work on the 707 – a civilian version of the KC-135 tanker it was building for the US Air Force. At that time Boeing was best known for its big, jet-engined, long-range bombers – the B-47 and the massive B-52, whose carpet-bombing missions in the Vietnam war were so devastating. As a maker of commercial passenger planes, Boeing, which ranked behind Douglas and Lockheed, was far less effective. The airlines looked at Boeing suspiciously: they regarded it, with good reason, as a company where military design led the way. Almost always, Boeing's commercial offerings were simply a modification of work commissioned (and paid for) by the military. This was true of the Stratocruiser, derived from the B29 Superfortress and built for the days when air travel was a luxury for the few who could afford it: cruising speeds were low, stops were frequent and passengers pampered. It was also true of the more utilitarian 707 – both planes started life as military transports.

Though the twin-decked Stratocruiser helped to raise the company's profile, it was not a commercial success. Launched by Bill Allen in 1945, the four-engined Stratocruiser was built with an eye for comfort and class. What captured the popular imagination was the circular staircase that linked the lower-deck lounge with the upper passenger deck and the seats that could be converted into sleeping berths. But the planes cost too much to build and were too expensive to operate.

By 1950, when the Stratocruiser programme was wound down, only fifty-six of the planes had been sold. When Bill Allen had been elected Boeing's new president five years before, he faced what Clive Irving describes as 'a crisis of peace'. He had to decide whether to continue to rely on the military or to look for new business with the airlines. The Douglas DC-7 was the plane to beat. It may have been propeller-driven but that was what the airlines liked: there was nothing showy or risky about the DC-7. It may, compared to a jet, have been slow, but it had a long range and was cheap to operate. What's more, the passengers liked it. It was plain that Boeing would have to work hard to convince the sceptics.

Boeing's first efforts to challenge Douglas's reputation as the world's most successful civil aircraft maker by building the jetliner of the future were not well received. Unalluringly code-named the 473-60C, the plane was not an impressive concept. It was, in effect, no more than a scaled-down version of the B-52 bomber with the same engines but smaller wings. Nobody liked it. 'The airlines recognized in it the old Boeing failings of partly cannibalizing a military design and not thinking an airliner through from scratch to what the airlines needed,' says Clive Irving.

'To be a serious contender, Boeing would not only have to show its unquestioned mastery of swept-wing technology, but to marry that to an airplane that would be economically irresistible to the board of an airline.'[9]

In 1950 the attractions of jet travel were by no means obvious. As the airlines saw it, the only real advantage of the jetliner was its speed. Its range was not as great as the best propeller-driven planes, its payload in passengers and cargo was small, the technology was unproven and, above all, its engines were remarkably thirsty. Many airline chiefs found it hard to see how the jetliner would pay.

Boeing listened to the sceptics. It scrapped its original plans for a two-deck cabin, a cocktail bar and a downstairs lounge; instead there was to be a single cabin of the same dimensions as the old Stratocruiser, with two seats on either side of a single aisle. The belly was given over to baggage and cargo – a recognition of the old airline maxim that payload means load that pays. But above all, the 707's defining characteristic was its ability to fly higher, faster and further than any other existing civilian aircraft, a function of the swept-wing technology which provided greater lift and the new bypass jet engines which supplied much greater power. In developing the B-47, Boeing had learnt a good deal about swept-wing technology from the papers of German aeronautical engineers captured after the war; and these lessons were carried over into what became the 707. And although, strictly speaking, the Pentagon may not have paid for the development of the 707, the fact that it was closely based on a specification for a military plane clearly was of enormous benefit to Boeing.

It cost Boeing $15 million to develop the 707 – about a fifth of the company's net worth at the time. But the gamble paid off – both for Boeing and Pan Am. In the first five years of the jet age, Pan Am's overseas traffic doubled and by 1963 the airline had become one of the world's best known and most profitable airlines, with an operating revenue of half a billion dollars. The success of the 707 thrust Boeing to the forefront of the world's planemakers. As a derivative of an existing plane, the 707 was, unusually, profitable almost from the start. But even before the first 707 was delivered to Pan Am in the spring of 1958, Boeing, in common with Douglas in the States and de Havilland in England, was taking a hard look at the short-haul market.

With a potential world market of 500 planes, it was a segment that had already attracted Boeing's rivals: Douglas was already hard at work on the DC-9 and de Havilland's Trident was already in the pipeline. Boeing was lagging behind in the race and needed to come up with something better. But what? Douglas was looking at four engines, the British favoured three, and all that the airlines would say was that they wanted more than two. It was not until late in 1959 when BEA signed a contract for twenty-four Tridents that Boeing finally concluded that de Havilland had got it right and that the Trident with its three, rear-mounted engines was the plane to beat. Six months later Boeing began the engineering work on what, because of the problems, it had nicknamed 'The Impossible Airplane'. At the time, the Boeing 727 seemed to be another great gamble: the company had already spent $130 million on development and orders were scarce. Only Eastern and United Airlines were interested, and half of their orders were subject to cancellation. By taking a decision to make no prototypes and go straight into production, Boeing upped the ante still further.

The 727 very nearly never happened. The board had decided that unless there were 100 pre-production orders by 1 December 1960, it would pull the plug. But on 30 November, the day before the deadline, Allen signed with Eastern and United confirming orders worth a total of $420 million – then the biggest single transaction in commercial aviation history. The board relented and the 727 went on to become the best-selling commercial jet in history. By the time the last 727 came off the production line in September 1984, a record 1,831 had been sold.

By the late 1960s, ten years after the 707 made its first commercial flight, Boeing had taken over the jet market as comprehensively as Douglas had once dominated the propeller-driven market. The strategy was clear and the execution clinical. With stretched and modified versions of the 727, the smaller 737 and the 707, Boeing set out to create a family of aircraft to cover as many segments of an increasingly complex and fragmented market in a way that none of its American or European rivals could match. Already the pace Boeing had set proved too much for Douglas Aircraft.

The son of a New York bank official, Donald Douglas had cut his teeth in the aircraft industry in the years after World War I by designing a heavy bomber for Glenn L. Martin in California.* In 1920 Douglas, backed by a wealthy aviation enthusiast called David R. Davis, left Martin to set up on his own with the aim of building a plane capable of flying coast to coast. The machine, a sturdy, single-engine bi-plane called the 'Cloudster', was on the point of taking off when news came that he had been pipped at the post. The mission was abandoned. But not everything was lost. The Cloudster became the protoype for a very successful range of torpedo bombers and lighter bomber/observer planes for the Army. In 1924 four Douglas bi-planes became the first aeroplanes to circumnavigate the world – a journey which involved two weeks of flying spread over six months. On the back of this success, Douglas persuaded a syndicate of Los Angeles businessmen, including Harry Chandler, the publisher of the *Los Angeles Times*, to fund Douglas Aircraft.

It was in the years immediately before World War II that the foundations of what was to become the world's most successful civil aircraft business were laid. In 1935, at the suggestion of American Airlines, Douglas produced the DC-3. Although

---

*   Now part of Martin Marietta, the defence company.

it seated twenty people, it became what Douglas described as 'the best-loved plane we have ever produced'. By 1940, the year before America entered the war, there were 300 DC-3s in service. Douglas aircraft dominated the trunk routes linking the major cities, and completed the task the railways had begun of knitting metropolitan America into a single nation. But it was during the war that the DC-3 really came into its own. As the Dakota, the plane became an essential piece of the American military machine. More than 10,000 DC-3s were made during the war, and Dwight D. Eisenhower named the Dakota as one of the five critical pieces of equipment that made worldwide war possible, the other four being the bulldozer, the jeep, the two-and-a-half ton truck and the amphibian DUKW.

When peace came in 1945, Douglas was unquestionably America's leading maker of passenger aircraft, easily outstripping its rival Boeing. Ten years later its propeller driven DC-7, which could fly the Atlantic non-stop, was regarded as the ultimate flying machine. But in 1953, the year before Boeing started work on what was to become the 707, Donald Douglas, whose family motto ironically was 'jamais arrière' (never behind), made a fatal mistake: he ordered that work on the DC-8, the company's first jet airliner, should be stopped so that everything could be concentrated on the DC-7. At a meeting to celebrate the 50th anniversary of powered flight, he said, 'In our business the race is not always to the swift or the first to start. I have always held the conviction that aeroplanes should make money as well as headlines.'[10] Douglas was not alone: Lockheed also abandoned work on a pure jet in favour of the prop-jet Electra.

Douglas never really recovered from this failure of judgement. It soon realized its mistake and resumed work on the DC-8 but it was too late: the initiative had been lost. In 1958, the year of the 707's debut, Douglas was producing more civil aircraft than Boeing, Convair, Lockheed and Fairchild put together. In 1959 Boeing delivered seventy-three 707s while Douglas delivered one DC-6, no DC-7s and twenty-one DC-8s.

As he got older, Donald Douglas became more and more eccentric. According to Bill Yenne's account of McDonnell Douglas, he spent much of what little spare time he had on board his yacht *Endymion* or alone at home in his large Spanish-style house near Santa Monica. He was fond of chocolate sundaes and playing the bagpipes. And although he handed over the presidency of the company to his son Donald Douglas, Jr. in 1958, he remained chief executive to the end. 'The Douglas Aircraft Company in the sixties was a jovial, but not entirely happy ship,' say the authors of *Destination Disaster*. 'All major executives were expected to gather at midday for martinis in the Heritage Room, where most days the founder would present a guest – sometime an aeroplane customer, but more often a film producer or a favourite writer.'[11]

For all the founder's quirks, oddities and miscalculations, Douglas Aircraft was a formidable operation whose products were much admired in the industry.

Paradoxically, it was the success of its DC-9 on which work started in 1963 to compete with France's Caravelle and Britain's BAC 1-11 that led to the company's downfall. After a slow start, the plane, one of the best civil airliners ever built, attracted more orders than the company could cope with. Anxious to secure the business, the Douglas salesmen had made reckless promises about configuration and equipment. A prospective customer was offered an absurdly wide choice: a hundred different galleys, anything between one and three fuel tanks, four different power ratings for the engine, and in the passenger cabin, a choice of colour for 800 different items. 'We have thirty-two different shades of white paint,' one visitor to the plant was told.[12]

At a time of acute labour shortages, Douglas was forced to hire untrained labour. As the labour force grew from 30,000 to 80,000, the time taken to build a DC-9 expanded from 48,000 man-hours to 80,000 hours. At the same time, the Vietnam war meant engines and sub-assemblies were expensive and hard to get. Douglas was forced to spend its dwindling cash reserves on buying its sub-contractors, and delays in obtaining equipment had a knock-on effect on deliveries, thus eating into cash flow still further.

By the autumn of 1966 Douglas, which only a few months before had announced that 'it was in one of the most satisfactory phases of its history', was in crisis. For forty years Donald Douglas, Senr. had written off the development costs of his aeroplanes as they incurred. But his son's decision to defer such write-offs until the planes were actually sold made the balance sheet look much healthier than it really was. A first quarter profit of $4.1 million became a second quarter loss of $3.4 million – a turnaround of just under $7.5 million in six months.

When the full picture became clear, the bankers told Douglas its only option was to put itself up for sale and wait for offers. Invitations were sent to five companies – North American Aviation, General Dynamics, McDonnell Aircraft Company, Lockheed and Chrysler. The first three accepted but the last two, Lockheed and Chrysler, declined. Of the three, the most serious contender was McDonnell Aircraft, whose founder James Smith McDonnell (better known as 'Mr Mac') had been eyeing Douglas since 1963 when Donald Douglas had turned down his offer of a merger. His offer of $43 million in cash – under half of what it cost the company to develop the DC-8 – might have seemed a trifle mean. But what made it hard to resist was that Mr Mac already had 300,000 shares against the 9,000 owned by the Douglas family. On 13 January 1967, after pushing the price up to $68.7 million, the Douglas board conceded. And though the terms of agreement stated that it was technically a merger under which the two companies preserved their separate identities, effectively Mr Mac was the man in charge.

Like Donald Douglas, James Smith McDonnell, whose father ran a grocery store in Arkansas and built a business financing cotton crops, learnt the rudiments of the aircraft business with Glenn Martin in California. He was following a plan he had conceived while a physics student at Princeton where he said that he 'would work with any pioneering aeronautics firm that would have him' until he was forty and then he would set up his own firm for the 'designing, testing and repair of aircraft and spare parts thereof.' In fact he was only twenty-eight when on 6 July 1939 he set up the McDonnell Aircraft Company. He had $165,000 in capital, one employee, a secondhand typewriter and a rented office at St Louis municipal airport.

Until the acquisition of Douglas, McDonnell had never built a civil airplane. Its fortunes rested on building fighters for the military, and by 1966, the year before the Douglas take-over, 90 per cent of its business depended on the Phantom II, one-time holder of the world's absolute speed record at 1,606.3 miles per hour. The first question facing James McDonnell was: should the new company commit itself to the great American airbus race? Douglas had already begun design work on a wide-body two years earlier in 1965 but had put plans on hold in April 1966 when Boeing announced it was going to build the 747. But as the airlines were showing little interest in a stretched DC-8 and as Lockheed had its own plans for a widebody, in November 1967, two months after Lockheed, Mr Mac decided to give the DC-10 project the go-ahead. It would, he thought, be a good opportunity to score over those arrogant people in Seattle. It was a decision that he would come bitterly to regret.

*

By 1973, as the Airbus A300 made its first appearance in North America, McDonnell Douglas and Lockheed were locked in a hugely unprofitable combat for supremacy of the wide-bodied tri-jet market. There was so little difference between the planes and so anxious were both companies to establish themselves that they gave massive discounts to airlines buying their DC-10s and Tristars. When McDonnell Douglas stole a march on its great rival by signing up American Airlines as its first customer for the DC-10 at a price of $15.3 million apiece for twenty-five aircraft, Lockheed countered by announcing the sale of 144 Tristars to Eastern and TWA at $14 million each. At that stage it looked as if Lockheed, with total sales of 168 to MDD's twenty-five was winning the battle hands down, but then United Airlines came to MDD's rescue with an order for sixty DC-10s. The president of United, George Keck, told Lockheed's Dan Haughton that 'the Tristar would be a fine plane but if the DC-10 isn't built, then McDonnell Douglas will be out of business. And I think that would be a bad thing for the airlines and a bad thing for the industry.'[13]

The struggle in Europe and the Far East was so intense that discounts were not the only inducement offered. According to evidence collected by investigators for the committee headed by Senator Frank Church of Idaho to investigate allegations of corruption and bribery by US aeroplane manufacturers, Lockheed, which was trying to sell its Tristars to the Dutch airline KLM and its Starfighter to the Dutch Air Force, paid Prince Bernhard of the Netherlands, who was a director of KLM as well as Inspector-General of the Dutch armed forces, a fee of more than $1 million. Precisely what the prince did in return for this money was never established. But Lockheed's president Carl Kotchian testified that the money was 'to establish a climate in which our product would be properly received and properly considered by people who would be active in making the decision'. He added, 'Some call it gratuities, some call it questionable payments, some call it extortion and some call it grease. Some call it bribery. I look at these payments as necessary to sell a product.'[14] As it turned out, KLM did not buy Tristars, though the Air Force did buy the Starfighter. But Prince Bernhard's reputation suffered badly. An official enquiry concluded that his denials 'cannot be reconciled with established facts' and that the prince had 'allowed himself to be tempted to take initiatives which were completely unacceptable and which were bound to place himself and the Netherland's procurement policy in the eyes of others in a dubious light'.[15]

In Japan, Lockheed spent even more money and met with even greater success. In this case their chosen middleman was not a European aristocrat but an obscure, immensely well-connected businessman called Yoshio Kodama. Officially Kodama was described as chairman of an insignificant colliery company and as an 'adviser' to a number of industrial concerns. In practice he was a behind-the-scenes fixer and, in some cases, bagman for some of the most important industrial companies in Japan, among them Fuji Steel, the Marubeni Corporation (Lockheed's official agent), Japan Airlines and All-Nippon Airways. It was this last company that was the focus of the Lockheed salesmen.

In 1969, while the plane was still in the development stage, All-Nippon, Japan's main domestic airline, had reached a provisional agreement with McDonnell Douglas to buy the DC-10. It was some time after this that Lockheed reached a 'consultancy agreement' whereby Lockheed would pay Kodama a straight fee of $138,000 a year. Six months later the contract was amended to give Kodama a $4 million bonus for the first six Tristars sold, with additional payments of $60,000 to $120,000 for each extra sale. Quite what Kodama did was never established, but on 30 October 1972 All-Nippon reneged on its DC-10 deal with McDonnell Douglas and announced that it was buying six Tristars at roughly $18 million apiece. Faced with accusations from the Securities and Exchange Commission, Lockheed eventually confessed that 'it had made $22 million in payments to foreign countries since 1970 to get lucrative aircraft contracts – a practice it termed necessary to meet the competition'. Some years later it owned up to making secret payments to Japanese government officials, including $1.8 million to the office of the then prime minister, Kakuei Tanaka.

Lockheed was not the only American aircraft manufacturer to pay bribes. After the SEC had threatened to take the company to court, it was revealed that McDonnell Douglas had made $21.57 million in questionable payments to sales agents in eighteen countries between 1969 and 1976. Among the countries in question were Pakistan, Zaire, South Korea, the Philippines and Venezuela. Boeing, too, was caught up in the scandal. Its first reaction was self-righteously to protest complete innocence. In 1975 it told its shareholders, 'All payments made with respect to foreign business have been clearly identified in the Company's accounting records, and no funds have been diverted, either directly or indirectly, to so-called slush funds.'[16] Later, after commissioning a special report by its outside directors, it told the SEC, 'The Boeing Company has made a complete disclosure of payments to foreign officials, and no further investigations are required.'[17] The SEC thought otherwise and continued to press charges. It was only in 1982 that Boeing finally admitted it had withheld information, and pleaded guilty to paying $7.38 million in 'irregular commissions' to agents in Spain, Honduras, the Dominican Republic and Lebanon. Ninety five per cent of the money went to Spain and Lebanon.

However embarrassing these disclosures may have been to the aircraft manufacturers, they had little or no impact on the fierce battle for sales being waged between McDonnell Douglas and Lockheed for the wide-bodied market. For McDonnell Douglas what was far more damaging were the disasters that overtook the DC-10. The first indication that the DC-10 design was flawed came in June 1972 when an American Airlines DC-10 suffered a problem while at 12,000 ft over Windsor, Ontario, on a flight from Detroit to Buffalo. There was a loud bang as a cargo door measuring some 12ft by 10ft blew off, immediately followed by explosive decompression as the rear deck of the plane collapsed, damaging the control cables. With great skill the pilot managed to return to Detroit and landed the plane safely by using the trim tabs on the wings. An investigation by the airline concluded that the cargo door had not been properly latched and recommended that a small hole should be cut in the door so that the latch could be inspected from the outside before the plane took off. The investigators also discovered that the wiring in the motor that activated the latches could not carry sufficient current to operate the latch, and they wrote to the FAA to suggest it put out a service bulletin.

Tragically, it seems as if word of this fault did not reach Hava Yollari, the Turkish national airline. On 3 March 1974 a Hava Yollari DC-10 crashed twelve minutes after take-off in the Forêt de Ermenonville about 30 miles north-east of Paris, killing all 346 people. It was an accident that was in almost every respect a carbon copy of the Canadian incident two years before. Like the American Airlines DC-10, the floor of the Turkish plane collapsed from the force of compression. With no means of controlling the plane, the pilot could not prevent the DC-10 plunging to earth at a steep angle. The official report into the disaster blamed an improperly latched cargo door and a defective warning light.

The Paris crash proved to be a crippling blow from which the DC-10 programme never really recovered. But even if Paris had never happened, it was clear that the oil shock had fundamentally changed the economics of the airline business. As the *Sunday Times* team pointed out:

> Nobody at the time forsaw the horrors of the energy crisis and general inflation that were shortly to end the great airline boom. Had anyone done so, the decision might have gone against building one, let alone two, American airbuses. Nobody, indeed, could have been expected to make accurate predictions about the effect on airline traffic of Middle Eastern politics, and of the unique circumstance of all the industrialised Western economies being depressed at the same time.
>
> Both McDonnell Douglas and Lockheed had airily predicted that there would be, eventually, homes for one thousand airbuses. Now they were committed to going out and proving the point, in order to make profits on top of development budgets that were coming out at $1 billion each. 'We're going to have to make an awful lot of money out there for an awful long time,' said MDD's David Lewis. 'It's a bit more exposure than we are used to.'
>
> In the wake of the oil crisis, the economics of the American airbuses, once so promising in the era of cheap fuel, began to look nothing like so attractive. Post 1973, airlines did their sums again and found that the Tristar and the DC-10 were a lot more expensive to run than they had imagined. The DC-10 crashes dealt a horrendous blow to the plane's prospects. A great deal of the cost was down to the third engine – which is where the twin-engined A300 scored. The development of its GE engines and the increase in the range meant that worries about it being able to fly coast to coast over the mountains began to evaporate.[18]

With the accent now on fuel economy, the decision by Lockheed and McDonnell Douglas to build a three-engined airbus instead of a twin began to look rash, while the decision to build two virtually identical airbuses instead of one appeared to be downright foolish. Airbus lost no opportunity to twist the knife. When the first advertisement for the A300 appeared in the autumn of 1973, it was what admen call knocking copy. In a clear reference to the American widebodies, it asked, 'Why pay for three engines when all you need is two?' And although many in the airline business still had their doubts about the Airbus offering, as time went by the attractions of the European wide-bodied twin began to be more apparent. Just as it became clear that Lockheed and McDonnell Douglas had got it wrong, so it began to dawn that Airbus just conceivably might have got it right.

The gap between the Americans and the Europeans was still immense: for all their problems the Americans still had well over 90 per cent of the world aircraft market but the balance of advantage was by the second half of the 1970s beginning to shift. Throughout the airline boom of the 1960s, the size and strength of their domestic market had worked to the benefit of the American plane makers. But by the same token, when the boom ended in the early 1970s, America's big three, Boeing, Lockheed and McDonnell Douglas, were forced to look overseas for business. Their search for orders took them into distant and unfamiliar territory. What's more, it brought the Americans for the first time face to face with a competitor whose product was well suited to the prevailing market conditions. For the Americans it was a battle for market share; for Airbus, it was a fight for survival.

CHAPTER SIX

THE SILK ROAD

I F THE AMERICANS WERE HAVING problems in the wake of the oil shock and the consequent recession, things were much worse at the Airbus headquarters in Toulouse. For a time it looked as if the bold adventure would be over almost before it had begun. When Bernard Lathière took over from Henri Ziegler as chief executive in February 1975, the number of A300s that had been sold but not yet delivered was exactly twenty. For a company setting out to challenge the Americans with an aircraft designed for world markets, it was not exactly an impressive start. As John Newhouse observed, 'Europe's Airbus appeared to be a typical European airliner – well-designed, well-built, and a commercial flop.'[1]

The bulk of the orders had come from the national airlines of the sponsoring governments – Air France, Lufthansa and Iberia – but not only was the number of orders far below the figure that ministers had laid down as a pre-condition of government support, but the commitment of the airlines themselves was less than wholehearted.

The previous autumn Iberia had cancelled its order for four A300s, invoking an escape clause that allowed them to do so if Airbus Industrie failed to sell fifty aircraft by a set date. And now Lufthansa, which had ordered three A300Bs with an option on a further four, was threatening to pull out also. When the news reached Toulouse, Lathière immediately set out for Frankfurt, where he demanded a face-to-face meeting with Reinhart Abraham, the head of Lufthansa.

Lufthansa complained it had had to pay the full price for its A300s while some insignificant charter company had benefited from a new law that gave companies a 10 per cent allowance on new investment. Lufthansa had told the federal government that unless it received equal treatment, it would cancel the Airbus contract. As this was a quarrel between a German airline and its government, there was not a great deal that Lathière could do except try and bluff it out. Which is what he did.

'Look,' he said. 'It's very simple. You know very well what will happen if you break your contract: it will put us in a phenomenal pickle. Everybody is going to say that you only took the plane because of government pressure. And now you want to cancel because you think it's so awful.' 'I have read in books,' Lathière continued, 'that when you are being blackmailed and have reached the point where you can't pay any-more, the only thing to do is take a knife and kill the blackmailer. So this is what I'll do. If you cancel the contract, the next day I'll hold a press conference and I'll say to the whole world that I'm stopping and I'll suggest to the government that the reason the Airbus programme is being stopped is because of Lufthansa's behaviour.'[2]

Abraham was thunderstruck. 'No one has ever talked to me like that before,' he gasped.

'Well', Lathière replied, 'It had to happen to you one day.'

Abraham was silent for a long three minutes before he said, 'OK, then, let's shake hands. If you are able to say things like that in front of me, it's because you are going to lead Airbus in the right direction.'[3]

Like Henri Ziegler and Roger Béteille, Lathière, who was born in Calcutta where his father worked for Michelin, was a member of France's intellectual elite. A poly-glot and a man of restless energy, he was fond of pointing out that French was his third language. Working as they did in British India, his parents conversed in English while his nanny spoke to him in Bengali; and it was only after the family returned to France ('born in India but made in France,' he says) that he learned French. As a graduate of the *École Nationale d'Administration*, Lathière was almost predestined to become a civil servant. It was therefore no surprise (least of all to himself) when he was hand-picked for the prestigious *l'Inspection Générale des Finances*. After a mete-oric rise through the ranks of the civil service, Lathière was made the director of the air transport ministry, where he had an overview of airline policy as well as of civil aerospace projects such as Concorde and Airbus. After a spell as head of the Paris air-ports, he moved across to private industry to become president of AirInter where he spent seven years before taking over from Henri Ziegler at Airbus. It was yet another example of the ease with which French technocrats moved smoothly back and forth between the public and private sectors.

In this respect at least, Bernard Lathière was typical of the top echelon of Airbus management. In other respects, however, Lathière was a very different character from the highly organized and self-controlled Roger Béteille or the suave, well-con-nected Henri Ziegler. Lathière's style was altogether more effusive. He liked cigars, fine wine and had a gift for self-dramatization. On his first meeting with Dan Krook, who came from Fokker to be his commercial director, he told the Dutchman over lunch that he had bought a Rembrandt drawing that day to show his confidence in Holland and Dutchmen. Of his job, he has remarked, 'I think that when you are at the top of an outfit like this, the president's role is not only to try and help the gen-eral director to run the show, but also to make myths.'[4] He was, needless to say, an excellent salesman.

Lathière had barely arrived at Toulouse before he was given an opportunity to display this talent. One of the last things Henri Ziegler had done before handing over to Lathière was to negotiate a deal for A300s with Air India. It was an important piece of business: the first contract with a major, non-European airline and won in the face of fierce competition from Boeing and Lockheed. As the final touches were being put to the deal, Ziegler phoned Lathière who asked, 'Have you thought that as Air India is the country's flag carrier you are going to have to get agreement from the supervising body, the Indian government?'

'Oh, that's a mere detail,' Ziegler replied.

What Ziegler apparently did not know was that when previously Air India had signed up with Douglas for some DC-9s, Indian government approval had taken two years and the business had gone to Boeing, not to Douglas. The story was that Boeing had tipped the deal its way by publishing a list of names of people in India who had benefited from the Douglas sales campaign.

Shortly after his chat with Ziegler, at 6.30 one morning Lathière's telephone rang and someone sounding like a policeman said, 'This is the cipher room of the ministry of foreign affairs. The ambassador in Delhi has telexed to say that you've blown it if you don't go right away. The Americans have returned and Lockheed has put $6 million on the table to stop the job.' Lathière immediately summoned Béteille to Paris and within thirty-six hours Lathière was in Delhi.

On arrival he was met by Air Chief Marshall P.C. Lal, president and chairman of Air India, whom the irrepressible Lathière greeted with the cry, 'Listen, thank you for being tough with us like that because you are letting me be in the country of my birth on my birthday.' To which Lal replied, 'What are you doing for lunch?' They went off to a state hotel where as luck would have it, there were fifteen Boeing men on one table and eighteen Lockheed on other. 'That looks like trouble,' one American was heard to remark when, as lunch ended, a birthday cake arrived and the president of Air India got up to sing 'Happy birthday, dear Bernard'. But worse was to come. Lathière fished in his pocket and produced a photo of an old lady, an old man and a small boy. His host had no difficulty in recognizing the old man and the old lady, but was stumped by the picture of the boy. The old man was none other than Mahatma Gandhi and the lady was a well-known Indian poet and a figure from the independence movement. 'In that case, you know everybody,' said Lathière triumphantly. 'Because the little boy is me.' He went on to explain that the picture was taken on board ship when Lathière was returning with his parents to France. Gandhi had befriended the family, saying he loved children. So during the voyage the young Lathière came to spend time with the great man and helped him to milk his goat. It was a *coup de théâtre* to which the unhappy Boeing and Lockheed men had no reply. As Lathière himself says, 'You can never avoid silliness in negotiations.' When, two years later, the two men met again as Airbus delivered the plane, the airline president said to him, 'Do you know what? It's the first time anyone has come to me to sell me a plane with a photo of Gandhi: how do you expect me to resist?'[5]

By the end of Lathière's first year in charge, Airbus had sold a further nine planes – including four to South African Airlines and three to AirInter. The South

African deal was a small but important step in Airbus's long battle to establish its credibility. At the time, almost no one took the consortium seriously, as the following story neatly illustrates. During the course of the campaign, South African had invited all the manufacturers to provide an economic profile of their own aircraft and then rank it and the rival aircraft in order. At this point Boeing was working on a short-haul version of its long range 747, so all four manufacturers were in the frame.

Unsurprisingly, Boeing's study concluded that its short range 747 was the best solution for SAA; the second-best solution was the A300, the third was the Lockheed 1011 and the fourth was the McDonnell Douglas DC-10. Lockheed's study put its 1011 first and the Airbus second, followed by the 747 and DC-10; McDonnell Douglas also ranked the Airbus second. Airbus itself naturally followed the others' lead and put its own plane in the top spot. When these studies were published everybody laughed. Seeing an opportunity to steal a march, the Airbus salesmen, with their tongues firmly in their cheeks, suggested a points system in which the winner got four points, the second, three points and so on. Under this system the A300 emerged as the clear winner. The lesson of this story was that the Americans were far more concerned about each other than they were about Airbus. But in this case they badly miscalculated.

SAA had a reputation as a very rigorous airline that left nothing to chance. Traditionally it was a Boeing airline. Its remote location, thousands of miles from Europe, meant that the aircraft and the after-sales service had to be first-class. The 'hot and high' African routes, as the industry called them, were particularly demanding. And but for a piece of brilliant improvisation, Airbus might easily have lost the business. Trials of the A300 by SAA revealed that on the run down to Capetown, the plane couldn't cope with Johannesburg's hot and high conditions. George Warde, the former president of American Airlines who went on to head up the Airbus sales operation in the States, called Béteille to tell him, 'Roger, we have a problem. We've got to increase the gross take-off load of this plane somehow.' Back in Toulouse, the engineers set to work. They concentrated on the leading edge of the wing which had a flap along its entire length, save for the last two-and-a-half feet. The solution, they decided, was to weld a piece of metal on to this end section to, in effect, extend the flap. The result was a dramatic increase in lift; and the engineers went on tweaking until the plane's take-off performance had been substantially improved. Reassured, in September 1975 SAA placed an order for four A300s with an option on another four. Airbus had made a modest but reasonably encouraging start; it now had orders from four flag carriers, even though two of them, Air France and Lufthansa, were, in all but name, members of the consortium.

But then came the drought. If 1975 had been a lean year, 1976 was to be even worse; in the company it is called 'The Black Year'. In May one plane was sold to

Transavia, the French domestic airline, after which fourteen months were to pass without a single order. Morale at Toulouse was at rock bottom and Béteille's vision of a European challenge to American hegemony in the sky seemed to be a mirage. In the first flush of enthusiasm Toulouse had believed that after a slow start, by the end of 1977 the A300 would have more than broken even, with production up to ten planes a month and total sales of more than 400. As it was, between 1974 and 1976 Airbus sold precisely fifteen aircraft.

With sales at a virtual standstill, the number of unsold aircraft (known in the industry as 'whitetails' because they were without airline insignia) parked on the field at Blagnac just outside Toulouse rose to sixteen. The consortium had reached the uncomfortable point where the number of 'whitetails' on the tarmac exceeded its total sales. Even so, the Europeans were reluctant to pull back. Until the spring of 1976, Toulouse kept the production line running at the rate of two planes a month. When bad times came, Airbus Industrie was much slower than Boeing to react. Unlike the Americans, it simply wasn't possible for the highly unionized Airbus Industrie (whose workers were, as they demonstrated in 1968, amongst the most militant in France) to react as quickly and as drastically as Boeing had done. Also, lacking Boeing's flexibility and astonishingly quick reflexes for such a big company, Airbus wanted to have its planes ready and available when the market picked up.

The drain on the company's resources and cash flow had become so great that the Germans felt that drastic action was required. The problem this time was not Lufthansa, but the German government itself, until now the prop and mainstay of the entire operation. By 1976 Helmut Schmidt, who came from the right wing of his party, the SPD, had succeeded Willi Brandt as chancellor, and economic policy acquired a more free market tone. There was also growing criticism in the German parliament about the cost to the German taxpayer of the Airbus programme. That October, when Jean Pierson took over as head of the factory, things had become so bad that only one airbus a month was coming off the line. A month later the Germans asked Airbus to stop production completely.

'It was a big, big fight between Airbus Industrie, with Roger Béteille and Felix Kracht on one side and the Germans on the other,' Pierson recalls:

> The Germans wanted to stop and my answer was that if you do that it will never start again. I have never seen aircraft reawaken once you have stopped the line – never. Finally we persuaded the Germans that the thing to do was to cut production by 50 per cent to half an aircraft a month and to wait until there was better news coming from the market.
>
> At the time I had no special knowledge of the market. For me it was normal common sense. We would never buy a car if we knew the manufacturer had stopped the line. It's the same with Airbus. The French government took its line from the industry which wanted to stay in. The industry people said, 'Look, you are at the end

of the line with Concorde. If you stop the Airbus line what do you do with the Toulouse plants?' It's as simple as that. That would be the end. We would have our backs against the wall. In Germany, it was different. At that time the importance of the aircraft industry was still being debated. There were different companies and no single, focal point.

The move to half a plane a month bought time for Airbus and for the French. The Germans said 'OK. We don't agree. But let's wait six months and let's look again. If it's still as bad then we'll say we have tried everything, and now we'll stop. After two, three, four, five meetings on the same subject, everybody's fed up and then you have to find a compromise.'[6]

Béteille told his staff not to panic and to concentrate on the job. Even so, the atmosphere at Blagnac was, so those who were there recall, rather like Britain in wartime when everybody crowded round the radio in the hope of hearing optimistic news from the front. In much the same way, messages from Airbus salesmen were eagerly anticipated.

But the good news was awfully slow in coming and there were very few crumbs of comfort to be had. 'We were newcomers,' says Jean Roeder. 'No one really trusted us and no one knew who we actually were, apart from the airlines we had actually worked with. There were doubts about our customer services ability; doubts about a plan financed by governments – or at least that's what it looked like. Among some airlines the fear that such a plane would become a political object was very strong. These were all unanswered questions. And also we were not very skilled in the way we came into the market. We had no sales experience. By comparison with Boeing and McDonnell Douglas we were tiny.'[7]

All that Béteille and Lathière could do was to use the time to build the organization, remedy its defects, establish the Airbus reputation as best they could, and hope, like Bernard Shaw's Joan of Arc, that the wind would change. The Airbus operation at this time left a good deal of room for improvement. Everybody agreed that the planes themselves were technically first class: well-built and well-designed. But the sales team was weak and inexperienced and the product support side of the business was poor. When George Warde first came to Europe to work as a consultant for Airbus, he told Béteille, 'You should thank God you haven't sold anything, because you are not ready to support. And if you don't support you are not going to be successful because Europeans have a history of not being very good at support – from Rolls-Royce up.' Warde complained that the people handling product support at Airbus were the same people who had done the same job with the Caravelle. 'And the Caravelle,' he remarked acidly, 'was known to have the worst product support in the States.'[8]

Béteille took these and similar comments to heart. The first thing he did was to strengthen his management team by calling in outsiders like Dan Krook from Fokker to head up the sales team. Krook was not wholly impressed by what he found. 'The situation was extremely difficult,' he says. 'There were many good people at Airbus but they were not working together as a team . . . The most difficult thing was to delegate responsibility and make people understand that they had to take a lot of responsibility for themselves and not wait for the general manager or the commercial director to tell them what to do. All these people had been there but they had never worked as a team together.'[9]

As the chief salesman, Krook was also worried that Airbus had damaged its reputation by doing leasing deals with second or even third division airlines. 'The Airbus aircraft were much too good for these kinds of operators,' he says. The problem was that with so few orders on the books, Airbus could not afford to pick and choose. It talked to everybody and anybody and was not above presenting leasing deals as hard sales in an attempt to talk up the numbers.

It was Lathière, Dan Krook and George Warde who devised what came to be known as the Silk Road strategy. As Warde himself says, 'I wanted to continuously be aggressive in the United States so that Boeing would constantly be trying to keep me out. In the meantime I wanted to go out into Japan, Korea, China and do what I called the old silk route that Marco Polo had done.'[10] Just as Marco Polo had opened the way for Europe's merchants and traders to central Asia, so Warde wanted to explore the Asian and Far Eastern markets before Boeing woke up to their potential. What Airbus was looking for were relatively new entrants to the market with no tradition of loyalty to US suppliers and relatively rich airlines in areas where traffic was expected to increase. 'These customers were absolutely key to Airbus strategy,' says Steven McGuire. 'While entry to the US was a must, over the medium term the consortium would have to be successful in selling in markets where none of Boeing, MDD or Lockheed had an advantage.'[11]

Of course, much of this was salesman's hyperbole and poetic licence. The Airbus strategy had nothing to do with Marco Polo or the Silk Road: the countries targeted were hundreds, if not thousands, of miles from the central Asian cities of Bokhara, Samarkand and Tashkent – the historic stopping points for the caravans travelling along the Silk Road that linked distant Rome with imperial China. But looked at less literally and more metaphorically, the comparison was not so far-fetched. Just as the merchants' caravans from Europe travelled to the Far East in search of fabulous wealth, so too did the Airbus salesmen.

The attack on the airline markets of the Orient and the Far East made a great deal of sense for a company in Airbus's position. For the most part they were places outside Boeing's sphere or influence. As Dan Krook says, 'The most important thing was to select the areas where we could possibly sell. Boeing would, of course, not allow us to get our first contracts in the United States and they would also do everything possible to prevent other big European customers from buying. But Boeing paid less attention to what was happening in the Far East.'[12] What Airbus had spotted but what Boeing had yet to realize was that countries like Pakistan, Singapore and

Thailand had by the 1970s already developed to the point where they were a growing and important market in their own right.

What Airbus was looking for were markets where European planes were already known and well-regarded and the cards were not marked in Boeing's favour, as in the States and many parts of Europe. Airbus was well aware that many countries in the region strongly disapproved of what the Americans were doing in Vietnam and was anxious to take advantage of the fact.

But even here it was hard going. And one reason was because the A300B was not perhaps the ideal plane for this market. It had not quite the capacity or, more importantly, the range that the region's fast-growing airlines, like Singapore, were looking for. Lathière was convinced that if Airbus was to succeed in the Far East, a stretched version of the A300B was what was needed. But Béteille had come to the same conclusion some time ago. Work was already in hand on the B4, a heavier and more powerful version of the A300B, with the range increased from 2,500 kilometres to 4,000. In the B4, ready by the spring of 1975, Airbus had a plane that was well suited for medium to longer distance regional trips like Hong Kong to the Philippines or the Philippines to India. It was bigger than every Boeing plane with the exception of the 747, and it was much cheaper to run than Lockheed's and McDonnell Douglas's tri-motored airbuses. By quadrupling the price of fuel, the oil sheikhs of the Middle East had inadvertently done Airbus a favour by carving out a niche in the market for the A300 family.

In the Far East the Airbus strategy was to identify the most promising prospects and then pick them off one by one. In such a relatively untouched market the idea was to play one airline off against another by exploiting local rivalries and jealousies. And the chances were that if they succeeded with one airline, then the others in the area would follow. It was the Airbus version of what the Americans were calling, in a quite different geo-political context, the domino theory: if one falls, the rest will follow. By moving from defence in Europe to attack in the Far East, Airbus was hoping to turn the tables on Boeing and the other Americans.

It was left to Ranjit Jayaratman, son of an Indian minister of transport who joined Airbus as general sales manager, to put this plan to the test. The first target was Singapore International Airlines which was making its mark as the region's leading player. In 1972 Singapore was a minnow among airlines, ranking no higher than 54th in the world. It started before the war as Malayan Airways, it acquired its own identity when Lee Kuan Yew, the prime minister and creator of modern Singapore, broke the Malaysian connection to create the country's own airline, and installed his own man, Joe Pillay, a London-educated engineer to run it. The airline, which had no more than a handful of Boeing 707s, was small, but as a natural stopping point between Europe and the Far East it was strategically located. In return for landing rights in Singapore, Pillay secured reciprocal rights in airports around the world. By 1975 SIA, which had bought 747s from the outset, was flying to Seoul, Hong Kong and Taipei.

Singapore showed little interest when Jayarathman first approached them in 1976. Undeterred, Jayarathman was content to bide his time. He knew that Singapore Airlines and Malaysia Airlines, both offshoots of the abortive marriage between BOAC and Qantas, were deadly rivals; and since 1972 Malaysia had been watching Singapore's meteoric rise with a mixture of admiration and envy. So, on learning a year after his rebuff by Singapore that Malaysia was going to replace three of its 707s, he innocently said that he could arrange for them to have some Airbuses before SIA. Were they interested? Having baited the hook, the fish duly bit and Malaysia Airlines became an Airbus customer.

It requires no great imagination to work out what Jayarathman did next. With the Malay letter of intent in his hand, he approached Singapore once again and told them that Malay was going to buy three Airbuses. And he asked, 'What are you going to do?' He was summoned directly to Singapore were he saw Joe Pillay, the head of the airline, who was, so it is said, on the point of buying a DC-10. Jayarathman explained that the Airbus could do everything that the DC-10 could do but for 30 per cent less.

'I don't believe you,' retorted Pillay.

'Well, let me try and persuade you,' Jayarathman rejoined.

On the way out, Jayarathman passed a GE representative who asked him what was going on. The Airbus man told him, 'Don't worry. You'll sell your engines. But they'll be on Airbus, not a DC-10.' He was to be proved right. On 11 May 1979 SIA bought six Airbuses equipped with GE engines.[13]

Singapore may have eventually succumbed to Airbus's wiles but the Silk Road strategy was far from being an instant success. 'When we screwed up in Singapore in 1976,' says Lathière, 'we had to change our target. We had reckoned that if Singapore takes it, the others will follow suit. But they didn't take it, so we changed tack and pounced on Thailand instead.'[14]

It was the Thai order in mid-1977 that finally ended the fourteen-month sales drought. But even here there was a last-minute panic. The Thais were on the point of signature, when there was an attempted coup. At home in France, Lathière read with horror the 'Revolution in Thailand' headlines in the papers the next day. 'This can't be true,' he said. 'We really are out of luck.' The next day Lathière met Dan Krook and Roger Béteille, who said, 'Listen, president. You must go over there right away in the next twenty-four hours to show the government that you are not afraid to go out there in the middle of a revolution because you have confidence in their stability. If, moreover, you can take Mrs Lathière, all the better.' So after telling his wife that she must 'be sacrificed on the altar', they set off for Bangkok where Lathière tracked down the president of the airline playing golf on a Sunday, followed him from hole to hole and finally persuaded him to sign at the 17th.[15]

*

Not all of Airbus Industrie's attention was concentrated on the Far East. There were also matters closer at home to attend to. Strangely enough, among the people Airbus Industrie talked to at this time were its deadliest rivals, Boeing and McDonnell Douglas. In the course of the black year of 1976, senior Airbus people went to St Louis to see McDonnell Douglas, while some months later a top-level Boeing delegation came to Toulouse. As the battle for sales raged in the Far East, in the United States and Europe the talk was of cooperation and joint ventures.

As we saw in the last chapter, the oil shock of the autumn of 1973 had had a profound effect on the thinking of the aerospace industry's planners. With the accent now on fuel-saving efficiency, the focus both in the United States and Europe had shifted: the airlines were telling the plane makers that what they wanted was aircraft that would carry between 150 to 200 passengers over the short to medium haul. By the mid-1970s Boeing, McDonnell Douglas and Airbus were all committed to building planes that would satisfy this demand. Of the three, Boeing's plans were the most ambitious. With sales of the 747 picking up, Boeing's 'T' Wilson decided that the time had come to take advantage of McDonnell Douglas's and Lockheed's weakness induced by the commercial failure of the DC-10 and the Tristar. At this stage Airbus was so far below the horizon that it simply didn't enter into Wilson's calculations.

From a financial point of view the Boeing plan was even more daring than the 747 decision had been. After a gap of more than ten years during which it had launched no new planes, Boeing was intending to build not just one brand-new plane, but two. In sanctioning the go-ahead for what was to become the twin-aisle, wide-bodied 767 (first known as the 7X7) and the long, thin, single-aisle 757 (initially the 7?7) 'T' Wilson was making what Boeing's historian describes as 'the boldest and most costly commitment in Boeing's history, nearly twice the net worth of the company'.[16] The decision made the business magazine *Forbes* exclaim, 'Nothing in the past compares with the multi-billion-dollar gamble the 757 and the 767 programmes represent.'[17]

Wilson was more relaxed. 'I don't agonize about that sort of decision,' he later told an interviewer. 'We seemed to be ready to take on something new. We had the disciplines and the organization to handle that . . . I don't stew and fret too much about the market. That's something over which we don't have any direct control.'[18]

When news of Boeing's plans reached Toulouse, Béteille and Ziegler knew that they had to respond if the A300 was not to be a nine-day wonder, just another example of a promising European initiative that had failed to make it. From the very beginning Roger Béteille and Henri Ziegler had been convinced that the only way for Airbus to survive and prosper was for the consortium to follow Boeing's example and build a family of aircraft to cater for every sector of the market. 'We were most anxious to develop a family of aircraft,' says George Warde, 'that would give people options right through the range. Also, the question of commonality was very important. Training, spare parts and ground support equipment are all very expensive and if these things were compatible it would save money and help you keep customers.'[19]

But what's a family? As Airbus saw it, the various versions of the A300, it had produced so far – the short-haul A300B2 and the medium-range, heavier A300B4 – were essentially variants on a single model. It argued that only when a plane appears that serves a completely new segment do you have the beginnings of a true aircraft family. It took some time for Béteille and Ziegler to convince the consortium's partners of the force of this argument. The first reaction of both the industrial partners and their supporting governments was that Airbus Industrie was an *ad hoc* creation formed simply to produce the Airbus, aka the A300. And it was not until mid-1975, eight years after the Airbus idea had taken shape and five years after the creation of Airbus Industrie as a formal entity, that the supervisory board formally endorsed the Airbus family idea. It was perhaps the most critical decision in the history of Airbus. 'At the beginning, very few people apart from Henri Ziegler, Roger Béteille and one or two of the industrial people realized you could not survive on one aircraft; that if you were going to be successful, you would have to have a range of aircraft,' says Bob McKinlay, former managing director of British Aerospace Commercial Aircraft, who became a member of the Airbus board when Britain rejoined in January 1979. 'If it was a failure, one aircraft type was enough; if it was a success, one was not enough.'[20]

Obtaining the board's support for the idea was only half the battle. What still had to be decided was what form the new member of the Airbus family should take. Béteille's first idea was what he called the B10 'minimum change'. Conceived in 1973 as a response to the changing economic conditions and the lack of demand for the A300, the B10 was first thought of as an addition to the nine existing variations of the A300B. Some of these versions, such as the B2 and the B4, were already in development; others only existed in Béteille's mind or on paper. The B10 was, in practice, a sawn-off version of the A300B. Béteille and Krook thought that rather than build a new wing to support a cut-down fuselage, the answer would be simply to put fewer seats in the A300. According to Bill Gunston, others strongly disagreed. 'The battle ebbed to and fro, and throughout the mid-70s Airbus Industrie's management was to a considerable degree riven in twain, with a strong faction known as the "antis". There was also uncertainty at the very top levels.' Gunston says that at Aerospatiale, 'almost all the board from

General Mitterand downwards were by late 1975 ready to hop into bed with Boeing'. [21]

The demand for a short-haul plane had come primarily from Lufthansa, with support from Swissair, an airline which Airbus feared and respected. The chance to add Swissair to its small roster of customers was an idea that made Airbus dribble. 'Swissair was very important to us,' says Jean Roeder. Lufthansa had already flown the A300. But Swissair was not only a famous airline, it was notoriously difficult to negotiate with. To win Swissair as a customer was a strategic goal. Airbus hoped that if things went well, Lufthansa and Swissair would be launch customers for the new plane.

Unhappily things did not go well. When the German and Swiss airlines saw the designs for what was still being called the B10, they hated them. The size of the wings meant that the plane was too big and too heavy. And eventually Lufthansa and Swissair told Airbus, 'We don't want this plane; it's not commercially viable for our purposes.' What gave their objections added force was that the Americans were offering brand-new planes with all the latest technology while the B10 was based on an A300 design that was already ten years old. There was no option but to go back to the drawing board and reconfigure the B10.

The work Airbus was doing on the B10 had not escaped the notice of the Americans. Both McDonnell Douglas and Boeing thought that there might be some technical and financial advantage to be gained from some form of collaboration or joint venture with the Europeans. If, for example, Airbus expertise on wide-bodied fuselage design – a key element of the A300 – could be combined with American technology and know-how, it might cut costs and even help overseas sales. It was a remote possibility but, they thought, worth exploring.

The first proposal came from McDonnell Douglas, who summoned an Airbus team to Los Angeles to discuss a joint project based on a proposed 200-seater called the DCX200. The technical discussions went very well – which is not surprising, as aerospace engineers the world over like nothing better than talking about aircraft design. But when the talks moved up a rung to the level at which hard decisions are made, this optimism evaporated. Later that same year McDonnell Douglas reached an agreement with Dassault to take a 15 per cent stake in its project for a twin-engined 175-seater – the self-same Mercure which had made its first appearance when Airbus was being debated nine years earlier. The plane was actually made but no more than forty were ever sold.

Shortly after the collapse of the Airbus/McDonnell Douglas talks, in the summer of 1976 a much more serious dialogue began with Boeing. The Seattle team, which numbered about thirty, was headed by Tex Boullioun, the head of Boeing's commercial aircraft division and one of Boeing's most effective operators. He had first made his mark in Boeing's guided missile division and had a reputation for being formidably numerate with a memory like a computer. Born in

Arkansas, he was nicknamed Tex because of his fondness for poker. With his cropped hair, he looked like a young Marine colonel. And though he was blunt and hard drinking, he claimed that as a young man he had had ambitions to be a priest.

As far as Airbus was concerned, Boullioun was an unbeliever. And though it never seemed to have crossed his mind that the Europeans would cause Boeing any problems, he also thought it could do no harm to distract Airbus from its work on the B10 by proposing some form of cooperation. It was never entirely clear to Airbus exactly what Boeing had in mind – because the talks ended before they could get that far. But what the Americans seemed to be proposing was that the two companies should work together on the Airbus B10 and Boeing's 767 as a single project. Tex Boullioun told Lathière, 'I can't work with either Lockheed or Douglas because they'll send me to prison. But with you we did our little calculations. We can't make your B10 fuselage any better so why should we pay for expensive research for a 767 fuselage. Let's make the same plane: you make the fuselage, and we'll make the wing.'[22]

At times the Airbus people found it hard to believe that during the day they were sitting down around the table discussing the definition of a common aircraft while in the evening they were taking calls from their chief salesman in the Far East who had spent his day going head-to-head with Boeing salesmen on the other side of the world. It all seemed rather surreal.

To help things along, the B10 project was, in recognition of the Boeing involvement, renamed the BB10, which led Bernard Lathière to suggest that Brigitte Bardot might be asked to be the godmother. But however alluring the prospect of the sexiest woman in France being involved in some way, the more Airbus heard about the sort of cooperation Boeing had in mind, the less it liked it. When Jean Roeder first heard the outline of the Boeing plan, he said, 'Gentlemen, if that's the way it is, many thanks but the meeting is at an end.'[23] After the talks had broken down, Roger Béteille was in no doubt about the reason why. He told Lew Bogdan, 'It didn't work because Boeing didn't want it to. If we had accepted their offer we would have become simply sub-contractors. But we were not ready to let go our fuselage which was the key element in the success of Airbus.'[24]

Meanwhile, the problem of making the B10 more attractive to Lufthansa and Swissair refused to go away. The more Béteille thought about it, the more convinced he became that what the plane needed was a new, smaller, reconfigured wing. As always, there were pros and cons. Designing aircraft, especially wings, is a business that always involves striking balances and making compromises. In this case, the advantage of a new wing was that, thanks to the advances in aerodynamic technology and dramatic increases in computing power over the previous ten years, it was possible to get much better lift and performance out of a smaller area. The drawback was that in modern aircraft the wings are also where the fuel is stored; so the smaller the wing, the shorter the range of the aircraft.

The redesigned wing was one hi-tech feature of the A310, as it came to be called. The other was the controversial two-man 'glass' cockpit. Up to now, all jet airliners had a flying crew of three, with the pilot and co-pilot side-by-side facing forward and a third pilot sitting on a seat at a right angle just behind them. It was his job to monitor the side panels. But by doing away with the side panels and replacing the traditional instruments with multi-colour, multi-function cathode ray tubes serving up information on demand, the designers eliminated the need for the third pilot. This did not go down well with the pilot unions, who put such pressure on the airlines that Air France, Sabena and Lufthansa insisted that their A310s should be equipped with a three-man cockpit. Opposition from the Sabena and Lufthansa pilots soon faded but Air France continued to fly with three air crew in the cockpit for some years afterwards.

The birth of the A310 was both prolonged and difficult. The design of the wing particularly caused intense debate and some infighting. It was a battle that the protagonists still remember more than a quarter of a century later. There are those who maintain that the reason why the A310 never sold as well as had been hoped was because its range was too short. Others maintain that the value of the A310 in underlining the presence of the Airbus family in the market place far outweighed any initial technical shortcomings which, in any event, were overcome as later versions of the plane were developed. If the A310 had not appeared when it did, some two years later, Airbus would have left the door open for Boeing's 767 to move in completely unchallenged.

Jean Roeder says:

> The A310 is a programme of very great significance for Airbus Industrie for two reasons. Firstly, it was the beginning of the family development. We showed the world that we were not sitting on a nine-day wonder, and that we wanted to realize a family of planes. Secondly, with this aircraft we won over customers we wouldn't otherwise have won. The A310 supplied us with a starting point for the A300-600 we would *never* have had without it. The A300 was gradually developed from the B2 to the B4 with its heavier weight and further range. But these versions still had the systems and the technology of the A300. What the A310 gave us was new systems technology, the efficiency and the productivity of the 'glass cockpit', and a new fuselage tail with a smaller elevator. All this helped us to modernize the A300 to become the A300-600, but I don't think it would have been possible without the A310. The A300-600 got the A310s shorter fuselage tail and two-man cockpit. With the new tail we could lengthen the cylindrical part of the fuselage, to accommodate 15 more passengers without increasing the overall length of the fuselage. And when GE brought a new generation of power plants on to the market, there was a big saving – some 7% – in fuel costs. So now we had two planes that had a great deal in common as far as systems and cockpits were concerned.[25]

Despite all that had gone before, it was by no means a foregone conclusion that Hawker Siddeley, Britain's sole remaining contributor to the Airbus programme, would make the A310 wing. With the British still on the outside and BEA showing not the slightest interest in the Airbus programme whatsoever, the consortium felt it was too risky to rely solely on Hawker for the A310 wing. 'We needed a new wing,' says Roeder, 'and it was evident that the English had the knowledge to make a wing but they were not in the programme.'[26] Last time, Hawker had made the A300 wing after it had agreed to bear a proportion of the cost itself (see Chapter 3 p.44). But Béteille and the rest of his team were by no means sure that Hawker, which was about to be absorbed into British Aerospace, would be prepared to do it again. Cunningly, Béteille proposed that Germany's VFW-Fokker and France's Aerospatiale should prepare their own proposals for a wing design and present the results in Toulouse. This they did. 'This put us in the precarious position of having to say which wing should be chosen which was not so easy if there are two big partners standing there with "a say" in the matter,' says Roeder. 'If you decide on one, the other doesn't look at you any more. Then something came to our aid. We realized the German wing was really better aerodynamically and the French one was structurally better.'[27]

At this point the machiavellian Béteille suggested that Airbus open a joint wing construction office in the north German city of Bremen to which the French would be sent to work with their German colleagues on the wing – one of the very rare instances where the French went north to Germany instead of the Germans coming south to France. By early 1978 there some eighty people of the so-called integrated wing design team hard at work developing a rival to the British wing. Inevitably, word of all this was not slow to reach Hatfield, just as Béteille had intended. Hawker Siddeley, which had started work on an A310 wing in 1977, realized that things were serious and stepped up its own efforts. But it was not just Hawker that was being targeted by Airbus: these wing games were part of a Franco-German plan to lure the British back into the programme. The consortium not only needed British wing technology. With little money coming in from the A300B and with the cost of putting the A310 into production already looming, Airbus Industrie also needed British government money.

*

For Airbus Industrie's sales team, as the year turned, excitement about prospects in the Far East was matched by acute disappointment in the United States. Knowing that it had next to no chance of seducing Boeing's major US clients, Airbus had decided to make a play for what Dan Krook describes as 'one of the smaller big airlines'. The target was the aggressive Texas-based Western Airlines, which was trying to steal business from its rivals with such gimmicks as steak and champagne for breakfast and broadcasts from the cockpit that allowed the passengers to listen to the pilots' commentary during take-off. Talks opened at the Farnborough Air Show in September 1976 when Western expressed interest in buying eight A300s. George Warde, who had just started work for Airbus in North America, went to see Art Kelly, the Western president whom he had known from his days with American Airlines, and it was arranged that one of Western's senior people and, incidentally, a representative of the Mormon Church on the board, should come over to Toulouse to look at the plane. Western was impressed and the serious talking began. There was huge excitement in the Airbus camp. As the negotiations continued, the Airbus sales team grew more and more confident that the vital break-through into the American market they had been looking for over the past three years was very close. 'We were given a lot of attention by Western Airlines,' says Krook. 'They played along very well and we were supported in the sense that we thought we had advocates in the company that gave us a good chance.'[28]

A decision was due in the first part of December 1976. But shortly before the crucial board meeting, word came that there would be no decision until after the turn of the year. George Warde thought that this was a bad sign. Time is in Boeing's favour, he said. The longer the decision was postponed, the more time they would have to come in and muddy the water. Which is exactly what happened. According to Warde, Boeing lobbied individual members of the Western board. Airbus people believe that Boeing used its influence with Salomon Brothers and Lehman Brothers. When in the final days before the decision Western asked the New York bankers for advice, both firms recommended that they should not go ahead. In the immediate aftermath Toulouse pointed a finger at Western's chief pilot, who was a great fan of Boeing's and also owned 20 per cent of Western's shares. The pressure had the desired effect. Shortly after Christmas, Western announced that it was not going to buy the Airbuses and intended to purchase Boeing and McDonnell Douglas DC-10s instead.

The loss of the Western order was a bitter blow to Dan Krook and his colleagues. 'The importance of the North American market, particularly in those days,' says Arthur Howes, 'could not be stressed highly enough. It was vital for the success of the programme that we broke into North America. Without that we could never go to the rest of the world and say our programme was confirmed.'[29]

Roger Béteille was not a man to brood on failure. A few days after the collapse of the Western deal there was a meeting in Paris at which Lathière, Béteille, Krook and Warde were present. As Warde remembers it, 'Everybody was being very straight and nice with each other.' Even so, everybody knew what the real agenda of the meeting was. It was Krook himself who took the initiative. 'Look,' he said. 'George knows more about Americans than anybody because he is one. And I – er – yield to him.' Lathière and Béteille turned to Warde and asked, 'What do you recommend?'

Warde replied, 'Well, I'll tell you what. Let me go. I've got a house here in Pibrac. I'll leave this house. I'll leave product support. I'll go back over there. I'll devote my full energy and effort to this and if I haven't sold any in two years . . .' His voice tailed away. 'I'll come back periodically . . . excuse me . . . I'll come back at whatever point it is logical for me to do that.'[30] And that was the end of it. Dan Krook continued as head of sales and George Warde left for New York to mount a renewed and concentrated assault on the American market and its airlines.

CHAPTER SEVEN

THE CAMEL'S IN THE TENT

IT WAS MAKE OR BREAK TIME. While the Airbus salesmen working the Far East were moving in on Thai Airlines, George Warde shut down his house in France and returned to New York as head of Airbus Industrie North America. As the former head of a major airline, Warde had a well-filled contacts book and a well-connected bush telegraph. Not long after his arrival, he learned that the Eastern Airlines president, Frank Borman, the former astronaut who had taken over the cash-strapped airline two years before, was talking to Lockheed, McDonnell Douglas and Boeing about new aircraft for the New York-Miami run. Using his contacts, Warde succeeded in getting Airbus invited to the party.

Airbus may have been a Johnny-come-lately, but as Warde saw it, this was an advantage. 'I'd rather be the closing act than the opening one,' he said. 'It gave me an opportunity to think about why they should have the aeroplane.' It also gave him time to prepare the ground. 'I had a few good friends at Eastern who were sympathetic to what I was saying; they liked the idea about the engine; and they liked the idea of the support programme.'[1] But although Warde felt that he was among friends, he knew that smooth talking would not be enough to clinch the deal. He would have to offer some real incentives.

It was at a meeting between Warde, Charlie Simon (Eastern's vice-president and chief finance officer) and Frank Borman that Warde came up with his bold 'fly and try' idea.

It was Borman who opened the exchange.

'What kind of proposal do you have?' he asked.

'Well, before I make a proposal, first you have to decide whether you want the aeroplane,' Warde countered.

'I don't know if I need it.'

'Well, you don't if you are going to die, because you can't make it with the Lockheed 1011. They have had a lot of engine trouble and what have you.'

Seeing Borman flinch, Warde decided to strike home.

'I'll tell you what I'll do. I'll let you have four aeroplanes free for six months.'

'Free?' Borman inquired incredulously.

'Yes. You pay for the training. You pay for the spare parts you use and you pay for your fuel and operating costs but you don't pay for the aeroplanes. And then in three months time you have to make a decision and I'll unwind the deal if you don't want it. If you do, we'll proceed on a firm programme.'[2]

Warde says that he thought of this on the spur of the moment while Lathière, whose father had been a car salesman, claims it was his idea. He says he told Warde, 'It's like lending a guy a Rolls over the weekend. Then on Monday he comes in and buys the car.'

Lathière was, as usual, gilding the lily. There was, as he knew, a huge difference between selling cars and selling planes. To lend a Rolls to a potential customer for a spin over a weekend would hurt nobody. To lend an airline four Airbuses over six months for nothing could cost millions.

'We were taking a huge risk,' says Lathière 'We were lending them new planes which once they had been flown would be worth nothing like as much. It was a gamble which could have cost us about $150 million to $200 million.'[3]

But Airbus was so desperate for business and Eastern was potentially such a huge prize that the risk was thought to be worth taking. Borman took the bait. Warde persuaded him to take Eastern's pilots and maintenance people off the airline's Tristars and DC-9s and send them to Toulouse to familiarize themselves with the plane and its systems. It cost Eastern some $7 million to train the flight crews, but Airbus agreed to pay for the maintenance and the cost of US certification.

One evening in April 1977 Lathière received a terse message from his sales team in Miami. 'Congratulations, you have got a blue-eyed baby.' The blue eyes referred to Frank Borman who earlier that day had agreed to the Airbus 'fly and try' proposal. On 2 May, Borman was in Toulouse to sign a deal in which Airbus was to lend Eastern four A300B4s on trial on the New York–Miami route for six months. By coincidence, on that very same day it was announced that Thai Airlines had ordered four A300s. It marked the end of a sales drought that had lasted fourteen months. It seemed that the twin-track sales campaign devised by Krook, Warde and Lathière some two years earlier was beginning to bear fruit.

Once Borman had agreed to go ahead with the trial, Airbus set about the practical details of importing the planes into the States and arranging what the industry calls 'product support' – training the pilots, supplying the spare parts and organizing the maintenance for an airline to whom almost every aspect of the Airbus operation was unfamiliar.

When the Americans threatened to impose a five per cent import tax on the planes, Warde reacted vigorously. He called Franz-Josef Strauss to complain, 'How can I be competitive? If I absorb the five per cent, my board will say that I'm giving the plane away; if I cut the five per cent, the Americans will accuse me of dumping.'[4] Franz-Josef agreed to come to Washington, where a meeting was arranged with the Vice-President, Walter Mondale. Strauss, whose style was hectoring at the best of times, went straight on to the attack. 'Look here,' he told the Vice-President. 'You are part of the NATO programme. If we in NATO buy one of your planes, we are going to charge you five per cent. That means that the NATO budget for American aircraft will remain unchanged but you will deliver five per cent fewer aircraft. If, on the other hand, you remove this requirement on Airbus, we won't do that.'[5] Franz-Josef was, of course, bluffing. Apart from the fact that he had once been West Germany's defence minister, he had no authority to speak for NATO. But his bluster had the desired effect: the five per cent import surcharge was removed.

To solve the mechanics of importing the planes into the States, Lathière, Bétielle and Warde set up a leasing deal whereby the banks would import the planes and then lend them, temporarily, to Eastern. A consortium, led by the Bank of America and supported by Morgan Stanley and the General Electric Finance Corporation, was put together to facilitate the arrangement in which Eastern itself had an interest. 'We tried to do everything right,' says Warde. 'It was a long-drawn-out, tough affair. I have always said I never had a white hair on my head 'til I did that deal because it was so complicated.' But the tactic of drawing Eastern into the arrangement worked just as Warde had hoped it would. 'It caused the people in Eastern to feel that they had invented the aeroplane,' he says.[6]

There then followed an agonizing pause while Airbus waited for the outcome of the Eastern trials. The planes had been flown to America by the end of August and were in service with Eastern by the Thanksgiving weekend. And though all the signs were good, it was not until the following March that the news came through. The trial had been a success: the pilots liked the plane and fuel consumption was three per cent under the promised figure. Eastern was prepared to buy.

Quite apart from its strategic importance, the Eastern order was massive: in total the package was worth a staggering $778 million. Not only had Borman put his airline's name down for twenty-three A300Bs with an option for a further nine, but he was, he said, also ready to buy twenty-five of the as-yet undefined and untried A310. It was a huge affirmation of faith in the Europeans. From Airbus's American rivals came a sharp intake of breath. As Boeing saw it, *the camel's head was in the tent*. The Eastern decision not only wedged open the door to the American market, but it served notice to the rest of the world that Airbus had arrived.

The decision may have been made but the deal itself was far from done. Borman was a man who drove a hard bargain and he was determined to extract as much, if not more, than Airbus was prepared to give. He had to be tough. Although Eastern, along with United, American and TWA, was one of America's Big Four, it had made next to no profit over the past ten years and was loaded down with $1.3 billion of debt.

However, the first problem Borman raised was not financial but operational. The question revolved around the strength of the runway at New York's La Guardia airport, which jutted out some 2,000ft into the East River and was partially built on wooden pilings. The fear was that the junction between the runway and the jetty would not stand the weight of the airbus as it landed and therefore the New York Port Authority would not grant the plane permission to land. Mysteriously, these objections were not raised about the heavier DC-10 and Tristars that also used La Guardia. Airbus offered to change the size of the tyres and modify the landing gear. But to no avail. It was only after Airbus offered to put up around $800,000 to pay for the runway to be strengthened that the problem disappeared.

The next objection raised another old bogey: the FAA's refusal to sanction any flight by a twin-engined civil airliner over water that lasted more than an hour. As Borman wanted to fly in a straight line from New York to Puerto Rico rather than following the eastern seaboard and then turning hard to port, this was a problem. But after George Warde, armed with all his documentation and a history of the engine, confronted the FAA and persuaded it to relent, this problem, too, disappeared

These difficulties, though real enough, were more in the nature of niggles than serious obstacles. As everybody recognized, the key to the deal was finance. Where was the money going to come from? In the past, aircraft financing in America had been a comparatively straight-forward business. The airlines were cash-rich, the banks were happy to lend and there was no need for Boeing, McDonnell Douglas and Lockheed to become involved in the complex and messy business of aircraft finance. As Steven McGuire says, 'This was not an important consideration for the American manufacturers. In the first place, their major customers were the relatively wealthy US-based carriers. At least until deregulation began seriously to affect their operations by the mid-1980s, these airlines were quite able to find finance for their aircraft purchases and did not generally need or want the intervention of Boeing, MDC or Lockheed. Second, the deep and well-developed US capital market was an ideal place to raise cash for aircraft purchases.'[7]

As we have seen, despite the size of the 747 jumbo project and the strain it put on Pan Am's finances, it was Pan Am's bankers, not Boeing, who put up the cash to enable the airline to buy the planes. In the course of the transaction a couple of million dollars did indeed pass from Boeing to Pan Am, but the cash was not an integral part of the deal: it was paid to the airline as compensation for delays and modifications.

For Airbus the situation was completely different. Eastern wanted the planes but had insufficient money. Airbus had the planes but insufficient customers. The only way to square the circle, so Bétielle and Warde thought, was to provide the planes *and* the money. With the help of some friendly banks and with the backing of the French and German governments' export finance institutions, Bétielle and Warde put together a highly ingenious financial package on terms so generous they knew the Eastern board would find it hard to refuse. The Bank of America was to lend $522 million over fifteen years at the modest fixed rate of 3.5 per cent a year at a time when the normal commercial rate was close to 9 per cent. Two European banks,

Crédit Lyonnais and Dresdner Bank chipped in with another $250 million in export credits, while Airbus itself came up with a $96 million bond issue and engine makers General Electric rounded things up with a $45 million loan. The prime reason why the rates were so attractive was because these loans had been guaranteed by the French and German governments.

However unwelcome to the Americans, there was nothing particularly sinister or untoward in the involvement of the French and the German governments in this deal. By the early 1970s both the European and American governments had quite deliberately fashioned their export finance bureaucracies into instruments of economic warfare. Although each institution had its own history, by the mid-1970s Britain's Export Credit Guarantee Department, France's COFACE (*Compagnie Française d'Assurance pour le Commerce Extérieur*), Germany's Hermes and America's Ex-Im Bank were all doing much the same thing: promoting the sales of their countries' products overseas by lending or underwriting at subsidized rates of interest. America's Ex-Im Bank, a child of depression set up in 1934 as a lender of last resort to finance projects bankers thought too risky, had, forty years later, become what was described as 'an export promotion institution of considerable force'.[8] Under its aggressive president, John Moore, it had dramatically expanded its lending and had begun to undercut, by a substantial margin, the rates charged by the European export agencies.

That the European camel should be nosing its way through the flaps of the tent at night to steal away an important customer with tempting offers of cheap money was bad enough. Even more provocative was Airbus's next move. When Borman indicated that the A300B4s were too big and that what he really wanted was a 170-seat plane, Bétielle said, 'OK, you can pay us for 170 seats and if you use more, you can pay us extra.' To the Americans, this was the last straw. As they saw it, not only was a cash-strapped Airbus, with the help of the export credit guarantees of the French and German governments, offering to underwrite the whole deal, but it was now pricing it to undercut the American competition. The critics were not far wrong.

Bétielle's offer was shrewdly calculated to put his plane on the same economic footing as Boeing's newest but much smaller offerings, the yet-to-be launched 767 and the 757. There were important differences between the Boeing planes: the 767 was a brand-new, twin-aisle wide-body, while the long, thin, single-aisle 757 was what many airlines thought to be little more than a souped-up, twin-engined version of the 727; the wings were new but the fuselage had simply been stretched a bit. The important point was that these planes could, depending on the exact configuration, seat between 150 and 190 people compared to 240 for the A300B and 224 for the A310. In other words, Bétielle was trying for two bites at the cherry.

Boeing was not amused by these games. Eugene Bauer, the author of the authorized history of the company, puts the value of Bétielle's promise to Eastern at $168 million. 'In effect,' he says, 'Eastern was compensated by Airbus for the difference between operating the 240-seat A300B and its smaller US competitor. Airbus then recovered those costs in full through a government subsidy.'[9]

When the details of the Eastern deal emerged, they created something of a storm on Capitol Hill. Accusing Airbus of 'predatory pricing', Boeing whipped up political support in Congress. The plane maker's case was taken up by Charles Vanik, a member of the Ways and Means Committee of the House of Representatives. The Eastern case, he said, raised 'a serious question of unfair trade practices and excessive export subsidies'; and a sub-committee was set up to examine the 'financial gimmickry' that had supposedly been used to close the deal.[10]

Airbus countered by saying that Boeing had made similar leasing arrangements when offloading some hydrofoil ferry boats a few years previously, and George Warde was wheeled on to try and limit the damage by pointing out that almost a quarter of the A300 was made in America, almost all of which was the GE engines. But tempers rose again when Eastern's marketing department promoted the new planes as 'The Whisper Jet'. Nor did Borman help when he boasted to *Newsweek*, 'The export financing on our Airbus deal subsidized this airline by more than $100 million. If you don't kiss the French flag every time you see it, at least salute it.'[11]

The Eastern deal marked a watershed. By giving Airbus a firm foothold in the American market for the first time, it triggered a bitter trade dispute between the Europeans and Americans that was to last for almost twenty years and was to come close to breaking out into a full-scale trade war (see Chapter 10). The financial weapons Airbus had fashioned to win the Eastern skirmish were over the years to become even sharper and more wounding. And it was not long before the Americans began to repay the Europeans in their own coin.

Initially, the attitude of the Ex-Im bank officials to Airbus ranged from neutrality to indifference. They thought that the A300 offered little or no competition to Boeing and other American aircraft. They considered it was too small to go head-to-head with the 747 and too big to be a real challenge to the 727 or the 737. The only possible threat, the Ex-Im bank thought, was to the DC-10 and the Tristar. But the Eastern deal changed these perceptions. As Airbus began to make inroads into the American market, the bank adopted what was called 'the Airbus waiver'. Crucially, this allowed the bank to supersede the protocols that prevented it from promoting domestic commerce. The effect of 'the Airbus waiver' was that if Boeing or any other US aircraft manufacturer could show that Airbus was its foreign competitor in a particular deal, then the US manufacturer would be eligible for a special cut-price Ex-Im bank loan. Furthermore, where Airbus was concerned, the Ex-Im bank was ready to match or undercut any terms offered by the French, German and, later, British governments. Boeing made such successful use of the Ex-Im bank in the late 1970s and early 1980s, when up to 50 per cent of the bank's lending was for aircraft, that the bank was nicknamed 'The Boeing Bank' or 'Boeing Savings and Loan'. The willingness of the Ex-Im bank to finance Boeing's business in this way did much to undercut the American case that Airbus was a creature of government, only kept alive by a diet of handouts and soft loans amounting to billions of dollars.

*

The controversy over the Eastern deal was merely the opening round in a long battle and it would take many years before this conflict reached its climax in Brussels in 1992. In the meantime, the spotlight was swinging back to Europe, where the main protagonists were engaged in one of those stately dances in which partners alternate as the music changes key. But when the dance ends and the music resolves, everybody is more or less where they were when they started, but the permutations can be interesting.

The possibility that Britain might rejoin the Airbus project had been in the air for some time. In Toulouse, Bétielle and Lathière had a healthy respect for Hawker Siddeley's technical ability and were anxious, as we have seen, to replace the somewhat ramshackle, *ad hoc* arrangement that had existed for the past nine years. As Toulouse saw it, the only guarantee that Hawker Siddeley would be willing or even able to continue designing and building wings for Airbus was if the British government would underwrite the work, as it had initially. The French and German governments were also keen for what had become British Aerospace to rejoin the group as a full partner. With Britain now a member of the Common Market, it made no political or economic sense for her to stand back from what was already Europe's biggest and most important politico-economic enterprise. Furthermore, with the initial sales of the A300 so disappointing and with millions of dollars needed for developing the A310, the idea that Britain might come back to share the load was attractive. The French were minded to attach conditions; BEA had by now been merged with BOAC to create British Airways, and the French deeply resented BA's refusal to buy the A300 and could never understand why the British government was so feeble in its refusal to order the national airline to do so. If Air France understood where its duty lay, why should British Airways be so different, the French inquired. The Germans, on the other hand, were more laid back.

The first overtures to the British had been made in the late spring of 1976 when formal talks in Paris opened between the two governments at official and junior minister level. There were also contacts between the plane makers: Lord Beswick, a former Labour minister and now chairman of British Aerospace, met General Jacques Mitterrand, his counterpart at Aerospatiale and the brother of France's future president, François. But the moves were exploratory and the mood cautious. The French indignantly rejected a tentative British suggestion that they might participate in the A310 project as a separate exercise outside the Airbus programme and responded by saying that if the British wanted to rejoin the club, they should pay a re-entry fee. The two sides agreed to differ. And it was not until 1978 when Boeing made an offer to British Aerospace to participate in the making of the 757 that the issue moved to the top of the agenda. Boeing's approach was carefully calculated. It was also well-timed.

Unlike the French and Germans, the British no longer had any emotional or financial commitment to Airbus. And though Britain was by now a member of the Common Market, the country's political and business leaders still looked as much to America as they did to Brussels for inspiration, identity and self-interest. Furthermore, Britain's aerospace industry was in an even weaker condition than it had been in 1967. Rolls was only just beginning to recover from the RB 211/Lockheed disaster which had plunged it into bankruptcy, while British Aerospace, the new state-owned entity that now embraced both the British Aircraft Corporation and Hawker Siddeley, was suffering from excess capacity and a lack of orders. Both Rolls and BAe, so Boeing thought, were open to any half-decent offer. Finally, there was British Airways who had weakened any negotiating position it might have had by rejecting the Airbus out of hand and expressing a firm preference for the 757 fitted, of course, with Rolls-Royce engines. It was a situation that gave James Callaghan, the British prime minister, a great deal to think about. It also gave Boeing considerable grounds for hope. If things worked out according to Seattle's plan, Boeing would delivered a serious blow to Airbus by wooing Britain away; it would have obtained the help it was looking for with the 757; and it would have secured an engine manufacturer and launch customer for the new plane on the best possible terms.

Boeing's 'T' Wilson had, in his thorough way, done his homework and had taken good care to bait the hook. He knew that by offering British Aerospace the contract to build the wings for the 757, by enticing Rolls-Royce with the promise of a large American order, and by luring British Airways ever more firmly into the Boeing camp, he would be widening the split that had divided Britain's political and economic establishment for the past thirty years, since well before the signature of the Treaty of Rome in 1957. His calculations were correct: the Boeing intervention triggered a debate that was more or less a re-run of that eleven years earlier when Britain reluctantly signed up for the Airbus adventure. Now, as then, the choice was Europe or America? Now, as then, the politicians tried to have it both ways while the businessmen had to face some hard decisions. The only difference was that this time it was Boeing, not McDonnell Douglas or Lockheed, that was the main actor in the piece.

The battle lines between the main protagonists were clear from the outset. Most observers agree that had Boeing made British Aerospace an offer of full partnership on the 757, the British would probably have agreed. But just as Airbus had turned down Boeing's offer of collaboration on the 767 a year or so before because they had no appetite to be a Boeing sub-contractor, so BAe felt much the same way. The company had been making good money on the A300 Airbus wings and looked like making even more on the A310, and was profoundly suspicious of Boeing's real intentions. Peter Jay, then Britain's ambassador in Washington, who teamed up with Sir Kenneth Keith of Rolls-Royce to press the Boeing case, says, 'There was the usual tooth-sucking about whether BAe would really get the work. Before long I was discussing it with McFadyean at British Airways and Kenneth Keith at Rolls. Pretty soon it was clear that while British Airways and Rolls were dead keen, BAe didn't want to know. There was a neurotic anxiety at the time that they would end up as merely tin-benders. But it wasn't tin-bending. It was full sharing of the work.'[12] Some at BAe worried that they would be unable to meet the stiff terms of the agreement. Studies had shown that British production costs were some 30 per cent higher than Seattle's, but at the end BAe was suspicious, just as Airbus had been, of the Americans' intentions. Was the offer of work on the 757 to be a one-night stand, they wondered, or was it to be the beginning of a long-term relationship? Boeing might be offering good terms for the 757 but there was no guarantee of work further down the line.

For the next six months the future of Airbus and Europe's civil aerospace industry was a question that was to occupy the full attention of the president of France, the chancellor of the Federal Republic of Germany and the prime minister of Great Britain. Britain, as so often, was in two minds. 'The situation was intensely political,' said James Callaghan. 'Had we not gone into Airbus, it would have been interpreted as a political act. Giscard would have used it against us and Schmidt would have drawn a similar conclusion. On the other hand, we wanted Anglo-American co-operation. American industry can offer us something. Britain had an important dowry to bestow on a suitor. The question was who would pay the right price for this dowry. Heads of government must interest themselves in this industry. There is a lot of politics in it.'[13]

One of the first indications that Boeing was looking to Europe for help with the 757 came in the shape of a message to Britain's new ambassador to the United States, Peter Jay, shortly before the Thanksgiving weekend in late November 1977. Apart from a reputation for brains (he was famously known as 'the brightest young man in England'), Jay, a former Treasury official and economics editor of *The Times*, also had the distinction of being the prime minister's son-in-law, having married his daughter Margaret. In an uncharacteristically flamboyant piece of political patronage, James Callaghan risked the ire of the Foreign Office professionals by sending Jay to Washington. On his arrival Jay decided that the first duty of a new ambassador was to visit all the outlying outposts of his new empire. It was while his staff was organizing this that Jay received a call from Boeing inviting him to make a flying visit to Seattle over the Thanksgiving weekend. As this holiday, is, apart from Christmas, the most sacrosanct in the American calendar, it was clearly intended to be more than a social visit.

Having arrived in Seattle, Jay was ushered in see Tex Boullioun, the head of the commercial airplane division. After a brief outline of the 757, Boullioun came to the point. 'We want partners,' he told Jay. 'We would be prepared to give British Aerospace half the work and we would be looking to British Airways for the launch order.' Quite what the exact nature of the partnership would be was not spelled out in any detail. There was nothing in writing. But the ambassador left with the impression that Boeing was offering British Aerospace a full partnership rather than a subsidiary wing-building role. 'I came away with this proposition in my head and reported it back to London,' he recalls.[14] From that point on, Jay, whose father Douglas (later Lord) Jay was one of the Wilson government's most Europhobic ministers and a strong opponent of the Airbus project, worked tirelessly to promote the Boeing cause both in Whitehall and in Downing Street. He is coy when asked whether he used the family connection to bend his father-in-law's ear. But he says that he did tell Callaghan the story on a visit to London in the spring of 1978. 'To my surprise he showed a lot of interest in this. He picked this up in a very serious way. Then, even more to my surprise, he announced that he wanted to come to Washington and meet the key players.'[15]

Having enlisted our man in Washington as a virtual member of the team, Boeing made its formal offer in February 1978. It turned out to be something rather less than the equal 50:50 partnership that Tex Boullioun had described so enthusiastically to Peter Jay a couple of months before. What Boeing proposed was that British Aerospace should design and build the 757 wing on a fixed-price contract and that, apart from an allowance for profit and expenses, British Aerospace should work to Boeing's own estimate of costs. In other words: if British Aerospace could not match Boeing's levels of efficiency, then it would have to cut its profits or, worse still, pay the difference out of its own pocket. Against that, the work would create 9,000 extra jobs for British Aerospace, 14,000 jobs for Rolls-Royce, and give Britain something like a 50 per share of the entire 757 project.

To the Treasury this seemed like a fair, if not generous, offer. As Sir Douglas Wass, permanent secretary at the time, told Ian McIntyre, the reason why the department came down against Airbus was that it was regarded in the Treasury as just another public sector investment that had gone wrong. 'We costed it, scrutinized the assumptions about volumes of sales, the price that could be obtained and so on, and concluded that it was a rather dubious investment . . . It seemed to us that we'd be locked into a gung-ho European enterprise, and that quite the best course would be to stay out and let British Airways buy in the best market – which was Boeing.'[16] This was a mandarin's version of that old saying, 'Nobody gets fired for buying IBM.'

If the Treasury and the Department of Trade were Boeing fans, the europhile Foreign Office saw itself as a founder member of the Airbus supporter's club. It was not that they knew or even cared much about the aeroplanes themselves. But having played a large part in cajoling Britain into the Common Market, it was the commitment to the European idea that the Foreign Office officials were excited about. As they saw it, rejoining Airbus was an important part of Britain's long-term European strategy.

One of the main protagonists of this view was Sir Nicholas Henderson, Britain's ambassador in Paris, who was as energetically pro-Airbus as his counterpart in Washington was anti. Henderson was an ambassador of the old school. His account of the luxury, the style and the gossip of the *Parisiana haute* who came to his frequent parties at the British embassy evoke a now-vanished era. As a political operator, however, he was surprisingly outspoken, opinionated and thoroughly contemporary. By his own confession his ardent support for Airbus caused some irritation in London and there was at least one major row with Sir Kenneth Keith, the sardonic and abrasive chairman of Rolls-Royce. .

Sir Kenneth had made his reputation in the 1960s by establishing merchant bankers Hill Samuel as a major force in the City. As an expert on mergers and take-overs, Keith was frequently called on by government for help and advice. Although he was not by any stretch of the imagination even faintly left-wing, neither was he a visceral Tory like the majority of City people. Labour politicians appreciated his direct and unstuffy approach to the problems of the day and in 1972 asked him to rebuild Rolls-Royce after the government had taken over the bankrupt company. Even now, some thirty years later, Keith (now Lord Keith and in his eighties), still cherishes his macho reputation. Over lunch, he told me the story of his first days at Rolls-Royce. He recalled an incident in which one unfortunate executive turned up early for an interview, only to be told to come back at the appointed hour. When he did so, Keith said, 'You're fired. Be out of the building by 12 o'clock and remember that how you conduct yourself over the next hour will have a bearing on how we treat you in any settlement we might reach.' As chairman, his manner was distinctly pro-consular. His deputy chairman, Don Pepper, remembers an episode when Keith, as part of a world tour of the Rolls-Royce dominion, was planning a visit to Iran which included a meeting with the Shah. In preparation, Keith asked his staff to inquire whether the Shah had ever met him.[17]

Like so many of his generation whose attitudes were formed during the war, Keith was unshakeably pro-American. When we met he reminded me that his wife was American and that as a lieutenant-colonel in the Welsh Guards he had been on Eisenhower's staff as part of the Anglo-American command planning the D-Day invasion. He explained that Rolls-Royce's links with the Americans went back to World War II, when the Americans were building more Rolls-Royce Merlin engines for the Mustang than the British themselves. He explained that Rolls-Royce never went for the French, whom they thought 'too difficult, too tricky'. And he added, 'I steered Rolls hand in hand with British Airways. Together we tried the Boeing route.'[18] It is worth noting that Keith was a member of the British Airways board before he took on Rolls-Royce. Given their very different attitudes but similarly patrician characters, Sir Nicholas Henderson, the diplomat, and Sir Kenneth Keith, the merchant banker, were bound to clash.

It was in the spring of 1978 that the Airbus question began to feature regularly in Henderson's telegrams. In the entry in his diary for 5 April, he writes, 'One of my main preoccupations has been Britain's economic and industrial decline. I have sent several dispatches on this subject over the past two years. My sphere of responsibility is obviously limited. I can point to the way the problem of the threat to Western European industry presents itself to the French (and the Germans) and how they are thinking of meeting it. The airbus is a typical example. We pulled out of this Franco-German project in the early stages. We can never make up our minds whether to be junior partners of American industry or equal partners in European industry. My fear is that even if a great many people in Whitehall are thinking and worrying about this issue, the decisions when they are taken will be *ad hoc* and piecemeal.'[19]

Henderson feared that if Britain chose the Boeing option, the decision would have an effect well outside the realm of civil aviation. 'It will not help the attempts being made to coordinate defence procurement in western Europe,' he wrote. 'I doubt whether we would in the circumstances get much of a share of a new European aircraft; and it would not help industrialized co-operation generally in Europe . . . The danger of going in with Boeing is that you become a junior partner and are eventually reduced to being a components manufacturer.'[20]

Some three week after writing this, Henderson had lunch with Keith at the Rolls-Royce headquarters in Buckingham Gate. Henderson was on his own but Keith was supported by Sir John Russell, Britain's former ambassador in Madrid, and Sir Peter Thornton, a former permanent secretary at the Department of Trade and a recent recruit to the Rolls-Royce board. It was three knights against one. 'It was an experience I will not soon forget,' Henderson writes. 'They hammered at me to try and make me understand the importance of saving Rolls from further bankruptcy . . . [Keith] is determined to bring off a deal between Rolls-Royce and Boeing. He is afraid that a decision by British Aerospace to enter Airbus Industrie will ruin his chances, largely because he thinks that a European deal can only come if BA are forced to buy airbuses instead of Boeings.' Henderson countered by saying that he had no desire to see Rolls-Royce go bankrupt again, but suggested that Rolls-Royce should avoid the anti-European image it seemed to be acquiring.'[21] The lunch ended on an acrimonious note, though Keith did agree to come to Paris and try and improve relations between Rolls-Royce and the French.

The longer the debate went on, the clearer it became that this was an issue that only the prime minister himself could resolve. As Callaghan himself observed, 'The interests of ministers seemed likely to pull in different directions.'[22] To help him find a way through the maze, Callaghan turned to Sir Kenneth Berrill, the head of the government's think tank. But as Berrill and his colleagues produced a report so even-handed as be of little use as a guide to action, Callaghan decided that there was nothing for it but to go to the States to see for himself. On the weekend of 24 June the prime ministerial party set off for Washington. By this time the pressure was mounting from both the Americans and the Europeans. Boeing's 15 May deadline for an answer to its proposal to British Aerospace had already expired, and while Callaghan was actually in Washington, the French government took the opportunity to announce that if the British decided to rejoin Airbus, it would only be allowed back if British Airways bought European rather then American planes. In mid-July, shortly after Callaghan's return from the States, the French president, Valery Giscard D'Estaing, and the German chancellor, Helmut Schmidt, turned the screw still further by announcing that the A310 would go ahead irrespective, with or without the British. It was now more than two-and-a-half years since the board of Airbus Industrie had given the A310 the green light, and with the launch of Boeing's 767 and 757 fast approaching, and Swissair and Lufthansa approval only days away, the consortium's patience was running out. The view in Paris was that the British could delay no longer.

During his three days in Washington, Callaghan was entertained by all three players. On his first day he lunched with Frank Borman who reassured him that he intended to buy Boeing 757s fitted with Rolls-Royce engines. In almost the same breath he told the British prime minister how happy Eastern was with its new air-buses and what good planes they were. That same evening Callaghan had dinner with Boeing's 'T' Wilson and Tex Boullioun. It was a tense affair. The British had scarcely bothered to conceal their suspicion that the 757 might never be launched and could be no more than a ruse to split up Airbus, while the Boeing people were nervous that the United Airlines board, which was shortly to decide between its 767 and the A310, might 'do an Eastern' on them. According to John Newhouse, Wilson told the British their suspicions were unfounded and that Boeing fully intended to go ahead with both the 757 and the 767, but he threw little light on what the nature of the relationship between Boeing and British Aerospace might be. Looking back, Callaghan said, 'Wilson dangled larger future projects before us, but the more he said, the less interested I became, because I felt Boeing wanted to swallow us. Wilson seemed to want British Aerospace as a sub-contractor, not a collaborator.' Subsequently the British complained that Boeing had talked down to them and Callaghan said he felt he had been treated like the head of some underdeveloped country.

The final meeting with Sanford McDonnell, now chairman of McDonnell Douglas, and John Brizendine, president of Douglas Aircraft, passed off pleasantly enough. For some time the British had been pinning their hopes on the MDD's plans for a new medium-sized plane the British saw as 'a third way' – an opportunity for a three-way collaboration between British Aerospace, Airbus and McDonnell

Douglas. But as the dinner progressed, these hopes faded. Callaghan himself summed it up when he said, 'Sandy McDonnell put forward an attractive concept, but it was never as hard as Boeing's offer. It was never really put hard as a concrete proposition on which you could build a negotiation.'[23]

The next few weeks were to be the toughest of all. As the debate raged over whether or not Britain should rejoin the Airbus project, behind the scenes the lobbyists at Airbus Industrie were hard at work trying to tilt the decision in their favour. Arthur Howes, the Englishman who had played an important part in setting up the US operation, left his post in charge of sales for Europe and Africa to return to Britain to help persuade the British government and British Aerospace to join forces once again with Airbus Industrie. Toulouse knew little or nothing about the black art of political lobbying at Westminster but it proved to be a quick learner. The members of the Labour Party's aviation committee were identified as a prime target in the hope that they would influence the Cabinet and the prime minister. There were thirteen members in all and the only drawback was that, to a man, they all believed in the Boeing solution. Howes persuaded them to come on a fact-finding trip to Toulouse. 'We put on a massive visit and spent a great deal of time preparing a rather detailed presentation,' Howes says. 'At the end of the presentation they asked if they could have a few minutes on their own, and we left them alone. And they came out of their room and said, "We have decided. We are unanimous. Britain must become a partner in Airbus Industrie." And they even asked me to help them write a letter to Jim Callaghan expressing this view.'[24]

The closer the British cabinet came to making a decision, the fiercer the battle between the government departments became. The crunch came early in August. On 2 August the cabinet bowed to the pressure exerted by British Airways and Rolls-Royce by giving the go-ahead for BA's purchase of nineteen 757s equipped with Rolls-Royce's RB 211-235 engine. The government also agreed to give Rolls the money it needed to develop the engine. There was never any doubt that Rolls-Royce and British Airways would get their way. But there was still a question mark over the fate of British Aerospace. By all accounts the cabinet debate was noisy, with the pro-Boeing camp doing most of the talking. In chairing the debate Callaghan adopted exactly the same tactic as Harold Wilson had in 1967 (see p.15). According to Henderson, 'the PM listened quietly and then summed up by saying, "Well, it certainly seems to me that the consensus is in favour of joining Airbus Industrie so we'll go in."'[25]

The French were less than delighted. Giscard described the decision of the Callaghan government to give BA the green light to buy Boeings while simultaneously applying to rejoin Airbus as 'bizarre'. And for a few weeks, with relations between Paris and London at freezing point, it looked as if the French and the Germans would give the British the cold shoulder. The French minister of transport came to London to protest to Eric Varley, the minister for industry, and there was a chorus in the French press saying the British were trying to have their cake and eat it while facing both ways. Varley responded to this explosion of Gallic mixed metaphor by repeating that HMG could not, whatever the French might say, force BA to buy the European aircraft against their will. From his vantage point in Paris, Henderson tended to blame Callaghan. In his diary entry for 1 October, he wrote, 'The appalling impasse we have reached over British entry to Airbus Industrie could have been averted, I think, if the PM and Giscard had been on easy telephoning terms, such as those that run between Schmidt and Giscard. I don't think it is a language problem . . . The main handicap is a lack of confidence and sympathy . . . Callaghan can inspire trust more than Wilson but he always displays an unequivocally non-Continental attitude. He is too English, too involved with his own domestic affairs and uninterested in unanchored political speculation, particularly about the future of Europe, to make much personal appeal to Giscard.'[26]

It was, of all people, Freddie Laker who saved the day. The year before, Laker had launched his cut-price transatlantic Skytrain service under the slogan 'Fly me. I'm Freddie.' It proved an instant success. And by under-cutting his competitors by nearly 70 per cent, Laker rapidly became the sixth largest carrier on the North Atlantic, bigger than the Swiss, the French, the Canadians and the Scandinavians. Having established himself on the North Atlantic, Laker then set his sights on the European market and, to general astonishment, in late September, just after the Farnborough Air Show, announced his intention to buy no fewer than ten A300s.

Coming hard on the heels of the Eastern order, the Laker deal was some consolation for the disappointing news the month before that United Airlines had chosen not to follow Eastern's lead and had plumped for Boeing's 767 in preference to the Airbus. For Laker himself, the decision to spend more than a hundred million dollars on a plane that he once described as a camel was a distinct *volte-face*. He was then of the opinion that, 'It's useless: since it would be like a horse designed by a committee, it would fly like a camel.' What caused him to change his mind were the generous terms offered by the British government and Airbus Industrie, both of whom were, for their own reasons, extremely keen to secure the recently knighted Sir Freddie's support. Even then, Laker's enthusiasm for the Airbus was a mite grudging. Sounding more like British Airways than the man who had just come to the rescue of the European consortium, he said, 'It's a terrible indictment that I'm having to buy a new aircraft built abroad rather than in Britain.'[27]

In truth, Laker, who had just ordered five new long-range DC-10s from McDonnell Douglas at a cost of £228 million, was in no position to buy more aircraft. Indeed, it was Laker's inability to pay the first instalment of the $131 million he had borrowed from the banks to pay for his first three Airbuses that led directly to the collapse of Laker Airways in February 1982. But this was in the future. At the time, with air travel booming, Laker was, as ever, super-confident. To those who questioned his wisdom of buying more aircraft than he could possibly use, and asked what would happen if something went wrong, Freddie Laker would reply, 'In that case, you'll simply get your fucking aircraft back.' What he – and everybody else, including his backers – did not foresee was the collapse triggered by the second oil shock of 1979 in which the price of second-hand aircraft fell by more than 50 per cent.

To the British government struggling to mollify the French, still furious at British Airways' decision to buy Boeing, the Laker 'order' was heaven-sent. Although Laker did not sign the contract until early in 1979 and was still negotiating the final details of the financing package right up to the day before the delivery of the first aircraft in January 1981, he skilfully played on the anxieties of the manufacturers and the British government to extract extremely favourable terms.

At $42 million apiece, Sir Freddie was paying more or less the full market price for his three A300-B4s. It is comparatively rare for manufacturers to give airline customers a big discount on the ticket price of new aircraft; the savings usually come in the details of the finance package and in the cost of ancillaries such as maintenance, pilot and crew training, spare parts and so forth. So it was in this case.

Sir Freddie was a hard bargainer. Arthur Howes, who took a room at a Gatwick hotel to conduct the face-to-face negotiations with Laker, has vivid memories of these sessions. 'Freddie was very adept at misapplying the rules of arithmetic to prove that your aeroplane was wrong for him, and it was too expensive. He would deliberately break the rules of arithmetic to develop a price that was a long way from the truth. There was the aircraft price, the engine price, the price of the equipment. He used to do his little sums. He would cover sheets and sheets of paper with these false calculations. He had a stack of them about that high by the end of the negotiations. It was wonderful. After several days of this rather difficult negotiation, I began to feel as though I was being hit over the head with a rather heavy stick because it was the same argument all the time.' Howes eventually trumped Laker's card by having twenty copies of a single sheet with the correct sums. Each time Laker presented his sheet of paper, Howes would respond with his version until Laker acknowledged it was stalemate.[28]

There was, however, still the endgame. And it was here that Laker scored. As a launch customer, Airbus Industrie offered Laker free training for three crews per aircraft, instead of the normal one and a half; letters of credit covering spare parts and ground equipment from other suppliers; and a postponement of the up-front 10 per cent down payment until the day of the first delivery two years hence. All in all, this package of concessions was worth around £7 million – about as much as Laker would have paid, so Howard Banks has estimated, as a down payment on his first three Airbuses. It was a cash-free deal ideally suited for an under-capitalized, over-borrowed small airline.[29]

If Airbus Industrie's terms were generous, so too was the British government's interest-rate subsidy on Sir Freddie's $131 million bank loan. The money was lent by a consortium of thirteen banks led by the Midland at market rates over ten years. But to sweeten the deal the Thatcher government agreed to subsidise a fixed rate of no more than 10.2 per cent per annum over the life of the loan. The government may not, as Mrs Thatcher insisted, have to put up any cash for the Airbus deal, but it was, nonetheless, the government that helped to finance it. Reluctantly, the French agreed that, at a pinch, Laker was a suitable substitute for British Airways as Britain's first Airbus customer.

The way was now clear for both sides to settle the terms of British re-entry. They were understandably much less advantageous than they had been almost eleven years before. Exactly who came out best from this long drawn-out and messy business is hard to say. Britain had quite plainly been demoted. Instead of being an equal partner with the French and the Germans, Britain had no more than a 20 per cent share of the consortium. And though, once again, she had a seat at the Airbus top table, the cost to the government would be considerable and the commercial benefits hard to quantify. It would be another twelve years before Airbus Industrie could report that it had made its first operating profit. Rolls-Royce too was hardly a winner. The company may have secured the engine contract for BA's 757s, but after the initial orders from BA and Eastern, the launch customers, there was a period of almost two and a half years when Boeing did not secure a single significant order for the plane.* And when orders eventually picked up at the end of 1980 when Delta Air Lines ordered sixty 757s, it was Pratt & Whitney who supplied the engine, not Rolls-Royce.

The player who probably emerged best from this imbroglio was British Aerospace, who joined the consortium as a full partner at the very moment when Airbus sales were beginning to take off. By 1978/79 the Silk Road strategy was paying dividends: among the countries of the Far East to buy were the Philippines, Malaysia, and Indonesia; in Asia and the Indian subcontinent, there was Iran and Pakistan. After selling only thirty-eight planes in its first eight years, by the end of 1979 Airbus had sold 256 planes to thirty-two different airlines and was supplying more wide-bodied aircraft than any other manufacturer. Measured in dollars, Airbus had captured just over one quarter of the civil aircraft market. This was a remarkable achievement, something that no European manufacturer had ever accomplished.

The following year, in the wake of the 1979 oil price hike, the focus switched to the newly enriched Middle East, where Airbus salesmen, strongly supported by the French President himself, Valery Giscard d'Estaing, notched up successes in the Lebanon and in oil-rich Kuwait and Saudi Arabia. The French had no scruples in using their industrial and economic leverage to promote Airbus. While he was in

---

*   The only customer during this period was Transbrasil, which ordered nine.

Kuwait, Giscard announced a joint venture in which France was to build a petro-chemical plant in the country while opening the door for the Kuwaitis to invest in property in France. Giscard also made a series of speeches urging the Israelis to withdraw from the occupied territories and supporting the Palestinian case for self-determination. These remarks were well received by Airbus's potential customers in the Middle East: they went down particularly well in Kuwait, where a high percentage of the working population is Palestinian. By the same token, the strongly pro-Israeli stance of the United States hurt Boeing badly.

Those in Britain who had supported the Boeing alternative in the great Boeing v Airbus debate felt that an opportunity had been missed. 'I was bitterly disappointed and cross,' Peter Jay said to me. 'It seemed a tragic, wasted opportunity. We would have had a chance to be a world class manufacturer. I think British Aerospace was taking the soft option in the hope and expectation of continuing government hand-outs.'[30]

Nonetheless, those on the winning side of the argument remained low-key. The decision to rejoin was not accompanied by any triumphalist, pro-European fan-fares. A comment from Dr David Owen, the foreign secretary, that he thought that the episode had made Jim Callaghan 'more of a European' was about as far as the more Europhile wing of the Labour party would go.[31] On the British side, at least, it was looked at as a practical matter to be decided by a calculation of commercial advantage by those companies most closely involved. It was agreed that British Aerospace should have a 20 per cent stake in the consortium, that the French and the German stake should be reduced to 37.9 per cent apiece, while the Spanish share remained 4.2 per cent. To prevent the two major shareholders ganging up to outvote the smaller two, the British and the Spanish, the majority needed in the supervisory board for major decisions was raised from 75 per cent to 80 per cent. And, critically, the British government agreed to find £50 million for British Aerospace to help the company fund an estimated £250 million contribution to the A310's development costs. On 24 October the three governments announced that an agreement had been reached. After more than a decade on the outside looking in, Britain was once again a member of the club.

CHAPTER EIGHT

FLYING BY WIRE

O N 25 MAY 1979 A DC-10, American Airlines flight 191, took off from Chicago's O'Hare airport bound for Los Angeles. Just as the plane was about to lift off, the number one port engine ripped loose, flipped over the top of the wing and fell on to the runway behind the departing plane. The DC-10 climbed to 300 feet and yawed sharply to port, the nose dropped, and the now rapidly descending plane continued to roll until its wings were vertical. Thirty-one seconds after take-off and less than a mile from the runway, flight 191 crashed into an open field killing all 274 people aboard. It was the worst single civil air disaster in American history and it sent a shock wave through the industry.

The first thought was that the bolts securing the engine to its mounting had failed and that the engine had simply fallen off. The truth turned out to be more complicated. The brackets that attached the engine pylon to the wing were cracked. Under the stress of take-off the engine came loose and sheered through the hydraulic controls of the port wing, causing the wing slats automatically to retract. As the controls to the starboard wing were undamaged, the starboard slats remained in their extended take-off position. With the slats out of balance the plane started to roll. If the pilots had been able to see that part of the wing from the cockpit, it would have been a simple matter for them to correct the plane – as pilots did without difficulty in the simulator afterwards. But as they could not see what had had happened and as the cockpit warning system that normally flashes when the slats were out of balance had also been knocked out, the pilots followed the normal policy when an engine fails – which made the problem worse and the crash inevitable. As one of the test pilots said later, 'There is no pilot in the world that would have been able to save that plane.'[1]

The official inquiry showed that there was nothing wrong with the plane itself. It was the airline that was at fault. To save time and money American Airlines had ignored McDonnell Douglas's careful instructions about removing the engine and its pylon in two separate operations and detached the engine and its pylon in one piece. Instead of using the special jig recommended by the manufacturers, they did the delicate job with a fork lift truck. Hence the cracks – and the crash.

The regulators wasted no time. Almost immediately all DC-10s registered in the US were taken out of service. And although they returned about six weeks later, the Chicago disaster spelled doom for the accident-prone DC-10 and effectively marked the end of the American wide-bodied tri-jet era. At the end of 1981 Lockheed killed the Tristar: with sales of only 244, the Tristar cost Lockheed $2.5 billion in its thirteen years. And while DC-10s continued to roll down the Long Beach production line for a further seven years, volumes were low and the losses enormous. Overall no more than 446 DC-10s were sold. As a business, McDonnell Douglas, which was taken over by Boeing in 1998, never really recovered.

In many respects McDonnell Douglas and Lockheed were the architects of their own misfortune. As John Newhouse has observed, 'McDonnell Douglas and Lockheed built the same airplane, although it was perfectly clear, even in that time of high exuberance, that the market could not sustain both planes. One of the two companies should have built a genuine airbus – a twin-engined double-aisle airplane. Indeed, the widebody era should have started at the low end, with a shorter range twin-engined airplane, and evolved toward the bigger and longer-range airplanes. Some of Boeing's decisions were as imprudent as those of its two competitors, but Boeing was spared disaster, almost as much by good luck as by the energy and determination it showed in overcoming its mistakes. Boeing also benefited from the chaos McDonnell Douglas and Lockheed made of their commercial-airplane programs. But the major beneficiary of the chaos was Europe's Airbus program.'[2]

The industry had moved on since the late 1960s when the DC-10 and Tristar were conceived. The American-built, tri-engined widebodies turned out to be too big and too thirsty for the medium-range routes and too small for the long-range market catered for by the 747. In the Far East many Asian carriers were beginning to sell their DC-10s or cancel new orders. The makers of the tri-jets were being squeezed between the Boeing 747 and the Airbus A300.

As the optimism of the 1960s faded to be replaced by the meaner-spirited, more price-conscious 1970s, the attention of both airlines and manufacturers turned to smaller, less ambitious projects. As we have already seen, by the mid-1970s Boeing's plans for what was to become the long, thin, single-aisle 757 and the short, fat, twin-aisle 767 were already well advanced, if not completely formulated. At Airbus, too, there was a consciousness that the market was changing. By 1976 Roger Béteille was beginning to think that if Airbus was to be a real threat to the Boeing hegemony then it was time to challenge the Americans' domination of the single-aisle market represented by Boeing's 727 and Douglas's DC-9.

The A300/310 had loosened the American's hold on the market for larger aircraft, but in the 140 to 170 seat category the Americans were unchallenged. And it was this segment of the market, so the surveys showed, that had the greatest potential for growth. The 727 and the DC-9 were, by modern standards, dirty and thirsty aeroplanes. They were also getting old. Forecasts indicated that by the end of the 1990s some 3,000 planes in this category would need replacing: it was a huge market, worth between $50 to $70 billion.

In planning his next move Béteille was influenced not only by the need to challenge the American's dominance of the single-aisle market, but also by a fundamental shift in the nature of the American airline market itself. President Jimmy Carter's decision in 1978 to deregulate the airline business and abolish the Civil Aeronautics Board had a profound impact on the structure and economics of the airline business. The effects were not immediate. The first signals were confusing and it took time for a pattern to emerge. But within a couple of years a number of important airlines had gone bust. The best-known casualty was Braniff, the Texas-based airline that flourished during the 1960s but was badly hit by the second oil crisis of 1979 and by the turmoil following deregulation. Part of the chaos arose because deregulation opened the door to a host of smaller airlines who were, for the first time, able to compete with the major carriers on price. During the recession of 1980/81 the losses of the majors mounted while the profits of the local airlines rose. 'The first effects of deregulation were dramatic,' says Anthony Sampson in his 1984 study of world airlines. 'A new breed of air entrepreneurs saw the chance to expand small companies or to establish "instant" airlines which could undercut fares on local routes; they could dispense with much of the superstructure and bureaucracy of the big airlines and could use their flexibility to hit the giants at their weakest points where they could make quick returns.'[3]

Prior to 1978 the CAB had run a cartel. Its strictly enforced fare structure had ensured that fares on long-haul, transatlantic routes were kept artificially high, much higher than on domestic routes. The big airlines then used the profits that they made on the highly protected long-haul routes to subsidize the prices charged on the short-haul, domestic routes, thus shutting out competition from the smaller operators.

With the outbreak of a price war on the North Atlantic, the majors turned away from the small local markets to concentrate on fighting off the competition on the trunk routes. Meanwhile, behind their backs a host of small competitors rushed in to take advantage of the new freedoms. Some of these new ventures, like New York Air and Air Florida which offered 'free rides for a kiss', were short-lived. Others, like US Airways and People Express, survived the second 1979 oil crisis to profit from the new era. New regional networks developed with the smaller airlines providing the links to the hubs served by the big trunk carriers. Known as the 'hub and spoke' system, this is now a familiar feature of air travel throughout the United States, Europe and the Far East. It was, of course, not unknown prior to 1978. Each major had its hub: Northwest Orient had Minneapolis, TWA was based at Kansas City, and booming Atlanta was home for both Delta and Eastern. But the 'hub and spoke' system was given a big boost by deregulation. And as it expanded, so the

France's minister of transport, Jean Chamant (left), and West Germany's minister of the economy, Karl Schiller (centre), sign the agreement for the development of the A300B at Le Bourget air show on 29 May 1969.

Roger Béteille, the driving spirit behind Airbus.

Henri Ziegler, first president of Airbus Industrie.

Bernard Lathière, president, 1975-85.
'When I took over, things weren't
that brilliant.'

Franz-Josef Strauss, former West German
defence minister and first chairman of
Airbus Industrie.

1972. The first sale. Air
France's president, Pierre
Cot (seated right), and
Roger Béteille (seated left)
at the signing of the order
for six A300B2s.
Air France's
M. Galichon is seated
between Béteille and Cot.

The first flight.
The prototype
A300B landing at
Toulouse on
28 October 1972

On the road. 1971. German-built sections of an A300 on the way to Toulouse.

First set of wings for the A300B are unloaded from the Super Guppy after a flight from Hawker Siddeley in Britain.

2 May 1977. Breakthrough in America. Eastern Airline's Frank Borman (centre) closes the deal for A300B4s with Airbus's Bernard Lathière (right) and Roger Béteille.

BAe assembling Airbus wings in its plant at Broughton, Cheshire.

The Pyrenees Bear. Jean Pierson, president and chief executive, 1985–98

Noël Forgeard, Airbus chief executive officer and head of EADS Airbus division.

An A320 takes off into the sunset at Minneapolis.

An A330 in TAM livery on the runway at Toulouse.

An A340 takes takes off from La Paz, Bolivia, in the 'high & hot' campaign.

The Airbus single-aisle family in formation.

A Beluga air transport over Auch in south-west France.

The first A340-600 wing arriving in Toulouse.

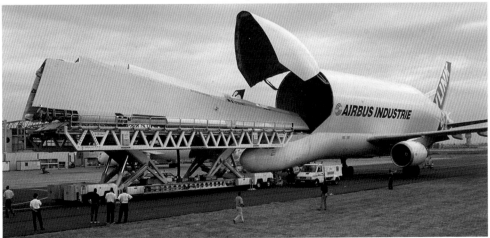

The A330/340 assembly line at Clement-Ader.

The shape of things to come. A mock-up of the A380 in flight.

The shape of things to come. A model of Boeing's SonicCruiser

demand for 150-seater, short-to-medium haul planes to ferry passengers from the sticks to the hubs simply exploded.

By the late 1970s the case for a new 150-seater was so strong that everybody wanted to get into the act. Even Airbus's own partners joined in. Airbus Industrie did not have the authority or the means to prevent its own shareholding partners from launching new projects outside the consortium. Not everybody shared Roger Béteille's vision of Airbus as a platform from which to challenge the Americans across the board. Several partners regarded the consortium simply as an *ad hoc* coalition to build the A300/A310 and were keen to do their own thing thereafter. This ambition led to the creation of the Joint European Transport group (JET). Its members were all Airbus partner companies and the plan was to create a new Airbus-type consortium to build a 150-seater. In a sense, history was repeating itself.

As we have already seen, European plane makers, led by the British Aircraft Corporation (now part of British Aerospace), had argued the case for a 150-seater ten years earlier. It was the key element in the noisy debate that preceded Britain's decision to join Airbus and to put up money for the A300. But the JET concept was not so much an old idea warmed up but an entirely new proposal to meet a new situation. And though JET's proposed structure and organization was similar to Airbus, its members regarded it as an entirely separate operation with its own funding and its own set of agreements. It was, in effect, Airbus Two.

The JET project eventually foundered and the baton was handed back to Toulouse. But one reason why the venture got as far as it did was because the Airbus Industrie partners were at loggerheads about what they should do next. The consortium was split. The French led the small aircraft faction while the Germans pressed for something significantly bigger than the A300.

One of the most striking features of the Airbus operation was that from the very beginning Béteille had mapped out the entire product range and had attached numbers from 1 to 11 for each. The A300 was B1, the A310 was B10 and the long-range, four-engined A340 was B11. One might say that with this chart to hand, Boeing should have been able to read Airbus like a book. But there was one important detail missing: what was not known was exactly when each new model would appear and in which order. Deciding when to press the start button on a new programme is perhaps the most difficult and most critical aspect of running an aircraft company. As a general rule, Boeing's reflexes were sharper and its top management more decisive than Airbus. With no supervisory board to second-guess them and with no shareholder partners to placate, once they had made their mind up, men like Bill Allen or 'T' Wilson rarely hesitated or prevaricated. Airbus's Roger Béteille and Bernard Lathière, on the other hand, did not enjoy the same freedom. They were constrained by the constant need to keep both their industrial partners and the bureaucrats and politicians of their government sponsors informed and happy.

Even the diplomatic Béteille admits that there was a rumpus. 'There were some divergent ideas within Airbus,' he told Arthur Reed. 'When we had to decide between the A320 and the A330/340, the Germans, under pressure from Lufthansa, were in favour of going for the A340, while the French, perhaps not completely unconnected with their part in building the CFM56, were in favour of the A320.*[4] Hartmut Mehdorn, one of Béteille's chief lieutenants at the time, is blunter. 'It was a huge battle,' he told me when I went to see him in Berlin some twenty years later.[5]

Mehdorn, a cheerful, approachable man, played a seminal role in the growth of Airbus. He is the antithesis of the conventional idea of the German engineer. He is outspoken and aggressive. He peppers his conversation with short, sharp remarks and describes anything he doesn't like as 'bullshit'. His style is more North American than north German and in the A320 v A330 argument he was firmly on the side of the French. 'What with all the talk from the Germans about stopping Airbus, things had been very negative,' he says. 'On top of this we had to spend a heavy amount of money over nearly three years before we could put the plane into production. So we had to be very strong and convince people we badly needed to attack Boeing's cash cow, the 727. With 1,700 727s flying around the world, there was a huge space in the market which we had to attack. Also there was the 737 fleet coming up which had to be covered. We had to attack Boeing's narrow body market.'[6]

The impression is sometimes given that Airbus is essentially a French project, conceived and led by France's brilliant engineers and technocrats. There is a good deal of truth in this. But it is also true that without men like Mehdorn, who developed much of the high-tech industrial infrastructure of the Airbus factories of north Germany, the operation would have been a great deal less effective than it is.

Mehdorn, who was born in Warsaw in 1942 and studied mechanical engineering in Berlin, was one of the first members of the post-war generation to become an aeronautical engineer – a prohibited occupation for Germans in the years immediately after the war. As a young production engineer, Mehdorn, like so many in Airbus, had cut his teeth on the 1960s Transall project in which the French and Germans joined forces to build a military transport plane. The Transall was not very successful but it gave the young engineers valuable experience of working together. In Toulouse and in Munich the engineers who had worked on Transall made up a sort of old boys club. Mehdorn says that the Transall way of working became a model for Airbus. 'One idea comes out of the design office in Hatfield, another comes out of Paris and another comes out of Hamburg,' Medhorn comments. 'And we had a meeting. And everybody had to explain. We take this good

---

*   This engine was developed by the American GE and the French SNECMA, a joint venture which
     had powered all Airbuses to date.

idea from Hatfield and another good idea from somewhere else. At the end of the day we had to go one way, but we had collected some good ideas. It's not the case that one idea is good and another is bad: everybody has good ideas. And this has driven Airbus quite early to a rather high performance.'

Mehdorn maintains that Boeing never understood this aspect of Airbus. He says that the way Airbus was organized made the Americans smile. 'Even though it had subcontractors all over the world, Boeing was organized too much on national lines. It had the Coca-Cola mentality and saw itself as representing the American way of life: put the bottle on the table and here's America. What it didn't see was that it was an enormous source of power to have young German engineers against young French engineers and British engineers against Spanish engineers. Nobody wanted to be in second place. It was an in-house competition.'[7]

In 1966 Mehdorn moved on to the Fokker Wolf plant in Bremen, which had made fighters for the Luftwaffe during the war and was now making components for the A300. Having made his mark as head of the A300 programme at VFW in Bremen, one of the five German companies working on Airbus, Mehdorn was summoned to Toulouse by Roger Béteille to help build up production from a very low level and to coordinate the flow of components from other suppliers. He arrived in 1978, just as Airbus Industrie was beginning to emerge from its long, dark tunnel.

Critics say that delay was inbuilt into the Airbus system. Certainly it took Airbus Industrie, on average, a couple of years longer than Boeing to bring new projects to market. The A300 took seven years from inception to its first commercial flight; while the birth pangs of the A320 lasted very nearly as long. But this was not necessarily a disadvantage.

In the aerospace business, luck is every bit as important as judgement. And the prizes do not always go to the swift: there are many examples of the tortoise overtaking the hare. As Hartmut Mehdorn observes, 'It's not speed that the aircraft industry demands. What matters much more is doing it right first time. If you get it wrong, it's very difficult to change it. If you get it right, six months either way doesn't matter that much.'[8] But in the case of the A320, what might be called 'Mehdorn's law' was stretched almost beyond breaking point. Promised for 1982, the A320 was not launched until 1984, did not fly until 1987 and did not enter service until 1988. In the interim both Boeing and McDonnell Douglas had made their bids for this sector of the market. As the delays to the A320 programme lengthened, so anxieties at Airbus Industrie mounted. At the time, no one could have imagined that the A320 would go on to be far and away the consortium's most successful plane.

*

By February 1981 when the A320 designation was used for the first time, the issue had been decided. Béteille had won his argument. But there were still many obstacles to be overcome and much to talk about. To force the pace the French government declared its support for the A320 at the Paris Air Show in June 1981. Air France joined in with an announcement that it intended to buy twenty-five A320s with an option on another twenty-five. As the plane had not yet even been defined, this was a remarkable act of loyalty. And it was not until that autumn that Airbus Industrie filled in the details. There were to be three versions in all: a 150-seater in a two-class configuration and a short and medium-range all-economy 164-seater. There was, however, no word from the Germans or the British. And it was not until March 1984 – almost three years later – that the A320 was formally launched. There were several reasons for this unconscionable delay.

Firstly, Lufthansa was not keen on the A320: it thought it was too small and the airline was tempted by the new propfan technology which involved two sets of counter-rotating propeller blades driven by a conventional jet engine. The propfan being offered as an option by McDonnell Douglas on its upgraded MD-80 was an ultra high bypass engine which promised startling fuel economies but was unproven. Airbus, too, had looked at the propfan but had decided, rightly as it turned out, that it was too risky.

Secondly, the A320 was held back by the reluctance of the engine makers, GE/SNECMA, who had powered the A300/310, to develop a suitable power plant for the A320. Although small, the aircraft needed at least 1,000 lbs more thrust than the 24,000 lbs its latest model, the CFM56, could supply. And it was only after Pratt & Whitney, Rolls-Royce, the Germans, the Italians and the Japanese formed the International Aero Engines consortium to produce the hugely successful V2500 that the GE/SNECMA partnership was goaded to upgrade the CFM56.

Thirdly, the partners argued fiercely among themselves for more than a year about who should do what. In Airbus language it was known as work-share and had been an issue right from the beginning. The Germans and the British view was that, whatever Toulouse might think, the French did not have a divine right to keep all the prestigious work to themselves and to leave the partners with the less glamorous pickings. As we have seen, the Germans felt particularly aggrieved that their role had been confined to the relatively simple business of putting the fuselages together. This had been an issue from the beginning, but with all the dramas over the A310 and with Boeing sniping around the edges to destabilize the consortium, the Germans and French closed ranks to get the job done. But with the Germans already in conflict with the French over the A320/330 argument and with the arrival of the British, the question of work-share began to loom.

The work-share battle was not fought in the first instance between governments, but by the partner/shareholders of the consortium. Although the governments may not have been in the front line, they were interested parties nonetheless. Government launch aid and development money was paid not to Airbus Industrie but to the companies themselves, and the amount was directly linked to the size of their contribution. Thus, for example, the greater the share British Aerospace had of the A320, the bigger the contribution from the British government would be. Politicians and government officials, therefore, had every reason to track the work-share negotiations extremely closely.

As we saw in Chapter 3, at the beginning of each new project the partners would assess the overall size of the job and would then negotiate what their individual percentage share of the work should be, based on an agreed assessment of the precise nature and extent of the work. Thus for the A300 and A310, Hawker Siddeley's contribution in building the wing was about 18 per cent of the gross. These percentages were freely bandied about during the negotiations. But what nobody was prepared to disclose to each other (or to anybody else, for that matter, including their own shareholders) was the net, i.e. how much money they made (or lost) on the job. According to Bob McKinlay, the A300 and A310 were profitable for Hawker Siddeley, while British Aerospace lost money on the A320 even though its share of the work rose to just under 25 per cent.

The work-share arguments were, so insiders say, as much about prestige as they were about money. Even though the work of final assembly accounts for little more than 6 per cent of the total cost of building an aircraft and accounts for a tiny fraction of the jobs, both the Germans and the British argued that it was their turn this time. A new production line meant, in theory, that everything was up for grabs. But that was not how the French saw it. 'Toulouse is the natural centre of Airbus activity, customers come to Toulouse and Toulouse is where the production line will be,' Airbus told *La Nouvelle Economiste* when the battle was at its height.[9]

At one stage the Germans pressed for a 40 per cent share of the A320 work as a reflection of their contribution to the Airbus project, while the British argued, somewhat disingenuously, that it was against the interests of the partners to specialize too narrowly and that the big jobs should be swapped around to give everybody experience of R&D and production. To get this idea off to a good start, the British suggested that they might build the nose and the fuselage as well as being responsible for the assembly and the flight testing. This idea, which managed to threaten the interests of both the other partners simultaneously, did not go down well, especially with Roger Béteillle, who said, 'we are strongly against the idea of people saying we have made a wing, now we want to make a fuselage'.[10] However, when the British realized how much their increased role would cost the Treasury, the idea was quietly dropped. Even so, it took the partners more than a year to sort out this who-does-what dispute. In the spring of 1986, with the first flight less than a year away, the argument was still going on.

In the event, the British share of work on the A320 was significantly larger than it had been on the first two Airbuses, mostly because some of the work the Germans had been doing on fitting out the wing after the British had pulled out in 1969 returned to BAe at Chester. 'Our share of the A320 work made good engineering sense because the sub-division in the first place was political,' says Bob McKinlay. 'The A320 wing was the neatest of the lot: it left Chester with everything on it.'[11] It was to be the first and last time that the British would have the responsibility for making an entire Airbus wing.

Frustrating as these delays were, the main problem was money. The politics of Airbus are such that decision-making can be slow and cumbersome. But the prime cause of the delay in this instance was the reluctance of the Germans and, particularly, the British to put up the money. Overall, it was estimated that the development costs of the A320 would be of the order of $1,700 million, most of which would have to come, as they did last time, from the sponsoring governments. What's more, the new Airbus was a late challenger in a sector of the market where the Americans were already firmly entrenched. It was therefore hardly surprising that the Germans and the English had their doubts.

Behind the scenes the French were becoming increasingly irritated and alarmed at the procrastination of their partners, but in public they tried to paper over the cracks. Bernard Lathière's comment on the situation to the *International Herald Tribune* in May 1983 was a model of restraint. 'We have mastered the technical, physical, political, industrial, and administrative problems of building an Airbus,' he said, 'but the amount of money involved in deciding to manufacture a third airplane does lead to some decision-making delays.'[12]

From the start the French were ready and willing to back the A320. Early in 1983 General Jacques Mitterrand, the head of Aerospatiale, had leaked a letter in which he accused the Germans and the British of not being sufficiently supportive of Airbus in general and the A320 in particular. As it was clear that both the British and the Germans were wobbling, that autumn Jacques' brother, President François Mitterrand, left no doubt as to where the French stood when he declared, 'The A320 will be built and I am its chief salesman.'[13] But the Germans were much less sure. Within the Kohl administration there were those, like Martin Grüner, the Airbus minister, who were doubtful as to whether the A320 would pay its way. Germany was the mainstay of the Airbus project, and although ministers realized that they were in for the long haul, they were well aware that they had seen no return on the billions of deutschmarks they had poured into the A300 and A310. The knowledge that sales of the new plane would, so they were told, have to be around the 700 mark for the government to get its money back did not fill them with confidence. Franz-Josef Strauss, chairman of the Airbus supervisory board and a director of Lufthansa, counter-attacked with the warning that if the A320 was not given the go-ahead, unemployment in Germany would rise.

In Britain, where Mrs Thatcher regarded the Airbus as unwelcome present from her Labour predecessor, enthusiasm for the A320 was, to put it mildly, lukewarm. When Sir Austen Pearce, who in 1980 on Mrs Thatcher's invitation had taken over from Lord Beswick as chairman of British Aerospace, made his first presentation about Airbus at Number 10, the Prime Minister replied, 'The last thing I wish to encumber myself with is another Concorde.'[14] The atmosphere became even more frigid when Sir Austen told her the British contribution to the A320 would be £480 million – roughly five times what Britain was asked to pay for the A300 fourteen years earlier. Undeterred, Sir Austen pressed on with his request for between £70 million to £80 million in launch aid plus a government guarantee on the loans for the remaining £400 million or so.

As a former international oilman, Sir Austen had been used to dictating terms to governments. Now it was he who was the supplicant. It was a harsh induction into the rough and tumble world of civil aviation. The company was in poor shape. His predecessor, Lord Beswick, an ennobled trade unionist, had made little impact. Beswick knew a lot about employment and labour relations but next to nothing about the aircraft business. He looked for his instructions to Gerald Kaufman, at that time number two to Eric Varley, the industry minister. Sir Austen, who had spent the previous eight-and-a-half years running Esso, also knew little about aircraft. But what he did know was that the company had too many people, too few orders and too little work. Like most industrialists in Britain, he had reservations about Airbus. He thought its management system was eccentric and its finances impenetrable. But as the company's civil aircraft programme was in disarray and as Airbus was, as far as BAe was concerned, the only game in town, Sir Austen thought it was essential to make the most of it.

'I started getting interested in 1981/82 when I started to go to supervisory board meetings,' he says. 'I was very concerned at the financial set-up at Airbus. My prime contact in government was Norman Lamont. He was the [aerospace] minister at the time and if anyone sat on the fence it was Lamont. He really wouldn't give an answer to anything. I kept asking when we were going to break even: how many do we have to make to break even? And nobody could tell me. Nobody knew.'[15]

Pearce says that the main reason why BAe became so keen on the A320 was that its own civil aircraft programme was stalled and the company badly needed the work to fill its empty plants. Within twenty-four hours of being told that its own HS146 was ready to fly, the head of the programme at Hatfield told Sir Austen that because of an electrical fault the plane would now not be ready for another three months. The longer the delay, the worse the situation would become.

It was at this point that Pearce stepped up the pressure. 'I knew that the French and the Germans had already got their money. The money was available. But Norman Tebbit [the industry secretary] was hanging back because he did not believe that this aircraft would sell. I don't know how many meetings I had with Tebbit on this, but I do know they were never on time – he was always at least half an hour late. I had a number of meetings with Franz-Josef Strauss and he gave me the message very clearly that if the British did not participate in the A320, that was the end of their involvement with Airbus. It was effectively an ultimatum to me. He finished by putting a date on it. He gave me about a month to get the money out of the government. I realized I was getting nowhere with Norman Tebbit and I realized the only thing to do was to go straight to the prime minister.'[16]

Pearce says that he knew that if he had talked to the DTI, they would have stopped it. He also knew that if he told his colleagues what he intended to do, the result would have been the same. 'They had other irons in the fire.'

'So I took it on my own shoulders and on the Friday I rang up Number 10 and said I'm up against a deadline and I want a meeting with Mrs T about the A320 Airbus as soon as I can.

'They said, "She'll see you on at ten o'clock on the Monday."

'On Sunday evening, my telephone rang. It was Norman Tebbit. He called me a bastard and all the names under the sun. I asked, "Do you want to come to the meeting?" and I said, "I'm sorry Norman but this is my company's future in the civil aircraft business and I'm going to fight for this as long as I possibly can."'

Pearce arrived at Number 10 on the dot of ten o'clock. 'I was told to go upstairs to Maggie's study and there she was sitting at her desk with Norman Tebbit beside her looking as black as thunder. She said, "You have 25 minutes." I said, "Prime Minister, I only want to tell you three key things. The impact on commercial position; the impact on our work force and on worldwide reputation as an aircraft manufacturer." I said, "If we don't get the money, British Aerospace is going to go down the drain. And it's your first privatization." She asked me a few questions, and after about twenty minutes, she said, "Norman, give him the money."'[17]

Sir Austen Pearce was not the only one to put intense pressure on Mrs Thatcher over the A320. At her summit meeting early in 1984 with President Mitterrand and Chancellor Kohl, Mrs Thatcher continued to insist that that the A320 had to yield 'a financial return commensurate with the risks involved', but she was left in no doubt as to just how important the A320 project was, not just economically, but politically as well. If Britain didn't contribute her share, she was told, then France and Germany were prepared to go on without her, leaving Britain out on a limb for the second time. This meeting proved to be critical. Shortly afterwards the Germans agreed to finance 90 per cent of Deutsche Airbus's £388 million development costs in return for a royalty of DM2.5 million for each Airbus sold, up to 600. If, however, the 600 target was not met, then there would be no royalties for the government, which meant that the full cost would be borne by the German taxpayer.

The British drove a harder bargain. The government agreed to put up £250 million in launch aid, of which £50 million would have to be repaid irrespective of whether the A320 sold or not, while the rest could be recouped by a levy on each plane sold. Furthermore, BAe was required to find £200 million from its own resources and there would be no government guarantee for any loans. It was not generous but in the circumstances it was the best that BAe could have hoped for. As things turned, it was also a good deal for both sides. Of the three governments, the

French offer was perhaps the most favourable to the contractors. The Mitterrand government agreed to meet 75 per cent of Aerospatiale's development costs and subsequently persuaded a consortium of French banks, led by Parisbas, to lend Aerospatiale an interest free loan of FF380 million until the A320 took to the air. It was also agreed that repayments would only start when the plane began to sell.

However tense the negotiations with governments might have been, the truth was that Airbus was in a much stronger position than it had been in the dark days of 1976 when the politicians wobbled and Airbus came within a whisker of being shut down. In 1984 one might say that Airbus had the governments over a barrel: the governments were in much the same position as the unwise bank. As the saying goes, 'If you have borrowed £200 from the bank, you have a problem; but if you have borrowed £200 million, the bank has a problem.' However reluctant the British and Germans may have been to finance the A320, they did not dare to pull the plug: the commercial future of Airbus was still too finely balanced. As Steven McGuire says, 'While governments were fearful about pouring money into Airbus, they were even more fearful that failure to do so would spell bankruptcy for the consortium . . . The possibility that Airbus could be on the verge of commercial viability, combined with the realization that failure now meant losing millions of taxpayers' money, increased political backing for the consortium.'[18]

One reason why Mrs Thatcher was prepared, as a last resort, to look kindly on the A320 was that at the time when she was making up her mind, the aircraft already had its first British customer in the shape of Sir Adam Thompson of British Caledonian. Like Sir Freddie Laker, Sir Adam was Mrs Thatcher's sort of businessman. Created out of a merger with British United Airways, Thompson had built up BCal to become Britain's second largest airline by shrewdly exploiting his company's Scottish origins: he dressed his stewardesses in kilts and adopted the saltire as the airline's logo. Based at Gatwick, he barged his way into the big time by obtaining licences to compete with BOAC on the London (Gatwick), New York and Los Angeles routes and also flew to Hong Kong and the Far East.

BCal was an obvious target for Airbus. It was looking to replace its fleet of BAC 1-11s and unlike British Airways had no hang-ups about the Airbus. With Sir Freddie Laker already in the bag, Sir Adam Thompson was obviously the next British target for Airbus's Arthur Howes. Having set up camp in a hotel close to Gatwick, throughout 1982 and 1983 Howes proceeded to lay siege to BCal's senior executives. It was hard going. The Americans were well ahead. Boeing and McDonnell Douglas had responded quickly to the changes in the market by revamping their existing smaller aircraft. The previous year Boeing had launched its 737-300, while McDonnell Douglas was offering a revamped DC-9 in the shape of the MD-80. With the world aircraft market severely depressed in the wake of the second oil shock and the effects of American deregulation, both companies had decided to play safe.

After the DC-10 debacle, James McDonnell had lost what little appetite he had for the civil aircraft business. On being told, shortly before his death in 1980, that a new 180-seater would fill a hole a market, he replied, 'Why should I fall into it?'[19] Boeing, too, decided to play for time. Rather than spend $2 billion on a brand new aircraft, which would steal sales from its existing and highly successful 737 range, Boeing calculated that it would be cheaper and probably just as effective to bring out an updated and slightly larger version of the 737 with a new, more powerful engine. By the time the Airbus board had given the A320 the green light, the revamped 737-300 had been launched and McDonnell Douglas had sold 280 of its DC-9 derivative, the MD-80.

When BCal's technical experts told the board it should buy Boeing's 737, Airbus's chances of landing the BCal order looked slim indeed. But Howes was not done yet. He responded with what he called a Launch Customer Incentive – Airbus jargon for the inducements routinely offered to the first airlines to commit themselves to buying a new plane. Howes attempted to paper over the fact that he was trying to sell a plane that did not yet exist and which he would be unable to deliver for several years by suggesting that Airbus pay for the cost of having BCal's old BAC 1-11s modified to meet new noise restrictions and proposing an ingenious financial package which involved a consortium of banks buying the planes and then leasing them back to the airline until the A320s were ready. As in the Laker deal, he also threw in some extra goodies like free pilot training. At the very last minute the deal was nearly undone by Air France's insistence that the A320 should have an extra six seats. As Air France was much the most important customer, having ordered fifty A320s against BCal's seven, there was no way Airbus could ignore this demand. But after Howes had agreed that Airbus should pay for the installation of an extra fuel tank on the BCal planes at a cost of half a million dollars per plane, the deal was done and BCal became Airbus's second British customer. As BCal was also the first independent airline to buy the A320, the deal supported Béteille's contention that there was a real future for the A320 – and, by extension, for Airbus as a whole.

Quite apart from its commercial future, there was a lot riding on the A320. The A300/310 aircraft were, apart from the A310's glass cockpit, conventional enough in the layout and design of their control systems. With the A320 Béteille decided to play the high-tech card and build a plane that was as close to the current state of the art as French technology could make it. His plan was to steal a march on Boeing by offering such a high level of technology that Seattle's planes would look instantly old-fashioned. For the Europeans to challenge the Americans at their own game was undoubtedly cheeky, but looked at as a marketing device to differentiate the Airbus brand from the competition, it had its merits, quite apart from questions of safety and reliability. 'The basic idea of Airbus,' Béteille says, 'has always been to compete against the established manufacturers. We had to bring something more. That something was daring to use advanced technology wherever it could bring economic results. We had to take more risks of failure than the established manufacturers.'

It was Béteille's decision to replace traditional controls with fly-by-wire that threw the spotlight of world attention on Airbus. It also provoked a storm of protest from traditional-minded pilots and their trade unions, and fuelled a fierce debate inside the industry about the safety implications of the new technology. Pilots who called it 'the Atari plane'† were incensed when Airbus took out advertisements which proclaimed, 'Anyone can fly this plane'. To some, it seemed as if the pilot was being pushed to one side in favour of the machine. As one Lufthansa pilot put it, 'For the first time in aviation history, pilots no longer had undisputed and direct access to the flight controls of the aircraft but were dependent on what the construction engineers programmed into the software of the steering computers. The pilot was in many aspects pushed out of the centre of the decision-making process.' Carl Sigel, Lufthansa's head of pilot training, was so concerned about the Airbus emphasis on computers that he insisted that the airline's pilots learned to fly the A320 as a conventional plane with the computers switched off before using the fly-by-wire system. 'Airbus oversold the idea,' he says. 'Pilots were encouraged to believe that they could do anything when, of course, they couldn't.'[20]

Since the days of Orville and Wilbur Wright, pilots had controlled their planes by hand. By pulling on levers or pushing on pedals connected to the ailerons, the elevator and the rudder by pulleys and wires, the pilot controlled everything from take-off to landing. But the A320 was a 'look no hands' aeroplane: there was no joystick and no mechanical controls. To fly the plane the pilot simply pressed buttons on a small sidestick controller which sent an electronic signal to the hydraulic units that drive the airlerons, the spoilers, airbrakes, flaps and so on. Predictably, many pilots, who are conservative people by inclination, proclaimed their undying attachment to the joystick, as did Boeing, who was not to introduce fly-by-wire for another ten years. 'I would never put a sidestick controller on any commercial aircraft,' growled Joe Sutter, the designer of the 747. And he added, 'Airbus is not going to sell a lot of airplanes by touting technology.'[21] To the traditional pilot the joystick was an integral part of flying. Just by putting their hand on the control column, old-timers claimed that they knew exactly what the aircraft was doing and, more importantly, what it was going to do. With fly-by-wire they no longer had this feedback and were, they felt, at the mercy of a machine.

In fact there was nothing so very new about fly-by-wire. Its developers, Aerospatiale, had made an analogue version for Concorde several years ago and it was already a familiar feature of military planes which flew so quickly at low level

† Atari was the name of a popular home computer with a joystick for playing computer games.

that a pilot's reactions would be too slow for him to control the plane manually. What was new, however, was the wholesale automation of the business of flying to the point where the pilot becomes almost redundant. With the A320 came not just a more sophisticated method of electronic flight control, but what Airbus called a 'flight management and guidance system'. The A320's computers both control the handling and the navigation of the plane and are also programmed to detect when the plane was flying outside what is called its 'envelope' and to correct it automatically, *irrespective of what the pilot is doing.*

In his study of Airbus, Bill Gunston, a veteran aviation writer, described how the flight management system works: 'To fly the A320 the pilot takes hold of a small SSC [sidestick controller] conveniently positioned ahead of his outboard armrest. Pulling a selector knob on the FMS [flight management system] glareshield display gives him control: pushing the knob in transfers control to the FMS. As in the big Airbuses this interface provides for immediate digital selection of heading, flight level, airspeed and vertical speed [rate of climb or letdown]. Integrating the FMS into the aircraft's AFS [automatic flight system] results in the A320 coming under the complete control of an FMGS [flight management and guidance system]. *In this mode the pilots . . . have nothing to do from take off to touch down but take an active interest* [my italics].'[22]

That modern planes should be able to fly themselves under the ever-watchful eye of the pilot was not in itself a particularly startling or controversial concept. Automatic pilots and automatic landing had been a feature of commercial airliners since the 1950s. What attracted attention – and controversy – were the claims that the A320's fly-by-wire system was so sophisticated and so safety-conscious as to make it virtually immune to pilot error. Airbus itself has never gone quite as far as to make this claim but others have allowed themselves to become so carried away by the wonders of the technology as to come very close to doing so.

Describing fly-by-wire, Arthur Reed, the former air correspondent of *The Times*, writes, 'EFCS, the electronic flight control system, ensures that the A320 is physically prevented from potentially dangerous conditions, such as stalling, being over-stressed, or over-controlled in manoeuvres . . . if an A320 pilot flying in the increasingly over-crowded airspaces of today, finds himself in a potential collision situation, he can, through the fly-through computer system built into the aircraft, apply instantaeous full control deflection, without worrying about stalling the aircraft, or damaging it structurally.'[23] Bill Gunston, whose enthusiasm for Airbus is unbounded, goes even further. 'The FMS computers are programmed to know the aircraft's permitted flight envelope, the limitations on its indicated airspeed, angle of attack and vertical acceleration,' he writes. 'Thus, as long as the pilot's commands stay within the flight envelope, they are relayed without modification: should they go outside it they are instantly inhibited, and those that approach the boundaries are progressively modified by being shaped to preserve safe flight.'[24]

From this one might reasonably conclude that the A320 was less prone to accidents than other less well-equipped aircraft. Unhappily, the first years of the A320's life were marred by a series of accidents that posed some awkward and embarrassing questions for the makers. The first accident happened at Habsheim, near Mulhouse in eastern France, on 26 June 1988, when an A320 on a demonstration low-level, low speed fly-past crashed after failing to clear some trees at the end of the runway. Just why the pilots, who survived, failed to apply the power in time is a question that has never been clearly established: but what is obvious is that although the plane was flying into danger, if the automated fly-by-wire safety system acted at all, it was already too late. There are those who claim that the computer, thinking the plane was actually landing, was in landing mode and thus effectively flew the plane into the trees. The inquiry blamed the pilots, saying they did not realize the plane was as low as it was. But since then, Airbus has changed the system to give the engines more power on approach.

The second serious accident was in February 1990 when an Indian Airlines A320 on a domestic flight from Bombay crashed three-quarters of a mile short of the runway at Bangalore, killing 90 of the 146 people on board. Again, opinions differed as to the cause of the crash but the consensus was that the pilot was inadequately trained and did not understand what was an extremely sophisticated system. One expert believes that the pilots had told the system to switch the engines into idle mode without quite realizing what the consequences of such a reduction in power during landing would be. Lufthansa's Carl Sigel says, 'If the pilots had switched off the fly-by-wire straight away and flown the plane manually, the crash would never have happened. They had plenty of time to fly the plane out of trouble. As it was they got confused and by the time they sorted things out it was too late.'[25]

Subsequently there were a number of other accidents involving the A320 and other by now equally heavily computerized Airbuses. In April 1994 there was the crash of a China Airways A300 just outside Tokyo which killed 264 out of the 271. The disaster was described by the *Los Angeles Times* as 'a terrifying battle between an inexperienced co-pilot and his airplane's super-sophisticated computer system'. While accurate enough, this is journalistic shorthand for what actually happened.[26]

In his study of air accidents Nicholas Faith reconstructs the sequence of events that led to the Air China crash. 'The plane was being flown manually on approach to landing by its twenty-six-year-old co-pilot. About two minutes before touching down, the A300 went into go-around mode, for reasons still unknown. Even though the pilot had warned the co-pilot three times in thirty seconds . . . the co-pilot continued to attempt to land the plane. The upshot was that the autopilot was trying to pitch the nose up while the co-pilot was trying to pitch it down. The crew then switched off the go-around mode, but the elevators remained set at a sharp angle. The crew, realising that the plane was too high to land, put the go-around mode back on. This caused the plane to climb sharply and approach a stall. The

A300 stall-prevention system automatically increased the engine thrust, but this merely increased the climb angle to 53 degrees. Unfortunately, the plane couldn't increase speed quickly enough. It stalled, the nose dropped and the airspeed increased to 150 mph at an altitude of 800 feet. At this point, the entire electrical system, including the flight data and voice-recorders, stopped functioning . . . and the plane crashed.'

What is common to these three accidents is that they occurred while the planes were either landing or very close to the ground, that there was a fatal mismatch between the actions of the computer system and what the pilots were doing or thought they were doing, and that the pilots themselves were either foolhardy or inexperienced. These adjectives, however, cannot apply to Nick Warner, Airbus's chief test pilot, who was killed in June 1994 while testing emergency procedures on an A330. The plane crashed before Warner had time to overcome a software error and regain manual control.

Even before the Warner crash, Airbus realized that its automatic systems were not perfect: in a statement issued in 1990 after the Indian Airways crash, the company acknowledged that there were limits and that pilots should use their own experience and discretion and not rely exclusively on fly-by-wire to get them out of trouble. In a notice warning pilots against over-confidence when flying the A320, Bernard Ziegler, Henri's son and head of engineering, said, 'We got the idea that some crews felt that they had God on their shoulders in flying the aircraft. They do not. What we've built is an aircraft that is very easy to fly. But the laws of physics still apply. If you don't have enough energy to fly over an obstacle, you will hit that obstacle.'[27]

In fitting the A320 with fly-by-wire, Airbus established a commanding lead over its rivals. It was quickly recognized to be a step-change in aircraft technology and was, in due course, adopted, although in a rather different form, by its rivals. In designing its own fly-by-wire system for the 777, the first of its planes to be fully automated, Boeing was careful to pay a great deal of attention to the pilots' concerns. 'The pilot always has the ultimate authority of control,' says John Cashman, Boeing's chief test pilot on the 777. 'There's no computer on the airplane that he cannot override or turn off if the ultimate comes . . . We make it difficult, but if something in the box should behave inappropriately the pilot can say, "This is wrong", and he can override it. That's a fundamental difference in philosophy that we have versus some of the competition.'[28]

Although more fuel efficient and more technologically advanced than its rivals, the A320's success was not immediate. In the first two years after its launch in 1984 the Airbus share of the single-aisle market averaged no more than 11 per cent, while Boeing's 737-300 notched up record sales. In 1985, as concern in the United States about the European challenge intensified, 252 of the 737-300 were sold – a record for a single model in a single year.

In playing the hi-tech card with the A320, Roger Béteille was gambling that he could beat the Americans at their own game. And he was to be proved right. What impressed companies like Northwest Airlines, who placed a $3.2 billion order for the A320 in 1986, was not the number of computers on board, but the numbers the technology could deliver in terms of operating and seat mile costs. Northwest was not alone. The previous year American Airlines had bought fifteen A320s, and six months before that Pan Am, as part of a giant A300/A320 package, had bought sixteen A320s with an option for a further thirty-four. With a year still to go, before it entered service no one could doubt that as far as the Americans were concerned, the A320 was Europe's *force de frappe*. Not only did it successfully challenge the American stranglehold on the traditional single-aisle market, but it gave the consortium the reach and the momentum it was looking for. The A300 and the A310 were, in their way, considerable achievements, but with the A320 the Americans recognized that the Europeans had become a force to be reckoned with. The Airbus family was taking shape. As early as 1978, when the A320 was still in embryo, the American business magazine *Dun's Review* made a highly prescient prediction, 'It is clear that Boeing will be the only American company producing planes (McDonnell Douglas had almost officially withdrawn from the race, and Lockheed simply does not have the financial resources), and it will compete probably with just one company, the French-English Airbus Industrie.'[29]

As much by luck as by judgement, the A320 was launched at a time when the market was booming. If it had arrived two years earlier, as originally intended, it might have been a different story.

CHAPTER NINE

THE PYRENEES BEAR

IN THE AUTUMN OF 1984 THESE triumphs were yet come. In truth, the situation looked bleak. Six years had passed since the launch of the 310; the years of delay over the A320 had sapped confidence and, worst of all, orders were flagging badly – the number of whitetails on the tarmac at Blagnac had reached fourteen, reviving uncomfortable memories of the sales drought nine years earlier. For all the successes along the Silk Road, the consortium was simply not generating enough sales and cash to sustain the momentum and keep pace with a confident and aggressive Boeing.

Once again, Airbus looked to America for salvation. In 1978 it had been Frank Borman's Eastern Airlines that had come to the rescue. This time, all hopes were pinned on Ed Acker's Pan Am. Much had happened to Pan Am since the days of Juan Trippe some twenty years before. It was no longer the proud force it had been in the early days of the jet era when it called itself, with some justification, 'the world's most experienced airline'. It was still a factor to be reckoned with on the North Atlantic and was still an international airline, but in the aftermath of deregulation it had lost much of its glory, to become a much smaller and much less profitable concern. With $1.2 billion of debt against $314 million of equity and with a cumulative loss of $564 million for the previous three years, Pan Am did not look like a good prospect. There were those in Toulouse who thought that Pan Am was such a basket case that it was not even worth talking to. But Bernard Lathière and his head of sales, Pierre Pailleret, were so anxious to shift the whitetails that they thought that no opportunity, however unpromising, should be neglected.

When word reached Toulouse in the spring of 1984 that Pan Am was thinking of replacing its fleet and was talking to Boeing, Lathière took charge. He despatched a team of forty Airbus salesmen to New York with instructions to close the deal no matter what. The stakes were high and Airbus was willing to be flexible. On offer were twelve A300s and sixteen A320s with options for another thirteen A300s and thirty-four A320s. 'It was a two-and-a-half billion contract and we were really head-on with Boeing,' Lathière recalls. 'Firstly, we had a better proposal than Boeing did. We said to Pan Am that if they wanted the planes right away, they could have them:

there were fourteen to hand ready and waiting in Toulouse. But secondly, we said to them if your traffic pattern changes and you find you don't need the bigger aircraft, we'll take them back and replace them with A320s.'[1]

Boeing's response, so Lathière says, was to make a matching offer with 767s and 737s. But he claims that Pan Am rejected this on the grounds that the A320 was a next generation plane, whereas the 737 had been around in one form or another for twenty years. While this account is probably true as far as it goes, it was only one ingredient of a complex deal. What swung Pan Am in favour of the Airbus package was not so much the actual contents but the alluring nature of the wrapping. Lathière insisted that there were no government subsidies of any kind. 'Not one centime, not one penny, not one deutschmark of European taxpayer's money is involved in the deal,' he protested. He was supported by the team leader, Pierre Pailleret, who said, 'We haven't accepted coffee beans, cocoa or bananas in return for planes, and we are not taking back any old Pan Am aircraft.'[2] However, neither would be drawn on precisely what terms Airbus had offered to close the deal. The suspicion was that, in deference to Pan Am's delicate financial state, the airline had been offered a generous leasing deal, with Airbus retaining some, if not all, of the equity in some, if not all, of the planes.

Offering airlines the opportunity of leasing rather than buying was a sales strategy Airbus Industrie had employed from the very beginning – for the simple reason that many of the airlines it was dealing with in the developing world had no money. One of the very first of these deals was with Air Siam, which was being run on a shoestring by Tony Ryan, the Irish entrepreneur who went on to found GPA, the aircraft leasing company. 'He had the planes for a ridiculously low rental,' says Airbus's Adam Brown.[3] Until their profits began to tumble in the aftermath of deregulation, America's major airlines were rich enough to turn up their noses at deals of this kind. In the past the big beasts of the American airline jungle, the Pan Ams and the Easterns, either bought their planes for cash or raised the money in the capital markets; leasing, they thought, was something best left to bucket shops. But as their profits started to crumble in the aftermath of deregulation, they became less sniffy. First, Eastern, then Pan Am were lured into the arms of Airbus with seductive leasing deals. For these highly geared, cash-strapped airlines the attraction was that it seemed to be a relatively painless way of acquiring something as expensive as a new fleet of aircraft. By leasing, the airline could keep the capital costs off the balance sheet while at the same time allowing it to present the leasing arrangements as tax deductible running expenses. And as the leased planes remained, in many cases, the property of the vendor, it was, in a worst-case scenario, the manufacturer who took the risk, not the airline. That this was one of the calculations in the Pan Am deal is supported by the fact that when Pan Am went bust, planes were returned by the administrators of the stricken airline to Airbus Industrie.

In Seattle and on Wall Street the Pan Am deal went down badly. It was the first time Pan Am had ever bought a plane from a non-American supplier and the order was one of the largest trade deals ever between Europe and America. Boeing grumbled that it had made a fair offer but added that 'we have to make a profit to survive', while on Wall Street the general opinion was that 'Airbus wanted the deal so badly that it was willing to make an offer that Boeing could not match as a publicly owned company'.

Oddly enough, the Pan Am deal was equally unpopular much closer to home. When the consortium's industrial partners realized what sort of a deal Bernard Lathière had done, there was a general demand for his head. Even before Pan Am, there was, said Jean Pierson, the man who succeeded him, a groundswell of discontent. It was felt that after ten years in the job, the strain of the constant travel, the glad-handing and the wheeling and dealing was taking its toll. His decision to base himself in Paris rather than Toulouse was unpopular. And although his home life was happy, he suffered a tragic blow when his grown-up son committed suicide. He himself bitterly regretted that he was away so much that he had missed the boy growing up. There was a curious incident on his return from America after the Pan Am deal which mystified his colleagues. As he came down the steps of the plane, he declared, 'My children, I have decided I shall stay with you!'[4]

The crunch came in October, just a month after the publication of Pan Am's memorandum of understanding which, in the aircraft industry, always precedes a formal contract. It has been suggested that it was Franz-Josef Strauss who demanded Lathière's head and delivered the *coup de grâce*. It is said that while on a private visit to France, Strauss paid a call on the French prime minister, Laurent Fabius, to tell him that making planes without orders and without any cost control was no longer acceptable and that Lathière had to go. But it seems that it was not the Germans but the French who undermined Lathière: as his drinking grew worse, his leadership had become increasingly erratic. Also, Airbus was only just beginning to emerge from its worst period since the mid-1970s.

The long wait for the A320 had taken its toll. In 1982/83 the consortium had taken orders for no more than twelve aircraft against Boeing's 262, and although things were beginning to pick up in 1984 with the controversial Pan Am order, the damage had been done. But who was to succeed Lathière? The very first idea was to have a government-appointed technocrat as the chief executive or *administrateur gérant*, with Pierson as Bétielle's successor as head of operations. But nobody, especially the Germans, was keen on that plan. The only thing that was certain was that the top man would be a Frenchman. There was nothing in the rules to say so. But that was how it was and that was, as far as the French were concerned, how it always would be. By the end of October there were three candidates for Lathière's job, each with their own sponsor. The minister of transport, Jean Auroux, was pushing the claims of his own man, a left-wing civil servant and technocrat in the classic mould; Béteille was supporting the claims of Pierre Pailleret, the commercial director, and Jean Pierson was Aerospatiale's man.

It was Aerospatiale's chairman who introduced Jean Pierson to the minister of transport, Jean Auroux. As it happened, the men already knew each other socially. So it was not a complete surprise when, of the three names put up by the minister of transport to the prime minister, it was Pierson who was chosen. The official announcement was duly made and that seemed to be that. But the supervisory board had other ideas. The political infighting was so fierce that another eight months were to pass before Jean Pierson's appointment was formally agreed.

On the very same day the minister of transport announced that Jean Pierson had got the job, the supervisory board met in Toulouse, and after considering the question throughout the afternoon, it announced that no decision had been made and that in fact no one had been selected. The board was split. While the British, the Spanish and the French wanted Pierson, the Germans, led by Strauss, had argued strongly for their man, Hans Schäffler, who was, as Deutsche Airbus's man in Toulouse, effectively Roger Béteille's number two. The French objected. The chairman of Aerospatiale went as far as to tell his boss, Strauss, that if he disagreed with the majority view, he had better discuss it with Laurent Fabius. When a few days later Strauss met Fabius, the prime minister made it quite plain that M. Pierson was not the candidate of Aerospatiale; he was the candidate of France.

Strauss, who had himself been prime minister of Bavaria, was not going to be brow-beaten. But equally, as chairman of the supervisory board, he knew that for the consortium to be divided so sharply on national grounds would do great harm to the Airbus image. So he proposed a compromise: Pierson would be the top man but his man, Schäffler, would share power as number two. Now it was Pierson's turn to object. 'It took a month to negotiate the wording,' he says. 'Finally we had something that was acceptable to me and my lawyer. But in the German mind – and this is constant to this day – there was the feeling "we have 37.9 per cent, the French have 37.9 per cent, so we are equal". He [Schäffler] was, in his view, number one bis.'[5]

However neat a solution this might have seemed to the politicians, to Airbus people, like Hartmut Mehdorn who knew both men well, it was an impossible idea. 'Pierson and Schäffler could never have worked together,' he says. 'Schäffler was a man for the nitty gritty. Very precise and a deep thinker. But not very decisive or strong. Jean Pierson was a factory guy; fighting with everybody. Jean was not a team builder: he worked by power. He was very French. He had his own little team and did not use the whole organization very precisely. He was also a market man. He had an extremely good relationship with key customers and had a fantastic feeling for selling. He had one thing that you meet in management very seldom: he can say "no".'[6]

Like Ziegler, Béteille and Lathière, Pierson was a product of France's elitist system of education. But unlike them he was not a *polytechnicien* or a graduate of *les grandes écoles*. Born in Tunisia in 1940, if he had followed his father's footsteps he would have gone into the army. As it was, he went to the *École Nationale Supérieure de l'Aéronautique et de l'Espace* where he studied aeronautical engineering. A military college created by Napoleon and restricted to the sons of officers, the school was just as competitive and almost as prestigious as a *grand école*. Entrance was by examination and only the top ten or twenty candidates were admitted. After national service, the twenty-five-year-old Pierson joined Sud Aviation, where he worked as a production engineer. When Concorde started he went to work with the BAC engineers at Weybridge as part of an exchange programme. In Surrey, Pierson acquired his wonderfully idiomatic and heavily accented English, and his intimate knowledge of the politics and practices of large and very complicated multi-national aircraft projects. Like many other senior Airbus people, he stresses just how important the collaborative experience on Concorde was and how many lessons were learned. Pierson concedes that Concorde had its problems. 'Concorde was difficult,' he says. 'The work-sharing was complicated and the work process involved a lot of committees. It was nothing to do with the English or the French. Another programme with other governments would have been the same. Technically, we did our job. Economically, that's another story.'[7] Nonetheless, for all his enthusiasm for multinational cooperation, in his attitudes to his job and his colleagues Pierson was as quintessentially French as any character in the TV soap *'Allo, 'Allo* so popular in the 1970s. On the whole, he liked the British, but did not conceal his reservations about the Germans.

In 1968, just as Airbus was beginning to take shape, Pierson came back to Toulouse, where as head of the Concorde production line he delivered the last two Concordes. Three years later he was sent to sort out the light aircraft factory at Tarbes, which he did with a ruthless efficiency that earned him the nickname 'The Pyrenees Bear' – an animal he closely resembles in both temperament and physique. Large and lumbering, he can be very quick on his feet when required. He is also remorseless when roused and relentless in pursuit, as the hapless Schäffler was to discover.

Pierson formally took over as Bernard Lathière's successor on 1 April. And his first task was to deal with unfinished Pan Am business. Pierson had his doubts about the wisdom of the deal Lathière had done. He believed that it was a good one from the Airbus point of view, but as he thought that Pan Am could go bust any day, he was worried about the knock-on effects of a collapse on Airbus. He says, 'We had the memorandum of understanding but the final, legal, binding contract was still in negotiation when I arrived. And my very first question was: are we going to the end or do I take the first opportunity to walk away?' In the end he decided that it would be bad for Airbus and equally bad for him, personally, if the first thing he did on arrival was 'to kill the only contract on the front burner'. After all, he only had to look out of his office window to see the whitetails, whose number had increased to twenty-four, parked on the tarmac. The contract was duly signed at the Paris Air Show at Le Bourget later that year. During the long summer break Pierson reflected on his next moves and brooded about his German deputy and not-quite co-equal, Hans Schäffler.

On his very first day back after the summer holidays, Pierson decided to broach the subject head on. Over lunch he told Schäffler, 'I am number one and you are number two. And if you are dreaming to be number one bis, you had better go and find a job in Germany.'[8] Pierson told Schäffler that he had that morning requested an interview with Franz-Josef Strauss in his office in Munich and that if the German side did not agree, he would hand in his resignation that coming Sunday. Evidently, Schäffler decided the best course would be to follow Pierson's advice, for six months later he left Airbus to take up a new job in Germany as head of Dornier.

Schäffler's departure was part of a much larger shake-up of the entire organization by the new managing director. The object was to improve Airbus's rather weak reputation among the airlines for product support and to sharpen up the sales effort in North America. 'When I arrived I got the impression, rightly or wrongly, that the work of the various directorates could be better organized,' he says. 'Everybody was overlooking the work of everybody else. Over the years, some people had built up mini-empires and these were cut down to size.'[9] Bernard Ziegler, for example, who had looked after both product support and flight testing, lost responsibility for product support, and flight testing was merged with engineering. When Ziegler protested that Airbus Industrie itself was the first customer for flight testing, Pierson shot back, 'We're not an airline.' Product support became a single entity and was completely reorganized.

In the year Pierson arrived, Airbus's record of product support was poor: when it came to providing spares, training and so forth, it had been voted the worst of all the manufacturers. Within three years, Pierson claims, it had so improved that Airbus's rating was better than Boeing's. The most noticeable changes, however, were in the face that Airbus Industrie presented to the world, particularly in North America, which now accounted for one-third of all sales. 'There was a need for a major investment in the US operation because what we were doing was Mickey Mouse,' says Pierson.[10] The sales team was moved out of its office on the 23rd floor of the Rockefeller Center in Manhattan to a more functional office block in Virginia close to Dulles International Airport. Two years previously Alan Boyd, who had served as transport secretary under Lyndon Johnson and was a civil aerospace negotiator for Jimmy Carter, had been recruited as chairman of Airbus's North America operation on a salary of $500,000 a year to replace George Warde, who had left to run Continental Airlines. But it was not until Pierson arrived that Boyd gained the freedom to hire the people he wanted. To many North American customers, Airbus still looked and sounded much too European to be really effective. Selling aircraft is a face-to-face business and those on both sides of the fence needed, quite literally, to talk the same language.

With Boyd fully in charge, the Europeans were sent home and replaced in the front line by native-born Americans like the young John Leahy, a New Yorker who was head-hunted from Piper Aircraft where he had been selling the little Cherokees, Aztecs and Cheyennes. The only Europeans to remain in the States were in finance and administration. 'The people who were making the opera were all Americans,' says Pierson. 'Of course, the finance and admin guys back stage were the ones with their hands in the grease, but airlines were looking at the people making the opera.'[11] The same principle applied everywhere: Arabs were appointed in the Middle East and Japanese in Japan. It might seem obvious, but for Toulouse it was a big cultural change.

'The main mistake that Airbus could make in the States,' Pierson states, 'is to say that now that we have arrived, we can appoint a German – no way. You have got to learn how do things the American way.' Pierson, whom everybody says was a brilliant salesman, schooled himself in the American way of doing business. 'I met the chairman of United six or seven times,' he says. 'We talked about the weather, the wife, shopping but never a word about business. Then one day the guy called me and said, "I'm coming to France. I'd like to come to Toulouse. Could you send a private jet?" That was done and for the first time, we speak business.'[12]

Pierson, the archetypal Frenchman, also invested a lot of time in becoming as American as possible. He joined the Wings Club of New York and became a member of the Conquistadores del Cielo (Conquerors of the Sky), the quasi-Masonic social club to which presidents and senior executives of American manufacturers and airlines aspire to belong.* The highlight of the year is a five-day beano in Wyoming the week after Labour Day. Everybody dresses up as cowboys, eats chilli con carne, drinks too much, and stays up far too late. Everyone's a good ol' boy, and the one rule is that nobody tries to sell anything to anybody. However, the moment the holiday is over it's back to normal. And when it comes to selling, whether or not you are a 'Conquistador' can make all the difference.

With Pierson's arrival came a change in business climate. After a bleak spell in the mid-1980s when new orders had virtually dried up, business in North America picked up dramatically, with blockbuster orders for the A320 from American Airlines and Northwest. This time there were no complaints, as there had been with the Pan Am affair, about tricky financing and sweetheart deals. As John Leahy was

---

*   The club was named after the title the Spanish adventurer Hernan Cortes had given to one of his three lieutenants after his conquest of Mexico: the other two were conquerors of earth and water.

to say several years later of the American Airlines order, 'We dumped the foreign accents, took off the gloves and got the deals done. Nothing underhand; we just learned to play as tough as the next guy.'[13]

In the space of twenty-four months Pierson and his team had sold as many planes as his predecessors had done in the first fifteen years of Airbus. While not a man to underplay his own achievements, Pierson says that this was not of his doing but were the fruits of a long-term strategy laid down by Béteille and others years before his arrival. 'The increase in sales in 1986 and 1987 was incremental and was a function of the growing size of the product line,' he argues. 'Thus the A310 builds on the sales of the A300. The A320 on the A310 and the A300 and so forth. The effects are both practical and psychological. In the first place, with more product we have more chance to attract airlines with their different needs. Secondly, every time you increase your product line, it is testimony to the fact that Airbus is here for the long term. The longer your track record, the more credible you become. The sales record was what it was not because there was a new team of people; it was not even because there were new aircraft. It was simply because the fruit was mature.'[14]

*

Shortly after his appointment, Pierson went to London to pay a call on his friends at British Aerospace. Already, at the back of his mind, Pierson was formulating his plans for building the next member of the Airbus family, a long- to medium-range widebody that would fill the gap between the A300/310 and Boeing's jumbo, the 747. As we have seen, Airbus had already taken a hard look at this idea back in the late 1970s and had rejected it in favour of the A320. But the market had moved on since then and there was renewed pressure from Lufthansa and the German contingent for such a plane. Pierson took the opportunity to sound out the British, and in particular Sir Austen Pearce and Sir Raymond Lygo, his partners at British Aerospace. 'We had a discussion about what was going on: Strauss, the Germans and all that,' says Pierson. 'And then one of them, I don't remember which, said, "Jean, please don't ask us for a new wing, we've got too much on."'[15] That same afternoon, Pierson paid a call on the minister in charge of aerospace, Geoff Pattie, who gave him the same message. It was agreed that the project would be put on hold for the time being.

Meanwhile, back at Toulouse arguments raged. There was general agreement that there should be a new plane, but should it have four engines or two? In the industry shorthand: should it be a quad or a twin? It was at this point that things began to get nasty. 'There was a fierce battle about whether to go for a twin or a long-range jet,' said Bernard Ziegler. 'People were not talking to each other in corridors.'[16] According to Pierson, Schäffler was being indecisive and Pierre Pailleret, who had returned from New York, was 'changing his mind every day about what plane to go for'. Frustrated and fed up, Pierson then had a brainwave. Why don't we have two planes, he asked his chief designer, but give them the same wing, the same cockpit, the same aerodynamic profile and 80 per cent of the same parts? The only real difference would be that one would be a quad and the other a twin. 'Could it be done?' he asked. 'That's an interesting question,' the designer replied. 'Give me three months.'

Before long, Pierson had the answer he was hoping for. 'Yes, it's feasible.' Very much as Roger Béteille had done years before with the A300B, Pierson turned to his closest aides. He called in Bernard Ziegler, the head of manufacturing, and told him to make up a small team of personal friends from Aerospatiale. 'You make a presentation and they'll be the jury. Let them decide which one to go for,' Pierson told him. When it came to the crunch, 70 per cent of the 'jury' were in favour of the long-range quad. It was at this point that Pierson decided to cut the knot. He said, 'Stop the debate. I have the solution. We launch the two together. The difference in cost is half a billion [dollars]. It's not that great. If you go to the government to request 3 billion or 3.5 billion, it comes to much the same thing. And the two camps, the long range and the medium range will be happy.'[17] These discussions continued for the rest of the year but they had progressed far enough by the beginning of 1986 for Pierson to be able to go back to British Aerospace to explain the concept in detail. This time the British were more receptive: British Aerospace was prepared to go ahead provided there were orders from five or six airlines. But there was one formality still to be concluded: the by-now ritual meeting with the British prime minister. Sir Raymond Lygo told Pierson that if the application for money from the British government was to go forward, he had to see Mrs Thatcher. Pierson remembers the encounter well. 'There was just a chair, no papers, and *le petit sac*. There was only one question: "M. Pierson. I hope this is not going to be a new Concorde."'[18]

By the end of the year, plans were sufficiently well advanced for the Airbus Industrie board to give Pierson the go-ahead to produce both the medium-range twin, the A330 which could carry 335 passengers in an all-economy configuration, and the long-haul quad, the A340 which would seat 295 people. The new planes were designed for what the industry called the 'long/thin' market: where the distances were as long as those covered by a 747 but where there were not enough passengers to fill a jumbo.

Airbus's intentions to renew its challenge by developing its biggest jet so far had triggered a lively concern both in Washington and in St Louis, headquarters of McDonnell Douglas. The US government was worried that, unlike the A320 market, the long/thin market was too small to support three competing manufacturers, and that of the three, McDonnell Douglas was likely to come off the worst. McDonnell Douglas did not disagree. Badly weakened by the DC-10's lack of success, it did not have the resources to build a brand new plane. Instead, it hoped that by revamping the DC-10 to make it larger and more efficient and by relaunching it as the tri-engined MD-11 it could steal a march on the competition. There was nothing very new about the MD-11. Its fuselage was a stretched version of the DC-10's, while the wing was identical in almost every respect: the only difference was a change in profile aft of the rear spar. The two planes were so close in design that McDonnell Douglas was able to say that when it produced the first MD-11, it was as if the 447th DC-10 was coming off the production line. The cost of developing the MD-11 was but a fifth of the money Airbus was spending on the A330/340. In 1987 McDonnell Douglas told a House of Representatives's committee that the development costs for the MD-11 were $700 million, compared to the $3.5 billion for the A330/340, and that three-quarters of the savings were the result of the experience gained in developing the DC-10.

For once Boeing was caught on the hop. 'When it became apparent that . . . the world's airlines would soon be able to choose from an Airbus plane or a McDonnell Douglas but not a Boeing, the company sat up and wondered whether this could be allowed to happen,' writes Karl Sabbach in his account of the making of the 777.[19] And although, Seattle, after talking to airlines, agreed with its rivals that the long/thin market had potential, it would be two years before its contender, the 777, made its appearance. With fifty-two orders and forty options for the MD-11 already in the bag, McDonnell Douglas was ahead on points. But only just. The A340 was more advanced technologically and, by all accounts, a good deal cheaper. The technical press reported that the ticket price Airbus Industrie was asking for the A340 was $10 million less than the MD-11. The news that Singapore Airlines had cancelled its order for the McDonnell Douglas plane after it had failed to reached its in-service target and that an American Airlines MD-11 had been forced to land on its inaugural flight after it had run out of fuel was also extremely embarrassing. It was therefore not surprising that Burbank, Lockheed's plant in Los Angeles, was uneasy.

History was about to repeat itself: the plot was the same, but the cast of characters was slightly different. Eleven years earlier, in an attempt to stifle the A310 at birth, Boeing had proposed a joint venture with Airbus Industrie to make the BB10, the so-called Brigitte Bardot plane (see Chapter 6). Now it was McDonnell Douglas's turn to see what it could do to disrupt the Airbus operation.

In the early winter of 1987 John McDonnell, who had just taken over from 'Mr Mac' as chairman of McDonnell Douglas, arrived in Europe. The Americans were thoroughly alarmed by Airbus's plans for an assault on the long/thin market. For McDonnell Douglas it was a case of do-or-die, but for Boeing, which was planning to launch its own contender in the shape of the 777, the stakes were also high. The manufacturers had convinced their friends in Washington that there was room for only two manufacturers in this market and that if Airbus went ahead with the

A330 and A340, the chances were that McDonnell Douglas would be forced to abandon the civil airline business altogether. It was not a question of market share, the Americans argued: it was a matter of survival. For the Americans the memory of what had happened when McDonnell Douglas and Lockheed simultaneously launched all-but-identical planes was still very vivid – even after twenty years.

In February 1987 the Americans launched a ferocious two-pronged American attack on Airbus. John McDonnell led for America's plane makers while the US administration mounted its own campaign. The two American delegations arrived in Europe within days of each other. And although the precise focus of the two was different – the McDonnell delegation talked about mergers and cooperation while the Washington delegates lobbied ministers about money and subsidies – the object in each case was the same: to destabilize Airbus and throw the A330/340 programme off track.

McDonnell called on ministers and senior officials in Paris, Bonn and London. His suggestion was that his company and Airbus Industrie should join forces in order to, as he put it, 'go after that big bear in Seattle'. As ministers in all three countries were acutely conscious of the seemingly endless expense of the Airbus programme, the idea that the Americans should take some of the strain was, they thought, an idea that had some merit. Accordingly, in March, Airbus Industrie was given permission to talk to McDonnell Douglas about the details of collaboration. One idea was that the two companies should build what would, in effect, be a hybrid. To be known as the AM 300, it would have an MD-11 fuselage and an A330/340 wing. Like the MD-11, it would have three engines, but by using the components from existing programmes it would, so it was thought, cost no more than $2 billion to develop.

How the plane should be configured was one question; how it would fit in with the product ranges of the two companies was quite another. Would it be an Airbus or a McDonnell Douglas? Would it compete against the A340 and the MD-11 or would it complement them? And if so, how? The questions were never answered, as the talks collapsed before they could be resolved. As with Boeing, the breaking point came over the old question of control. Airbus set a limit of 35 per cent on the American share of the consortium. But this was rejected by John McDonnell, who was looking for a 50:50 partnership, and the talks collapsed. McDonnell Douglas had not quite reached the end of the road. For a time it flirted with the idea of building a four-engined plane that would have been bigger than anything in the sky with the exception of the 747. But the company lacked both the resolve and the resources to make it happen. On the back of the success of the MD-80 series – essentially a relaunch of the DC-9 – McDonnell Douglas was to carry on as a maker of civil aircraft for another eleven years until it finally disappeared after the purchase by Boeing in 1998.

From the Airbus point of view the problem with the A330/340 was not so much competition from the Americans, but the ever-pressing question of finding the money to launch it. The A320 was not due to take to the air until early in the following year and although the order book was looking very healthy, the partners were feeling the strain. In May 1986 *Flight* magazine reported Aerospatiale as saying that it had insufficient cash flow to fund the production of the A320 and the development of the A330/340 programme simultaneously, and British Aerospace announced that without 100 per cent government aid for the new planes, it would have to withdraw from the consortium. At the same time, Deutsche Airbus was complaining of a severe cash crisis, as, it said, funding the A320 had soaked up all of its financial resources. It also urged a speedy approval of the A330/340 programme so that the Airbus family could be completed.

Deutsche Airbus was not the only one. Lufthansa, too, was becoming very restless. Its deputy managing director, Reinhardt Abraham, told the author Ian MacIntyre that he was so angry over delays in specifying the engine that Lufthansa came close to cancelling its commitment to the A340 and choosing the MD-11 instead. Abraham said that the consortium's delays in 1986 gave McDonnell the opportunity to launch the MD-11 and put their nose in front. He stated, 'It was possible for McDonnell Douglas to organize a conservative clientele who were sceptical of whether Airbus would make it and whether the programme would be approved, and this also meant passing up the possibility of getting together and competing jointly against Boeing.' Lufthansa would have liked Airbus to be much quicker on its feet. And Abraham was echoing a general complaint when he said, 'The top management in Toulouse has not enough power to make the crucial decisions. They have to go to the partners for confirmation of decisions about major changes, decisions about pricing.'[20]

To soothe the governments' anxieties about the cost of funding the A330/A340, Pierson went on the record to pledge, quite wrongly as it turned out, that this would be the last infusion of cash the consortium would ever need. With the new jets in place, he argued, Airbus would reach its declared goal of 30 per cent of the market and self-sufficiency would be assured. That was the upside of the Pierson argument; the downside was that if the consortium was not given the money it needed, there was a strong chance that Airbus would never reach its desired target and the governments would never get their money back. It was an argument that had worked when Airbus was fund-raising for the A320, so why not try it again?

As it turned out, the financing of the A330/340 was not quite as hard a struggle as finding the cash for the A320 had been. The success of the A320 had, to a large degree, calmed government fears that Airbus was, financially speaking, a bottomless pit into which taxpayers' money disappeared without trace. Also, the percentage the governments were being called on was lower than before. Whereas the Germans and French had bankrolled up to 90 per cent of the development costs of the first three planes in the Airbus family, this time the figure was down to around 65 per cent.

As before, the governments' launch aid went to their own national champions: France's Aerospatiale was lent a refundable 60 per cent of its share of the cost, which came to FF5.65 billion; Germany's Deutsche Airbus received DM3 billion; and the British government paid British Aerospace a grant of £450 million, covering 60 per cent of its development costs to be repaid by means of a levy on the future sales of the aircraft. French officials were quoted as saying that the French government would lose money if the sales of the planes did not exceed 700, and it is fair to assume that the British and Germans lent their money on a similar basis.

If the funding arrangements followed a by now familiar pattern, so too did the ructions about how the work should be shared out. The impending launch of a major new Airbus revived old German and British ambitions to play a larger and more significant part in the scheme of things. The Germans were particularly vocal. At meetings of the supervisory board they not only made a strong pitch for transferring the work of assembling the A330s and A340s from Toulouse to Hamburg, but argued that they should take over the new A321, a stretched version of the A320, as well. Not to be outdone, the British renewed the request they had made three years earlier during the row of the work share on the A320 that all the big Airbuses should be built in Britain. As before, the British backed off when they realized how much government money this would involve, but the Germans were more persistent. 'There was a tremendous battle with the French,' says Bob McKinlay, who, as one of the two British Aerospace representatives on the Airbus Industrie board, was chairman of the working party set up to look into the vexed work-share problem. 'We came up with an analysis that showed that building the A330/340 in Germany was a pretty bad idea – the costs were enormous.'

The Germans had lost their battle to build the A330/340 in Germany but there were some very real consolations. In the first instance, they were given a larger piece of the A320 action in that they now built the middle section of the fuselage as well as the front and rear. But what was much more important was the decision early in 1988 to build and assemble the A321 at Hamburg. 'It was something for which I was driving very hard,' said Hartmut Mehdorn, a member of the supervisory board and the man in charge of the German end of the operation. 'The German strategy was that every time a new aircraft came along, we would try and change the work-share a little bit to increase our understanding of the building of airplanes: not to be the idiot who makes the landing gear and maybe the cargo hold and maybe the wing tip. And since we had no independent aircraft development in Germany, I thought it was good to have a situation whereby at one time we make the wing box, the fin, and in the next aircraft we make the rear tail and in the next aircraft we make the centre section. It was a softly, softly approach and the aim was to be a competent Airbus partner; and not to be the bullshitter who knows only one thing.'[21]

In pursuit of his strategy Mehdorn used two arguments: the first was to do with money and the second was about logistics. He argued that if the French continued to monopolize the operation, the German and British governments would refuse requests for money on the grounds that most of it would go to the French. 'We had to organize things in such a way so as to keep everybody in Europe happy. If you want everybody to take part, there has to be something for everybody,' he says. The second argument was that with the A330/A340 just round the corner, the numbers of planes coming off the line each month would be so great that the operation in Toulouse would collapse; it would no longer be able to cope. 'We had to divide. There was simply no other option,' he argues. 'Ultimately it was about prestige, not money. We made big pressure. And today everybody agrees we made the right decision.'[22]

The Germans had, of course, been making fuselage shells for the entire Airbus range at the former VFB factory at Nordenham at the mouth of the river Elbe since the beginning. But the decision to shift at least some of the final assembly work to Germany was a big victory for the Germans. It was the first time in the history of Airbus that Toulouse had conceded that the final assembly of an Airbus could be done outside France. In some quarters it was not a popular move. 'This was not the decision of the guy you have in front of you,' Jean Pierson told me when I interviewed him in Nice. 'It was a purely political gesture by Aerospatiale. I don't know why. I even remember a debate inside Airbus with the Spanish saying they didn't want to pay for it.'[23] The Germans overcame such objections by offering to pay for the tooling costs of the new factory themselves.

Now the biggest aircraft plant in Germany with a workforce of over 8,000, the factory at Finkenwerder builds all Airbus's single-aisle planes with the exception of the A320. The smaller A318 and A319 as well as the A321 are all essentially German-made planes. Sheltered from the river by a high dyke, the former fishing village of Finkenwerder lies just downstream from the main port of Hamburg. Despite the presence of the factory on its doorstep, it is still a very small place. The streets are so narrow there is barely room for the Airbus lorries carrying huge sections of fuselage to squeeze by, darkening the front rooms of the houses. Though they have been making the big planes there for more than ten years now, life in Finkenwerder still seems slow and parochial. For night life and entertainment the locals have to take a ferry to the bright lights of Hamburg just across the river. From the windows of the factory's staff canteen in which, unlike Toulouse, even the most senior executives eat, there is a grandstand view of the giant container ships as they slide silently by. Twice a day an ungainly Beluga transporter (a descendant of the Guppy) lumbers into the air carrying fuselage sections the 1,200 kilometres to Toulouse for painting, finishing and final assembly.

'The single aisle programme was an essential step in the creation of a family of aircraft,' says Gerhard Puttfarcken, senior vice-president of the single aisle programme. Launched with the A320 in 1987, the single-aisle family's sales now exceed 2,700. 'No one expected to have such success,' he says. 'We had to compete against an established family. The decision to go for the A320 was not easy. We had a long, intense discussion about the product and its development.' He says that the company split into two camps, with one side supporting the single aisle and the other the long-range.[24]

The German workers at Finkenwerder say they feel every bit as much a part of the Airbus family as the French in Toulouse. Manfred Porath, the head of final assembly at Finkenwerder, comments, 'Once you are in the Airbus system, you can't lose it. It's like catching a virus.' He says the importance of the final assembly work coming to Hamburg was that 'we get the complete competence. We can incorporate all the techniques. We get the best part of the cake. With Hamburg and Toulouse having the same competences, we support each other.'[25]

The two assembly lines are housed in a vast hanger with seven planes at various stages of construction. As each stage is completed, they are moved up the line to the next station. When I visited Finkenwerder in the summer of 2000, the plant was producing twelve-and-a-half aircraft a month. Productivity has improved to the point that the time it takes to build an aircraft – from definition to delivery – has been cut from fifteen to eighteen months, to nine months. Despite the high level of automation, it's a little startling to see that operations like attaching the wings to the fuselage are still done by hand, with workmen tightening the nuts on the bolts with what looks like an old-fashioned spanner. The one hi-tech element in this operation is that the spanner is programmed so that it tightens each nut to precisely the same degree.

The story of Airbus's German operations is that of Germany's economic history in microcosm. Formerly a shipyard, Finkenwerder was converted, as Nazi Germany began to rearm in the mid-1930s, to build military aircraft. As Hamburger Flugzeugbau, it built the HA 135, a cloth-covered biplane with a steel tube fuselage and wooden wings. In the photos on the factory wall you can just see, if you look carefully, the swastikas on the tail fins. On the adjoining loch, soon to be the site for the A380 superjumbo factory, the company once tested its military seaplanes. These days, Finkenwerder and its sister plant on the North Sea coast at Nordenham are the twin showpieces of Germany's newborn civil aviation industry.

The launch of the A330/340 marked a new and significant stage in the evolution of Airbus. It could now match Boeing in every major sector of the market – bar one. The A300/310 was well established, especially in the Middle East and the developing world; the best-selling A320 had shown that the Europeans could play the high-technology game just as successfully as the Americans; and the new medium and long-range A330/340s had great potential. The consortium was no longer considered as a nine-day wonder or a seven-stone weakling. Starting from zero, its market share of the civil aviation business had grown to around 20 per cent and its position in the widebody sector of the market was a good deal better than that. By the end of 1987, with ten airlines already committed to buying 130 of the new aircraft, Airbus Industrie's overall share of the widebody market had risen to a remarkable 47.9 per cent. The world market for civil airliners was on the eve of one of the biggest booms in its history. For Boeing, if 1987 had been a record year with sales of more than $15 billion, and a cash mountain of $3.4 billion, then 1988, when sales doubled to reach $30.1 billion and orders reached a staggering 636 planes, was to be even better. Boeing was not the only beneficiary. Airbus, too, profited from the boom. And the better it did, the more determined the onslaught was from Airbus's enemies in the United States.

CHAPTER TEN

THE AIRBUSTERS

FOR AIRBUS INDUSTRIE 1987 WAS a year for fireworks and celebration. It marked the 20th anniversary of the Lancaster House agreement that was, in effect, Airbus's birth certificate; it was the tenth anniversary of the 'fly and try' offer to Eastern Airlines; and it was the year of the roll-out of what was to be the consortium's most successful plane, the A320.

As one commentator has remarked, 'The launch of the A320 was a watershed. It was the vehicle for getting the British back in to the programme, and established Airbus Industrie as the centre for large scale civil aircraft production in Europe . . . Taken together the Airbus family would move Europe into a scale of production and investment in civil aerospace hitherto unknown outside the United States.' Airbus was not slow to congratulate itself.[1] 'A classic year of achievement,' a press handout noted. 'The Airbus family is completed as sales continue to increase.'

In contrast to the low-key roll out of the A300, Airbus turned the introduction of the A320 into a showbiz spectacular. It made its appearance in a cloud of dry ice on St Valentine's Day, 1987 and was given the traditional champagne send-off by the Prince of Wales and Princess Diana who were returning from an official visit to Portugal. It was left to Franz-Josef Strauss, the chairman of the supervisory board, in one of his last public appearances before his death the following year, to punch the message home. When the A300 was introduced, he said, there were a mere fifteen commitments from the airlines. At the same point in the A320's career, there were, he exclaimed, no fewer than 439.

Strauss was followed by the French Prime Minister, Jacques Chirac. In a speech that was both triumphalist and defiant, he said: 'The Airbus consortium will not be daunted by the Americans who killed off the Concorde. The A320 has already been a spectacular success. We will fight any trade war blow-for-blow, as the future of the aeronautical industry and the employment it brings are at stake.'[2]

That Chirac should choose to raise the stakes by talking so undiplomatically about a trade war was an indication that the transatlantic trade dispute, which had been simmering for the past two years, was hotting up. On the very day of the A320 roll-out, a high-powered American government delegation, led by the deputy trade representative, Michael Smith, and Bruce Smart, under-secretary for international trade at the US Department of Commerce, arrived in Europe to air American grievances and to protest about how European governments were propping up a loss-making Airbus at the expense of their own virtuous and thrifty aircraft companies.

This time it was McDonnell Douglas, not Boeing, that was the focus of attention. At a press conference in London, ambassador Smith said his cabinet believed that Airbus and McDonnell Douglas could not possibly split this market and make money. And he added that Airbus's chances of profiting were 'almost zero' because of the greater cost of developing the A330/340 line against the MD-11, a DC-10 derivative. This was a transparent attempt by the Americans to undermine the financing of the A330/340 by playing on the instinctive misgivings of the Thatcher government. Earlier that day the Americans had paid a call on Britain's minister in charge of aerospace, Geoff Pattie, who received them coolly. The meeting was described as 'diplomatically frank', and later Pattie said that he thought the Americans should stop 'whinging and moaning'.[3]

The question of aircraft subsidies had been an issue between Washington and Brussels, since the end of the 1970s, but now, eight years later, the air had become distinctly frosty. 'The pressures really started in 1987,' says Mogens Peter Carl, the quiet-spoken Dane who led the European negotiating team and who is now, as director general of trade, the European Commission's most senior trade official. 'There were accusations earlier from the Americans about the misuse of Airbus credits, but it never went very far,' he told me. 'In those days Boeing and McDonnell Douglas were . . . riding high. So there was no reason for them to push. It was only in the latter part of the 80s that Airbus's growing market share and technology really started waking them up to the fact that here was something they should be worried about.'[4]

*

Initially, the transatlantic dispute had been no more than a squabble between Airbus and Boeing about the economics of civil aviation. But as the battle developed, it became something much more than that. As the Americans saw it, it was a black and white clash between two diametrically opposed economic philosophies: liberal, free-enterprise America on one side versus interventionist, state-supported Europe on the other. In this scenario the plain-speaking, plain-dealing Americans were the good guys while the devious Europeans were the bad guys. Specifically, the Americans complained that as private companies, Boeing and McDonnell Douglas were obliged to finance their programmes with their own money or with money borrowed in the market place at commercial rates, while as a creature of government, Airbus was cushioned by subsidies and orders from national flag carriers. What's more, the Americans argued, the American companies had shareholders to satisfy, while Airbus Industrie was not even obliged to publish proper figures, let alone make a profit. In supporting Airbus in the way they did, the Europeans were in breach of the 1979 GATT agreement on trade in civil aircraft. It was, the Americans said, simply not fair.

The Europeans reply to all this was suitably robust. What the American argument ignored, they retorted, were the massive sums Boeing and the other American manufacturers received from the US government and the military in indirect subsidies. John Hunt, director of aerospace for Britain's department of trade and industry, who had a ringside view of the dispute from his post at the British Embassy in Washington in the mid-1980s, says, 'The Europeans could always blunt the attack by referring to the huge subsidies the American manufacturers received in the form of military contracts.'

No serious student of the history of the American civil aviation business could fail to notice the decisive role played by the federal government in its development. During the 1920s and 1930s Bill Boeing built his company on the back of the American government's efforts to encourage the burgeoning mail business. At the same time, the government played a seminal part in the building of the nation's airlines by creating a regulatory environment that strongly favoured the growth of large trunk carriers capable of carrying passengers as well as mail. Under Walter Folger Brown, postmaster general during the Hoover administration, the government forced through a series of mergers designed to give the nascent airline business the necessary critical mass of capital and resources.

As the distinguished economist Lester Thurow has observed:[5]

America's commercial-aircraft industry grew up in a symbiotic relationship with government. The production of military aircraft financed research and development on products and processes that could often be carried over into commercial products . . . Regulated airlines were guaranteed the fares necessary to pay for high-tech engineering staffs and to finance rapid shifts to more sophisticated aircraft. Most of the markets for commercial aircraft were in the United States, and suppliers and users worked together much as if they were in the same business groups.

Technologically sophisticated users pushed technologically sophisticated suppliers . . . Given the enormous amounts of up-front development money (between two billion and four billion dollars), long periods of negative cash flow (five or six years), and even time lags until costs are covered (ten to fourteen years), no private company was ever going to break into this market against the entrenched American position . . . Without government help, Airbus could not have gotten started and could not have survived. The Europeans claim, however, that they are only doing overtly what the American government had done covertly twenty-five years earlier through military procurement.

Successive American governments intervened extensively to ensure the health of American aircraft manufacturers. They did so by creating an environment where manufacturing firms could expect to receive a steady flow of money to develop new civilian products. And US airlines assisted in the process by acting as reliable and eager launch customers for the new aircraft being developed. They would pay a deposit on several planes and this money would be used by the manufacturers to underwrite expenses for the project.

Valuable as the efforts of the US government were in creating the right environment for the aircraft manufacturers, the spin-off from building the huge jet bombers and military transports for the US air force was of even greater importance. Its procurement policies, particularly the requirement for large transports and bombers, says Steven McGuire, created a demand for large, heavy, jet-powered airframes. Military procurement acted as a safety net for these firms: by providing military contracts when the civilian market was lean, the government encouraged firms to stay involved in the civilian side of the business. The military, as well as NACA and its successor, NASA, also conducted generic research programmes whose results often benefited civilian products. This R&D support significantly reduced the burden on the manufacturers. Government sponsored R&D also aided firms by reducing their exposure to financial risk in the applications of new technologies to aircraft.[6]

In Britain there was surprisingly little communality between commercial and military work, but in America the pattern was very different. We have already described how Boeing's 707 grew out of a military tanker called the KC-135 and how Boeing's bid to build the C-5A giant military transport paved the way for the 747. What was of even greater importance was the access Boeing engineers were given after the war to the captured papers of German scientists who had been working on the aerodynamics on the swept wing – the key to high-speed, jet-powered flight.

What Boeing learned from this material and from the tests they were allowed to make in government-owned wind tunnels led directly to the B-47 and B-52 bombers of the 1950s and 1960s, which in turn were the parents of the KC-135 and the 707. A study by a firm of Washington-based consultants commissioned by the European Commission at the height of the trade dispute reckoned that between 1986 and 1991 US government spent between $18 billion to $22.05 billion supporting the commercial side of the American aircraft industry. These calculations are based on historical dollar valuations. If current figures are used, the range of total benefits rises from $33.48 billion to $41.49 billion. As this study was prepared for one of the protagonists and was designed as a riposte to another piece of research commissioned by the US government to illustrate Airbus's chronic dependence on government hand-outs, these figures should be taken with the usual helping of salt. The subject is so wide and the details so subjective that precision is impossible. Nonetheless, the general thrust of the argument is undoubtedly correct, however hard the Americans tried to deny it. 'The Americans were absolutely obsessed at imposing disciplines on the reimbursable loan arrangement (commonly known as "launch aid"),' says Mogens Peter Carl. 'The question of indirect subsidies was something they simply refused to acknowledge.'[7]

*

The first round of hostilities opened in 1978, when Boeing accused Airbus of 'predatory pricing' in order to secure the Eastern Airlines deal. Boeing complained that Airbus had arranged for European governments to extend $250 million of export credits to the cash-strapped airline. The terms were generous: interest rates were not fixed but varied according to Eastern's profitability. The arrangement was that the more money Eastern made, the higher the rate, and vice versa. Boeing also said that Airbus had put up $96 million of its own money to help Eastern on terms that, it claimed, violated the OECD agreements on export financing.

In referring the matter to GATT, Boeing was upping the ante. The dispute was no longer a spat between two aircraft manufacturers: it had now become a government-to-government matter. The General Agreement on Tariffs and Trade, known as GATT, was signed in 1947 as part of the new, post-war world order, which embraced the Marshall Plan, the founding of the United Nations, the International Monetary Fund and the European Iron and Steel Community, the forerunner of the European Common Market.

The underlying principle of GATT was a liberal belief in the virtues of free trade and in the evils of protectionism. Signatory countries agreed that as a general rule they would not impose tariffs or any other major barriers to international trade and they would not do bilateral deals with each other to discriminate against everybody else. Trade would be as open and as even-handed as possible. But in difficult cases, the architects of the GATT agreement acknowledged there would always be a need to negotiate special arrangements. As a mechanism for regulating international trade, GATT is far from perfect. The Geneva-based GATT has no legal personality of its own, unlike the EC where the contracting parties have transferred negotiating and decision-making powers from the national to the supra-national level. In GATT the best that can happen is that binding decisions will emerge by agreement after annual plenary meetings or after multi-lateral rounds of negotiations, like the Kennedy round, the Tokyo round, the Uruguay round, which can last for years. Where there is no general agreement or where the issues are limited to a few countries, special deals are sometimes tacked on as a kind of appendix to a general round. The aircraft accord is a case in point.

Until then, the GATT negotiators had paid little attention to the aircraft industry. With the business so dominated by a single country, there had seemed little point. But things were beginning to change. By the end of the 1970s, when the GATT Tokyo round was being negotiated, the aircraft industry had forced its way towards the top of the pile. It was not just Airbus: Brazil, Canada and Japan were all developing aerospace industries of their own. And the question was, how much government support should be allowed under GATT rules to ensure that the guiding principles of free trade and free competition were not unduly compromised? The Americans grumbled that foreign plane makers were undercutting them and that European governments were arm-twisting their national flag carriers to buy Airbuses instead of Boeings, while the Europeans complained against the duty the Americans imposed on imported planes.

In April 1979, in the aftermath of the Tokyo Round, the parties sat down to negotiate the GATT Agreement on Trade in Civil Aircraft. The aim of the Americans was to draft an agreement that banned government subsidies; the object of the Europeans was precisely the opposite. There was much hard bargaining but by the time they went home each side thought they had got what they wanted. The key section was article six, which dealt with government support, export credits and aircraft marketing. The paragraph dealing with government subsidies was, quite deliberately, a study in ambiguity. While it brought aircraft subsidies into the overall GATT framework, they were not banned as such. Those handing out subsidies were merely obliged 'to seek to avoid adverse effects on trade in civil aircraft'.[8]

The paragraph on aircraft pricing was equally opaque. It was agreed that 'pricing of civil aircraft should be based on a reasonable expectation of recoupment of costs, including non-recurring programme costs, identifiable and pro-rated costs of military research and development on aircraft, components, and systems that are subsequently applied to the production of such civil aircraft, average production costs, and financial costs'. Stephen Piper, the head of the American negotiating team, acknowledged there was no specific ban on government subsidies, but he thought that the 'reasonable expectation' proviso gave him what he was looking for.[9]

The Americans believed it was no longer possible for Airbus, or any other foreign competitor, to sell planes at low prices, safe in the knowledge that its home governments would cover the losses through subsidy. As Stephen Piper put it, 'Just as nothing in the agreement imposes obligations on government-industry relationship or prohibits domestic subsidies, nothing diminishes the obligation to avoid adverse effects on the civil trade interests of other signatories . . . How a nation organises its industry is a sovereign matter, but how a government-owned or supported firm competes in the marketplace is a matter properly of concern to the United States and to other nations.'[10] What the Americans seemed to be saying was that the Europeans could subsidise until they were blue in the face, but it didn't matter, provided the subsidies were not used to undercut the prices of competing American planes in the market place. But if it could be shown that Airbus was using its subsidies for price-cutting or dumping, then they would be, the Americans maintained, in breach of the GATT agreement.

George Prill, a leading spokesman for the US aviation industry, went even further when he told the House of Representatives Ways and Means Committee, only days after the signature of the agreement, that it had established the 'basic principle' that governments should not subsidise aircraft programmes.

The Europeans interpreted the agreement quite differently. Steven McGuire notes, 'The Europeans flatly rejected the American view that subsidies were severely restricted because of the accord's requirement that the pricing of aircraft be done with a reasonable expectation that non-recurring costs be recouped. In several places the accord positively affirms the right of signatories to use subsidies. The continued ability to use subsidies was the cornerstone of the European position. As far as subsidies to Airbus were concerned these were vital . . . For Airbus to work, it had to learn to do what the Americans had done via the B-52 and the C-5A in the 1960s.' McGuire argues that Airbus needed development subsidies to learn what Boeing and MDC had learned from the US military programmes years before. Direct subsidies to Airbus were – from a European perspective – the functional equivalent of US military R&D. And he says that the Europeans regarded any suggestion that the US industry, with over 80 per cent of the world airliner market, could be adversely affected by Airbus as absurd.[11]

The Americans may have failed in their attempt to outlaw European subsidies, but by bringing civil aircraft into the GATT regime they had nonetheless put down a reference point that was to be useful in the later, more ferocious stages of the battle. Already, the Europeans believed they could detect a distinct pattern in American behaviour: whenever Airbus scored a notable success or was about to launch a new model, the Americans reacted with a protest about subsidies. At first, Airbus's attempts to break into the American market with the A300 created little interest and even less concern, despite the massive government subsidies and launch aid.

The first protests coincided with the Eastern deal which, as we seen, led directly to the 1979 GATT accord. There then followed a lull of about six years when the issue remained on the back-burner. There was a brief flare-up in 1983 when the manufacturers went to Washington to lobby Malcolm Baldridge, the secretary of commerce in the Reagan administration. But although the government was sympathetic to the industry's request that it use its muscle to open markets and crack down on illegal subsidies, nothing much happened until the start of Ronald Reagan's second term in 1985. It was in that year that Airbus secured its famous Pan Am deal, followed shortly afterwards by equally spectacular coups with American and Northwest. At the same time, the consortium had signalled its intentions to go after Boeing's single-aisle market by giving the go-ahead for the A320 programme.

Up until now it had been the US manufacturers who had been leading the anti-Airbus campaign. But the events of 1985 galvanized an administration already alarmed by the apparent erosion of American economic power. By the mid-1980s, America was no longer the most productive country in the world: in terms of GNP per head she had been overtaken by the Japanese, the Germans, the Swiss and the Swedes. As Lester Thurow wrote in *Head to Head*, his influential study of the changing economic world order, 'The United States no longer leads in everything. In some areas, such as automobiles, it is a follower, and in others, such as consumer electronics, it is not even a player. Where American firms used to dwarf their competitors, they now find themselves increasingly on the small side.'*[12]

The 'rust-belt' industries in the heartland around Pittsburgh and other steel towns were in decline; the Japanese were threatening America's automobile and electronics industries and Far Eastern imports were crippling her textile business. As foreign imports poured in, America's trade deficit reached record levels. Nor could the European challenge be discounted. The signature of the Single European Market treaty in 1986, which set a target for integration that was only six years in the future, caused great disquiet in Washington. There was much talk about the growing challenge of 'Fortress Europe'.

The reaction of a Reagan administration elected on a free market ticket was to increase the rhetoric about the virtues of free market economics abroad while practising protectionism at home. Already the United States had reached a series of bilateral agreements with Japan whereby limits were placed on the imports of cars, textiles, semi-conductors and steel. In 1985 the administration turned its attention to the civil aircraft industry, America's largest earner of foreign exchange. America's indebtedness was alarming enough, but if anything or anybody threatened the ability of the aircraft industry to pull in the dollars, the situation, so the administration reasoned, might easily spiral out of control.

'Perhaps we should have done something to nip this whole thing in the bud way back, in 1978 or earlier,' Ray Waldman, Boeing's director of government affairs and a veteran of government trade policy under three presidents, told Matthew Lynn. 'It was really only in the early eighties that there were meetings to urge the US government to pay attention to the industrial targeting of this industry. Then in the fall of 1985, when the president was looking for targets for an unfair trade strike force, Airbus was singled out as a manifestation of industrial targeting in Europe that was causing harm in the US. There was a great deal of concern in the US about the deteriorating trade balance, and . . . about the future of the aircraft industry . . . if Airbus was not checked.'[13] Under instructions from the White House, officials of various government departments banded together to make up this task-force. They called themselves 'The Airbusters'.

---

*   In *Head to Head*, Thurow, writing in 1991, forecast that the main challenge to the United States for world economic hegemony would come from the European Community and Japan. Subsequent events have shown that the threat from Japan has been much weaker than anticipated.

The creation of the Airbuster team came only a month or so after the appointment of Clayton Yeutter as US trade ambassador. A former president of the Chicago Mercantile Exchange with a law degree and a PhD in agricultural economics, Yeutter was also well schooled in the ways of Washington, having served in both the Nixon and Ford administrations. His brief was to crack down on what the Reagan administration regarded as unfair trade practices. After some inconclusive meetings with the Europeans that autumn in an attempt to find some common ground on subsidies and other questions, the following spring Yeutter raised the ante by writing a stiff letter to the ministers of the Airbus countries. 'Our own preliminary economic analyses,' he wrote, 'do not persuade us that there is a solid economic basis to providing government aid to launch these aircraft programs. The market potential appears to be too small to allow for recoupment of such government aid, including interest charges, in a manner consistent with Article 6.2 of the GATT Aircraft Agreement.'[14]

Had he but known it, he was touching on a tender British nerve. Shortly after his appointment by Mrs Thatcher as trade and industry secretary in 1985, the new minister, Leon Brittan, whose views on economic questions were as dry as his instincts on social policy were wet, asked his officials to justify the practice. His first question was: how many aircraft have paid for themselves? To which the answer was: one – the Viscount. 'If the results are so poor, why do we go on doing it?' the minister inquired. The answer was worthy of Sir Humphrey himself: 'We need the jobs, we need the technology, and besides everybody else is doing it.'[15] However much launch aid may have violated Thatcherite economic doctrine, Brittan (and Mrs Thatcher herself, for that matter) were politicians enough to see that pragmatism outweighed dogma. Within weeks Brittan was writing to Yeutter defending government launch aid for the A320 on the grounds that it was not, in the opinion of the British government, in breach of the GATT aircraft agreement.

All the Europeans took the same line. Of the four, the French were the most pointed. After referring to the R&D money the American industry received from NASA and the Defence Department, Michel Noir, the French trade minister, effectively told Yeutter to mind his own business. The funding of the A330/340 (the main burden of Yeutter's complaint) was, the minister said, a matter for internal decision on which France and her partners would employ their own judgement. The main effect of Yeutter's intervention was to make the Europeans close ranks. With the informal talks approaching deadlock, Paris, Bonn and London passed the responsibility for the negotiations to the European Commission in Brussels. If there was going to be a transatlantic trade war, it would be Brussels that would carry the flag for Europe. It was a task Brussels accepted with alacrity. As the European trade commissioner Willy de Clerq roundly declared, 'Not only is Airbus a success story for European technology but, more importantly, it is an example of industrial co-operation within the European Community, and as such it deserves our strong support and we must defend the idea and the concept with all the means at our disposal.'[16]

For the next five years there was to be head-to-head confrontation between the European Commission and the US government. For the Europeans the battle was led by Willy de Clerq, who liased closely with the French, German and British governments and with the officials of Airbus Industrie to coordinate Europe's defences and to orchestrate the counter-offensive. 'It was the pressures of 1987 during which the Americans were trying to derail the A320 or at least make our governments grant support on more stringent terms that brought us into the process,' says the civil servant who led the team, Mogens Peter Carl. 'And that went up and down and up and down. There was quite a long period when nothing was happening.'[17] But there were other times when it looked as if the dispute would break out into a full-scale transatlantic trade war.

The Americans had several weapons to hand. They could trigger GATT anti-dumping measures, which allows the injured party to impose special duties on the offending imports; they could block access for the Europeans to US markets; or, most serious of all, they could initiate a so-called Super 301 action which, under the US trade act of 1987, would enable them to take countevailing measures against the Europeans. They could, for example, retaliate against Airbus subsidies by imposing punitive duties on German cars or French wine. Under pressure from Senator John Danforth of Missouri, the lobbyist for McDonnell Douglas, article 301 was specifically extended to permit retaliation against Airbus.

In the trade war games played by both Brussels and Washington, this threat of retaliation was described as 'the nuclear option'. But although the Americans frequently threatened to use it, somehow they never actually did. 'In the final resort the Americans recognised that there was always a danger that if they played the nuclear card and invoked 301, then the Europeans would use other items and commodities as a counter-weapon,' says John Hunt, the British official who was watching closely from his post at the British embassy in Washington.[18] Furthermore, the Americans were unable to maintain a united front. The engine makers Pratt & Whitney and GE were never as keen to pursue Airbus as Boeing and McDonnell Douglas for the obvious reason that the Europeans had been buying good customers for more than twenty years, and if the American firms joined in too vigorously, the only beneficiary would be Rolls-Royce.

By 1987 the dispute was hotting up. To counteract growing hostility on Capitol Hill, Airbus Industrie decided in mid-summer that the time had come to launch a peace-offensive. It despatched Alan Boyd, the head of its North American operations, to testify before Congress. Boyd had a surprise up his sleeve. He admitted something that Airbus had hitherto always denied: namely, that it had deliberately lowered its prices in North America as a device to gain market share. 'It's done by Proctor and Gamble; it's done by everybody,' he declared. 'If you are not in a market and you want to get into a market, you sell at whatever price you have to get into the market – agree or disagree, that's the fact.' Boyd followed up this candid admission that Airbus had been price-cutting with the unsurprising but perhaps incautious disclosure that the A300 and the A310 would never be profitable.[19]

This outburst of unaccustomed European candour signalled a change of tactics designed to forestall the threat of direct American trade action. The Europeans never denied that government subsidies had been from the very beginning an essential part of the Airbus operation. But they argued that the Americans never understood what the GIE was or how it worked. Jean Pierson says he spent an enormous amount of time meeting all the department of commerce officials in Washington, all the US trade ministers and the American ambassadors in Paris, London and Bonn trying to correct their misconceptions about the GIE. 'But the trouble is,' he told me, 'the United States has some very simplistic people. They said that to develop your aircraft, you have money from the government and you used this money to subsidise your sales – which was [long pause] let's say, stupid. They were right to say that without money from the government at the time, when we were at zero we could never have beaten Boeing. What bank would have been stupid enough to have lent us the money. They were right about that. Where they were wrong was to say that I was giving the aircraft away. How could I do that when British Aerospace was saying "Jean, I want this amount of money from you for our wing."'[20]

By conceding that its early models were unprofitable while declaring that the later ones were going to be money-makers, Airbus was signalling that it was ready to move away from its hard line on subsidies and was willing to accept some restrictions on condition that the Americans conceded some ground on indirect subsidies. With the financing of the A330/340 now in place, the American campaign to shake the resolve of the French, German and British governments had plainly failed, and Airbus felt it could afford to make some concessions. In May the Thatcher government had approved a $750 million loan to BAe for its share of the A330/340 programme and a month later the programme was formally launched. Before the year was out, there were what the industry calls 'letters of intent' from ten airlines for a total of 130 aircraft. And although it would be another two years before this interest was converted into firm orders, it looked as if the A330/340 would be a success. 'Once again,' says Mogens Peter Carl, 'the Americans had missed the boat in terms of timing. They had missed the launch of the A330/340 which had already been done. That was bad for Boeing. At the same time it helped us in the sense that we could be much more forthcoming in respect to the conclusion of an agreement that had to do with future funding.'[21]

However robust Jean Pierson's defence of the GIE may have been, within the Airbus family itself there were increasing doubts about the system. The rows with the Germans the previous year over the delays to the A330/340 programme and the

continuing bickering between the partners over work-share all helped to focus attention on a system of management and organization that everybody realized was far
from perfect.

Mike Turner of British Aerospace, who took over Airbus responsibilities in the
mid-1990s, is scathing:[22]

> I quickly learned that the management of Airbus was a disaster. There were the rows
> that went on between the partners; and the interfaces were almost impossible to
> manage. The products were fantastic. So was the family idea with the communality
> between the A320/330/340. But I was going to supervisory boards which were a
> joke. Nobody listened. Everybody talked during a presentation. Us Anglo Saxons,
> we'd sit there and listen and take notes. But during a presentation, they all start talk-
> ing, doing other things and ignoring what was going on. It was awful. Of course
> underlying all this we had the partners who where both shareholders and suppliers.
> And we still haven't agreed the partners' share on A330/340. We still do not have an
> agreement on which each partner gets paid. That situation had been going on for six
> years. So the system was becoming impossible. And once it had grown into a $15 bil-
> lion company it had become completely unmanageable.

The Germans, the British and even the French recognized that if the consortium was
to compete effectively against the Americans, it would have to streamline a decision-
making process that was agonizingly slow and cumbersome. In a fast-moving and
cut-throat business like the making of commercial jetliners, a system in which a
single partner could hold up development of a new plane for months, if not years,
was unacceptable. There was also pressure from Airbus's paymasters, the member
governments, for greater transparency and accountability. One of Airbus Industrie's
greatest weaknesses was a complete lack of any centralized system of financial control. And although Airbus Industrie could – and did – make estimates as to the
likely profitability of its programmes, they were just that: only guesses. As a way of
running a very large, highly capital-intensive, hugely competitive international business, it was, to say the least, eccentric. Above all, it frightened the bankers to whom,
increasingly, Airbus Industrie were looking to in order to finance its new projects. It
was no accident that the A321 was the first Airbus plane for which there was no government support at all.† The more commercial the consortium became and the
nearer it moved towards break-even, the more reluctant its sponsoring governments
became to go on providing the same level of funding to support the venture. It was
one thing to guarantee loans or provide strictly limited launch aid. To continue

---

†   Launched in November 1989 at the cost of half a billion dollars, the 186-seater plane was financed
     with the help of a 150 billion Italian lire bond issue. At the time of its launch it had secured 107
     orders, with options on a further 74.

funding up to 80 per cent or more of a complete programme was quite another. The success of the A320 underlined the force of these arguments.

In the autumn of 1987 the governments decided that the moment had come for a shake-up. A committee was appointed to investigate Airbus Industrie and to make recommendations as to how its organization and management might be improved. Each country chose its own representative. The French, the Germans and the Spanish picked people who knew the industry and Airbus well. Only the English chose a complete outsider. The Frenchman was Jacques Benichou of the French Aerospace Industry Association; the German was Peter Pfeiffer, a former director of Bayerische Vereinsbank and a former member of the supervisory board of Deutsche Airbus; the Spaniard was Emilio González Garcia, deputy general manager of Banco Español de Credito and former chairman of Airbus's Spanish partner, CASA; and the Englishman was Sir Jeffrey Sterling, a former property developer, chairman of P&O, and one of Mrs Thatcher's business cronies. Inevitably, they became instantly known as the Four Wise Men. Altogether, they spent the first four months of 1988 interviewing everybody at Airbus, including Franz-Josef Strauss, Jean Pierson and his colleagues at Toulouse, as well as the senior managers of all four partners.

Their report, when it came that April, was far from complimentary. It acknowledged Airbus's 'remarkable' commercial strategy; it paid tribute to its 'technological achievement' and successes; and it praised the vital part it had played in keeping for Europe what it called 'its rightful place in the sky'. It conceded that in trying to break into a market dominated by the Americans, Airbus had faced enormous inherent problems and that 'it was still at too early a stage in most of its programmes to have reached a break-even point'. Even so, the Wise Men said, problems have arisen from 'a certain lack of adaptability and organisational efficiency in the Airbus organisation'. However desirable, they felt it was perhaps too early to convert the consortium into a fully-fledged plc, but they concluded, in effect, that the GIE had passed its sell-by date and they called for a complete revision of the Airbus Industrie structure and rules.

Turning to the detail, the investigation found that there was 'a lack of correlation' between the marketing of Airbus programmes and their financial aspect; they criticized the absence of an overall balance sheet and described the organization as 'unwieldy'. There were too many committees and the clause requiring the approval of decisions by the partners holding 81 per cent of the shares meant in practice that all decisions had to be unanimous. 'What is required,' the Four Wise Men said firmly, 'is an Airbus Industrie structure which would be more responsible for all parts of the programmes, more concerned with profit and loss, and less dependent in its day-to-day operation on each industrial partner. The partners, on the other hand, need to control more closely Airbus Industrie's decisions, since they bear all the risks.'

The Wise Men had also had hard words to say about Airbus management. 'It is imperative to establish as soon as possible a system in which decisions, the power to take them, and the background knowledge appropriate to the decisions vest clearly in particular managers or groups of managers inside a tightly defined reporting system.' The authors went on to warn the consortium that unless these changes were made immediately, problems for Airbus would only increase, 'leading . . . to serious production delays, severe extra costs and, worst of all, the loss of goodwill of major airlines'. It was very important, they said, that relationships between Airbus Industrie and the partners were simplified and streamlined.

Although they did not say so in so many words, the Four Wise Men clearly felt that Jean Pierson and his team in charge of day-to-day management at Toulouse had grown too strong and the supervisory board too weak. 'The supervisory board should be the main instrument of overall policy control of the whole Airbus project,' they declared. Accordingly, the report recommended a series of changes and reforms designed to impose a more conventional form of discipline on both Airbus Industrie and its partners. It suggested that the supervisory board should be drastically reduced in size; that reporting lines between the managing director and the supervisory board should be made much clearer; and that a central accounting system should be established under a finance director with powers 'to require from all four partners full details of their programme costs, invoiced prices and profits and losses arising from work contracted to them by AI'.

As the Wise Men themselves pointed out, this last requirement was the key one. For the first time the partners would be forced to reveal their most closely guarded secret – the amount of money they were making out of Airbus. 'If Airbus Industrie does not take steps to constitute itself in the organisational manner we propose and to introduce full transparency of costs and profits together with producing comparisons between AI and its partners,' the report's authors warned, 'we doubt whether Airbus can ever reach long-term profitability.'[23]

Unsurprisingly, the report did not go down well in Toulouse. If implemented, its proposals would, if nothing else, have curbed Jean Pierson's swash-buckling style. He was sufficiently put out to tell colleagues that he was thinking of resigning. But this turned out to be no more than a fit of Gallic pique. Following the death of Franz-Josef Strauss later that year, the time-honoured tradition that the chairman of the supervisory board should be German was observed with the appointment of the former Free Democrat politician Hans Friderichs. The supervisory board was reduced in size and a British accountant, Robert Smith, was brought in from British Aerospace to be the new finance director. He was not, however, given the sweeping powers recommended by the Four Wise Men, and within eighteen months he was gone, having failed to extract any meaningful financial information from the partners (which included his own company). He also complained that he had been sidelined during Airbus Industrie's talks with the banks about the financing of the A321. With the departure of Robert Smith, the report of the Four Wise Men was put quietly to one side as the top management at Toulouse concluded they had more urgent things on their mind than the restructuring of the company.

In Seattle the Wilson era had come to an end with the emergence of Frank Shrontz, Boeing's eighth president but only the second lawyer after the redoubtable Bill Allen, the architect of the modern Boeing, to hold the job in the company's history. All the others had been engineers. After graduating in 1954 from the University of Idaho College of Law, Shrontz moved on to study business administration at Harvard. In 1958, the year he gained his MBA, he joined Boeing as a contract coordinator and began his slow and patient climb through the ranks of the organization. By 1967 he had become assistant to the vice president for contracts and marketing. But in the early 1970s he left Boeing for Washington, DC, where he became assistant secretary of the Air Force in the Nixon administration and later assistant secretary of defence. In 1977, with the Republicans out of office, Shrontz returned to Boeing. His time in Washington certainly helped his career. By the early 1980s he was, as head of sales and marketing, the force behind the highly successful 737-300 sales campaign. In 1985 he had taken over from 'T' Wilson as president; three years later he completed the transition when Wilson stepped down as chairman.

Unlike Bill Allen, Shrontz was not a man inclined to bet the company: his style was cautious and conservative. He favoured the traditional Boeing incremental approach to making airplanes. Instead of building brand new models, Shrontz, like his patron and mentor 'T' Wilson, preferred to extract as much as he could by modifying and stretching existing planes. This had been Boeing's response to Airbus's A320 when it launched the 737-300. And for a time it was Shrontz's answer to the twin challenge of the A330/340 and the McDonnell Douglas MD-11. 'We started out looking at a stretched 767,' says Phil Condit, who was in charge of the programme and was eventually to take over from Shrontz. 'But it would not have enough capability. We looked at a 767 with a new wing, or a 767 with a partial double deck, but in the end we decided we needed a new plane. Stretching a plane is relatively economic, but the more you change the more it costs.'[24]

Boeing's answer was the 777 – a twin-engined widebody designed to go head-to-head with the Airbus and McDonnell Douglas offerings – the A330 and MD-11. Launching a new aircraft is such an expensive business that no manufacturer builds a single model for a single market. Just as the A330 came with a range of options and configurations, so did the Triple Seven. It was, in a sense, a mini-family within a family. The first member was designed for medium-range routes across the north Atlantic, the US and throughout Asia for routes with too few passengers for the 747 but too many for the 767. The second was built for the so-called long/thin routes with distances of between 5,500 to 7,000 nautical miles but with a with a much lighter passenger load than the 747. The final version was intended to be a really long-range machine capable of carrying 300 passengers for up to 8,500 nautical miles, the equivalent of flying non-stop from Chicago to Hong Kong.

Although Boeing was the last entrant in the race, there was not much to choose between the three contenders. They were all brand-new and all had much the same capacity and capability. It therefore stood to reason that the battle between the three manufacturers would be even fiercer than usual. As one of America's largest airlines and one of Boeing's oldest and most loyal customers, United Airlines was a prime target for all three sales teams. Between them, they were offering a bewildering thirty-three plane/engine combinations for United to choose from. And then there was the money. Jean Pierson remembers all too clearly a call from Steven Wolf, the chairman of United, just before the launch of 777. Both men were staying over the weekend at the Meridian hotel in Nice; Pierson was lunching with his wife and her parents when Wolf called. 'As Boeing was about to launch the Triple Seven, would Pierson be willing to renegotiate the price of the A340?' Wolf inquired. For once, Pierson was caught at a disadvantage. 'I gave him something, but not what he wanted,' he recalls. 'But just think! For just $2 million per aircraft, I'd had a chance to spoil the launch of the 777. But I was in a hotel. It was a weekend. And I was thinking short-term.'[25]

As it was, when the crunch time came, the battle was hard-fought. 'We went into seventy hours of negotiations and it was very emotional because we could tell by the faces of the people coming out of the inquisition chamber that things had not gone well,' says one United Airlines observer who had been called in from San Francisco to give technical advice on the engine options. 'What was happening was that somebody would go in there from one manufacturer and present a deal, and then he would be dismissed and the next person would come in, and we'd try and better the deal. So it was a ratcheting process through those seventy hours, trying to get the best terms.'[26]

In the end, honours were even. Airbus Industrie may have lost the United Airlines order, but for the first two years, sales of the Boeing 777 and A330 were level-pegging. Where Airbus scored was that in the longer-range four-engined A340 it had a second arrow in the quiver.

As Jean Pierson saw it, the successful launch of the A330/340 was the culmination of the Airbus adventure. The consortium had not only survived but had proved it could match Boeing blow-for-blow in every sector of the market, bar the jumbo. Even there, the A340 could fly as fast and as far as the 747. In a lecture in the spring of 1991 at the Cranfield school of management in Britain, during which he revealed that the venture had made operating profit for the first in its history, Pierson waxed lyrical about Airbus as a symbol of European achievement.[27] It was no accident that he made his speech at a time when the trade war with the Americans was reaching its climax. He declared:

Airbus Industrie stands as a symbol of what Europe can accomplish when it combines its forces around a common project. A forerunner of the concept of globalisation in the aircraft industry, Airbus Industrie has spurred a large number of projects in cooperation across a broad spectrum of the industry. It stands, today, as the only recourse against a monopoly of the civil aerospace industry by US manufacturers. Our products come in over one hundred different colours – the colours of our customers around the world. That is the real commercial power that is now back in European hands.

With much patience, our partners chose to invest in what they know to be a very long-term business activity and accepted fully that it would take a while before they saw a return on their investment. In doing so they generated wealth in Europe, the wealth that comes from skills retention, employment and career opportunities, import substitution, export earnings. The determination of the partners to keep the damaging demons of intra-European rivalry at bay was a key factor in the success of Airbus Industrie. It is in the interests of Europe that this determination should prevail. If there could be one lesson . . . to be learned from the Airbus Industrie experience, it would be that cooperation is the key to prosperity and that there simply is room no more for narrow nationalistic endeavours.

With these words Jean Pierson nailed Europe's colours to the mast and threw down the clearest challenge yet to the Americans.

*

The launch of the Triple Seven ushered in the final and most bitter stage of the transatlantic trade dispute. From 1990 onwards, urged on by Boeing, the US government stepped up its campaign to persuade GATT that Airbus Industrie's government subsidies were illegal and its sales' tactics were improper. As Frank Shrontz told the US Council on Foreign Relations, 'Boeing and McDonnell Douglas have a strong case for retaliatory action under US law. We see such action as a last resort because it would be protectionist in nature and because we believe that GATT and other multinational mechanisms are more consistent with meeting our goal of resolving the issue under international law. But Airbus and the EC should understand our position. The issue must be resolved. Twenty-one years of subsidy is far too much. Enough is enough.'

In April 1990 the Americans made a formal complained to GATT about German government foreign exchange subsidies to Deutsche Airbus, and the following year they broadened the attack with a second complaint about Airbus subsidies in general. The Americans were the first to draw blood. But the Europeans were quick to repair the damage. 'We lost the export subsidy case,' says Mogens Peter Carl. 'But it was settled immediately afterwards. We agreed with the Germans that they had to change their system. But what happened in reality was the way the German government simply changed the way in which it handed out very substantial amounts of money to Deutsche Airbus. Instead of going by route A, it went by route B.'[28]

To provide ammunition about subsidies, the US department of commerce commissioned a firm of consultants called Gellman Research Associates to conduct a detailed survey of Airbus finances from the beginning. The report, which was designed to heap fuel on a fire that was already blazing merrily, was published in September 1990. 'The aircraft manufacturing industry is characterized by both high sunk costs and significant learning economics,' it said. 'A firm entering this industry must be prepared to commit billions of dollars to develop a single product even though only a relatively small number of aircraft will be delivered each year, with deliveries beginning some years after the initial commitment. Once spent these billions are sunk and cannot be recovered either fully or easily by selling off the underlying assets.

'The large size of the investment required, the limited number of units sold each year, the difficulty in liquidating assets in the event of financial difficulty and the learning curve effect make the aircraft manufacturing industry both risky and oligopolistic,' Gellman said. 'By creating and sustaining AI, the governments of the AI-member companies have ensured that at least one of the limited number of civil aircraft manufacturers will be European.'

The report's description of the economics of aircraft manufacture was remarkably objective and even-handed. But as an analysis of Airbus's finances, the report is more partisan. The authors concluded that over the past nineteen years, France, Germany and Britain had committed about $13.5 billion in support of AI's aircraft programmes, up to and including the A330/340. Of this, the authors say, the Germans had contributed 58.9 per cent, the French 25.1 per cent and Britain 16 per cent. But this sum, large as it is, does not include financing charges. If the cost of government borrowing in each country is applied, then the figure rises to $19 billion. And if commercial borrowing rates are applied, then the initial $13.5 billion, at a conservative estimate, almost doubles to something close to $26 billion. Of this, the report concludes that the Airbus partners had, by the end of 1989, repaid no more than $500 million or just about 4 per cent of the total. From this the consultants conclude, 'AI has avoided the traditionally high financial barriers to entry into the aircraft manufacturing industry through the receipt of substantial – and continuing – government support. Such support has ensured that AI will be one of the world's limited numbers of aircraft manufacturers.'

If the study had stopped there, there would have been few – including top management at Toulouse – who would have disagreed. The consultants' conclusions about the profitability of the planes themselves were more contentious. They constructed an elaborate model to calculate the profitability of each type of aircraft in the Airbus range from its inception to the year 2008. There were six in all: the A300, the A300-600, the A310, the A320, the A330 and the A340. The confident tone of the report served to disguise the fact that the consultants were, in fact, only guessing. For figures on Airbus costs, for example, the authors were forced to rely on estimates provided by Boeing and McDonnell Douglas to the US department of commerce! The authors say that they did see the individual estimates but were given the DOC's merged version, which they reviewed for what they describe as 'reasonableness'.

Estimates of Airbus revenues were equally speculative. The authors reached their conclusions by multiplying the number of planes that had been or were likely to be sold over the period by their own guesstimates as to what the airlines might have paid for them. Then, after making a stab at working out how much it would cost Airbus to repay government launch aid and adjusting the cost of loans to commercial rates, the report triumphantly concluded that 'none of the AI aircraft programs . . . is commercially viable'.

By this, the consultants meant that, in their opinion, the returns were not and, never would be, large enough for the Airbus companies to repay the investment, including government subsidies at market rates of interest. The A300 had, they concluded, 'sustained significant negative cash flows even with the provision of government launch aid. These losses have been compensated for, in part, by additional government support in the form of production subsidies and equity infusions to AI member companies.' Overall, the A300 was reckoned to have lost at 1990 prices an astonishing $15.4 billion; its derivatives, the A300-600 and the A310 fared almost equally badly, losing $12.9 billion; the A320 and A321 were thought to have lost $3.5 billion and only the A330/340, so the consultants believed, were likely to produce a positive return, though not large enough to be commercial.‡[29]

Time has proved the Gellman estimates of Airbus profitability to be wrong. The A300/310 were certainly heavy loss-makers. But the A320, which has gone on to sell almost twice as well as Gellman assumed it would, is a money-spinner, while sales of the various versions of the A330/340 have exceeded the Americans' expectations. Nonetheless, as a weapon in the trade war, the Gellman report served its purpose. It certainly threw a useful shaft of light on the nature and extent of government subsidies – a subject on which everybody concerned has been extremely evasive. The governments have used the fig leaf of commercial confidentiality to deliberately conceal from their electorates the true cost of the European Airbus adventure. When I asked a very senior British civil servant why the public could not be told how much the British government had lent in launch aid on each programme and how much had been repaid, he replied, 'I have to be very careful here. We do know. But we don't tell.'[30]

‡   As the authors themselves say, the exceptionally large losses for the A300 and A310 programmes are misleading. In a footnote they explain that they result 'in part from expressing losses incurred in the 1970s and 1980s at 1990 price levels'.

As tempers rose across the negotiating table, privately Airbus Industrie began looking for a compromise. With the launch of the A330/340 safely under way, Jean Pierson reckoned that the time had come to put out some feelers to Boeing. At the annual Conquistadores del Cielo jamboree in Wyoming in the summer of 1990, Pierson button-holed Boeing's Frank Shrontz and said, 'Look, let me know when you are next coming to Europe. Call me privately by phone. Come to Toulouse. I can assure you that your visit will be personal, low profile, no announcement, no communications. Just a private meeting with me and Alan Boyd.' In September that year Shrontz duly turned up. Pierson offered Shrontz a deal. Airbus was ready to accept a lower level of government subsidy if America would agree to cap the indirect subsidies they received from government contracts. 'We have to do two things,' Pierson told Shrontz. 'Firstly, we have got to stop all this argument and secondly, we have to convince our governments.'[31]

Shrontz was receptive. Although he had been a strong advocate of using the GATT rules as an anti-Airbus weapon, he was coming round to the view that it was more practical to limit and cap European subsidies rather than try to eliminate them altogether. In Washington, too, there was a reluctant recognition that Airbus was something the United States would just have to live with. Laura Tyson, chairman of the Council of Economic Advisers and a senior adviser on economic and industrial matters to the Clinton administration, has observed, 'Airbus had sold too many aircraft, had too many airlines . . . as customers and enjoyed too much political support in Europe for the US to succeed in obtaining all its objectives . . . The issue became not to stop Airbus, but rather how to cope with Airbus.'[32] Even so, it was to take another eighteen months before there was a formal agreement along these lines between the European Commission and the US trade representative. The outline of a deal had been clear for some time: the haggling, as Mogens Peter Carl describes, was over the restrictions that would be imposed on American indirect subsidies:[33]

> There was a hellava rearguard action by the Americans over the provisions dealing with the so-called indirect subsidies. All of a sudden they woke up to the fact that this was something that could impose strictures on their side. The Americans were absolutely obsessed at imposing disciplines of this reimbursable loan arrangement. Firstly, because our governments had been supplying Airbus with 100 per cent of development costs which gave it a heck of an advantage and secondly they were arguing that the conditions under which this money was supposed to be reimbursed was extremely lenient.

In April 1992 the parties finally agreed that on the European side, direct subsidies on new aircraft programmes would be limited to 30 per cent of total development costs, while the Americans would restrict indirect subsidies to no more than 5 per cent of the value of a manufacturer's civilian sales turnover. As well as conditions about the timing of the repayments, it was agreed, in a clause directed primarily at the French, that governments would not put pressure on other governments to buy aircraft.

After so much fuss over so long a time, the result was modest. The American effort to use GATT machinery to destabilize Airbus had plainly failed: it was a case of too little, too late. The Europeans, on the other hand, felt that they had won. 'There were gunning for two things: quantity and quality,' says Mogens Peter Carl. 'What they got – but only up to a point – was quantity but only with respect to reimbursable loans. They didn't get it in respect of other loans.' Carl maintains that the provisions of the agreement regarding repayments are less stringent than they appear at first sight. 'They are merely predictions, not an outright obligation.'[34]

From Ronald Reagan to George Bush, Senr., American administrations had fought to change a system they thought unfair. However, the aircraft companies on whose behalf they were acting were less consistent. The attitudes of Boeing and McDonnell Douglas were determined by two factors: how well Airbus was doing and how big a threat Airbus posed to their own products. In that last regard the 1992 agreement had not come a moment too soon. By the autumn of that year Airbus had began to develop its plans for a superjumbo so big that it would eclipse Boeing's 747. As both companies saw it, this was the beginning of the largest and possibly the last campaign in a war that had already been going on for more than a quarter of a century.

CHAPTER ELEVEN

THINKING BIG

THE FARNBOROUGH AIR SHOW, which takes place once every two years in a small Hampshire town some forty miles from London, is the shop window of the international aerospace business. It is the place where the industry gathers in the late summer or early autumn to display its wares, show off its latest toys, exchange gossip and, occasionally, to do deals in the chalets that line the airfield. But as the rivalry between Airbus and Boeing has grown ever more intense, so Farnborough has acquired a somewhat synthetic atmosphere. For weeks the rival public relations teams lay plans to capture the headlines by releasing carefully prepared announcements of orders from important airlines who may well have tipped the manufacturer the wink months before. The presidents and chief executives of the world's most important airlines are flown in to deliver a few well-chosen words as to why their company has decided to bestow several billion dollars worth of orders on the manufacturer in question. Each day the figures are totted up. And the bigger the numbers, the bigger the headline – or so the theory goes. At the end of the show the manufacturer with the most column inches is declared the winner. As far as real news is concerned, Farnborough is, more often than not, a non-event. But not always.

For Farnborough 1992, Airbus Industrie had decided that it would use the opportunity to showcase its new A340. But that was before it had heard what Phil Condit, who had become Boeing's new president only a month earlier, had to say. After delivering the standard pitch praising the virtues of the Boeing approach – 'The issue is not which manufacturer has the newest airplane . . . The question is have we met customers' needs and added value?' – Condit dropped a small nugget of hard news. 'Some airlines,' he said, 'have expressed an interest in an airplane larger than the 747-400 for entry into service around the end of this decade. Boeing is meeting with interested customers to identify requirements and define possible configurations. These are both 747 derivatives and all-new airplanes, with seating capacities up to 750.' Did this mean that Boeing was thinking of building a Super-Jumbo? the journalists inquired. 'Everything is under consideration,' the new president replied.[1]

After this, Airbus's Jean Pierson had little option but to respond. After an extended plug for the A340 and several sideswipes at American indirect subsidies,

Pierson addressed the question of what he called, in Airbus jargon, the UHCA – the ultra-high capacity aircraft. He said the Airbus plans for a 600-seat plane were well advanced and that the consortium had been talking with ten airlines about putting together a programme that would be launched in a couple of years. 'We are in dialogue with airlines to finalize a project that will be a great success.' In fact, this was not the first time Airbus had mentioned that it was thinking of challenging Boeing's big aircraft monopoly. The previous year Stuart Iddles, Airbus's senior vice president for commercial affairs, had said much the same thing at a *Financial Times* aerospace conference, but it was Pierson's remarks that caused the stir.

Had the air correspondents known about what happened next, the story would have been even bigger. The following day Pierson paid a brief private visit to the Boeing chalet to discuss with John Hayhurst, the Boeing vice-president that Shrontz and Condit had appointed to mastermind the super jumbo, the possibility of the two companies working together on a joint project. The idea did not come from Pierson, nor was he keen on it. The man at Airbus who was pushing it was Jürgen Schrempp who, as managing director of DASA, the German wing of Airbus, was a senior member of the supervisory board and chief representative of the German faction. 'Schrempp wanted to play a role in the aircraft industry in Europe more important than the one he believed he had in Airbus,' says Pierson.[2]

In the world of Airbus politics Schrempp was a new and, as Toulouse saw it, disruptive force. From the beginning Schrempp had his own agenda, and it was one that Pierson, who had grown used to running Airbus Industrie his own way, found hard to accept. Everybody in Toulouse knew all about Pierson's idiosyncrasies and foibles and made allowances for them. 'When Pierson is put in charge of something, he doesn't want to share responsibility,' says Jürgen Thomas, the veteran German engineer and father of the A380. To make the point, Thomas tells a favourite Airbus story: Ziegler appears before God who asks him what merits he had on earth. Ziegler does his best to explain. Then Pierson appears. God asks the same. Pierson replies, 'Why are you asking me these nasty questions? And besides, what are you doing sitting on my swan?'[3]

Schrempp first made his mark as an ambitious young Daimler-Benz executive. He had caught the eye of the chairman Edzard Reuter when working as the head of the truck division in South Africa and the United States. Schrempp's chance came when, after much debate and fierce opposition, Reuter, the son of Ernst Reuter, the former mayor of Berlin, succeeded in his plans for diversification by gaining approval for his take-over of Messerschmitt-Bolkow-Blohm, Germany's main aircraft contractor and the leading company of the Deutsche Airbus grouping. It was a deal that aroused much controversy. The left was concerned that it would give Daimler-Benz a near-monopoly of the German aerospace business, while the Daimler shareholders fretted about taking on MBB's Airbus losses even though MBB as a whole was profitable. It was only after the German government had given undertakings that it would take over the Airbus debts and offer guarantees against foreign exchange losses on sales that these worries abated. Quite apart from the financial and monopoly concerns, the union of two companies such as Daimler and Messerschmitt, who played such an important part in the building of Hitler's war machine, revived unhappy memories of the Nazi era. The news magazine *Der Spiegel* had a cover story with a picture of an airplane festooned with rockets and a caption which read, '*Mercedes-Benz – Waffenschmiede der Nation*' ('Armourer to the Nation').

With the acquisition of MBB, shortly to be renamed DASA, power inside Airbus shifted further towards the Germans and in particular towards Schrempp, the newly appointed head of Daimler's aerospace division. From the beginning Schrempp, who did not disguise his ambition to succeed Ezhard Reuter as chairman of Daimler-Benz, made it clear that he had no taste for Airbus's collegiate style of management.

The first clash with Pierson came at a meeting of the supervisory board when Schrempp vetoed a proposal for what was to be the 150-seater A319 on the grounds that everything under 150 seats was, so he claimed, not Airbus territory. And he announced that DASA would launch its own 100-seater under its own name, with Pratt & Whitney as the engine supplier instead of Airbus's long-time associate, GE. Pierson brushed this idea aside quite easily: he asked Adam Brown, the company's chief strategist, to prepare a paper showing just how uneconomic Schrempp's proposal for a 100-seater was and then presented the result to Schrempp's boss, Reuter, when he came on an official visit to Toulouse. Schrempp responded by buying Fokker against the advice of the man he had displanted as the most senior German on the Airbus board, the long-serving Hartmut Mehdorn.

The next clash came at a meeting of the supervisory board in Seville on 15 December 1992, three months after the meeting with Boeing at Farnborough. The superjumbo was at the top of agenda. According to Pierson, Schrempp told the partners that Airbus was not going to do the big plane because it would involve co-operation with Boeing and DASA had already discussed that with the American company. Schrempp announced that a committee would be formed and invited the other partners to join it. He added that if they were not convinced, he was prepared to go it alone. Faced with this ultimatum, the board reluctantly agreed to go along with the Schrempp plan. But Pierson was so furious that Dick Evans, then chief executive of British Aerospace, had to intervene to calm things down. 'Don't play games,' he told Schrempp. 'Let's have a break. It's very important to have a break in these sort of international meetings.' Pierson was not to be mollified. 'Look, Dick,' he protested. 'This guy is against Airbus. The best thing is for you to be with him. Don't let him alone.'[4]

Less than a month later, Pierson's worst fears seemed to be confirmed when Jeff Cole of the *Wall Street Journal* revealed that Boeing was planning to link up with the German and British members of the consortium to build the superjumbo. The headline, 'Boeing and Two Members of Airbus Plan Jet Venture', was bad enough. But the story was even worse. An agreement between Boeing, Daimler-Benz and British Aerospace to pursue development of a 600-seat airliner was expected in February, it said. And it added, 'The companies' participation in the venture with Boeing would not require them to pull out of the Airbus consortium because they have no agreement with Airbus to produce jets of this size . . .' Cole then indulged in some damaging speculation on the likely effect of this new alliance on Airbus. He wrote, 'The agreement would present a new threat to the cohesiveness of the four-nation Airbus consortium by stealing some of its most powerful players in the potent market segment for ever-larger jets that eventually could carry as many as 800 passengers. At the same time it would probably prevent Airbus from attempting any similar development in the near term.'[5]

The cat was well and truly out of the bag. And it was, more likely than not, Boeing that had untied the string. For Seattle it was a perfect opportunity to sow disorder and dissension in Airbus ranks by picking off one or two members of the consortium and setting those partners at odds with the others. It was a tactic it had already tried with the British. So why not the Germans, especially on a project as big and important as this one? That same day Boeing issued a statement that confirmed the accuracy of the *Wall Street Journal* piece. Mischievously, the Americans omitted any mention of Aerospatiale or Airbus Industrie.

Pierson attempted to repair the damage by putting out a statement that insisted Aerospatiale and CASA were also taking part in the discussions. A noisy row then ensued. Boeing said it had not mentioned Airbus Industrie because it was only a marketing organization; Airbus retorted that it was thinking of asking the Japanese to help build the giant plane. But eventually things quietened down: a joint committee consisting of Boeing people and Airbus people, headed by Jürgen Thomas, was set up, and work began to evaluate every aspect of what was called, in the low-key language of the industry, the Very Large Commercial Transport – VLCT for short.

Just as they had seventeen years previously when they met to discuss the 'Brigitte Bardot' plane, the BB10, the top brass of Boeing and Airbus were talking to each other across a table. But this time, so Thomas says, they were talking not as contractor and sub-contractor, but as equals with a view to a genuine 50:50 partnership. According to Thomas, 'Earlier merger and cooperation talks with Boeing had been profoundly influenced by the fact it was not a dialogue of equals. In the '70s and even later, Boeing was convinced that Airbus planes would suffer the fate of all other European planes that had gone before and that Airbus would die. We were regarded as dwarfs. But in the VLCT project it was a study of equals.'[6]

Even without the presence of so many lawyers, the atmosphere would have been rather awkward and formal. The Boeing people were strictly instructed before each meeting as to what to say and what not to say, what to reveal and what not to reveal. The Airbus people had a bit more freedom, but not much.

Both sides were very careful about what they said to each other. 'We were very conscious of anti-trust legislation,' says Thomas. 'We had our lawyers at all our meetings and the other side had theirs. Each company had its own law firm. Each document that was issued was checked by the lawyers and we were not allowed to exchange any commercial information. There were a lot of things off-limits.' Carefully, and methodically, the two teams examined, step-by-step, the feasibility of the project from a technical and a commercial point of view. 'The first thing we looked at was whether there was any "show-stopper" to this affair,' says Thomas. 'It's very easy to look at this sort of thing for months and suddenly you discover something that is a complete killer: the plane is not certifiable or that it is impossible to get that number of people out of the plane in nine minutes in the case of an emergency.'

The teams met regularly at roughly three-month intervals. And over the next two years they had ample opportunity to exchange information and examine their cultural differences. Thomas remarks:

> We were surprised about the one-dimensional thinking of the Boeing people. If you had a structural man, he was thinking structures; if you had an aerodynamics man, he was thinking aerodynamics and if you had a finance guy, he was thinking finance. Whereas the Europeans are much broader-thinking. When I looked at certain results and I talked to my counterpart and I said, 'I know that if in three months we marry all these results, the technical results, the financial results, and the marketing results, the end result will be very bad for you.' My counterpart said, 'How do you know this? We haven't even done the exercise.' If the aircraft is bigger, you produce less units. And because of its other characteristics, I can tell that the business case will be bad. They are only one-dimensional thinkers until you make the final cooking. But then you put everything into the pot and everyone is surprised that the soup is as good as expected. But with a little bit of experience, you can already guess the taste of the soup.

That the two companies should pool their resources to build the world's largest and most costly civil aeroplane was not such a foolish idea.* From past experience Boeing knew that if it went down that route on its own it would be 'betting the company', just as it had done nearly a quarter of a century earlier with the 747. Furthermore, the capacity of such a plane, which theoretically could carry up to 1000 passengers, was so great that there might be a market for only one, just as there had been for the 747. If that were indeed the case, it would make a great deal of sense, so Shrontz and Schrempp reasoned, to share the risks and expenses.

In 1993 the volatile aircraft market was in the middle of the worst cyclical downturn for ten years, and although Airbus was to be much harder hit than Boeing,

---

*   It would not be the biggest. That prize belongs to Howard Hughes' flying boat, *The Spruce Goose*, which flew only briefly and then only as a prototype. The plane never went into production.

Seattle was nervous. Boeing was just launching its 777 and the ever-cautious Frank Shrontz, so Thomas says, was extremely reluctant to commit the huge sums that would be needed for the superjumbo. While the 747 had cost a total of $2 billion, the building of the new giant could easily take $2 billion dollars a year out of the company's cash flow for up to five or six years. Even making allowance for the fall in the purchasing power of the dollar over twenty years, this was still a very large amount of money.

Many in the industry, like Airbus's Hartmut Mehdorn, thought that the project was so huge as to be beyond the resources of any single company. 'With the super jumbo, we had to over-jump the 747,' he says. 'This aircraft is so expensive that maybe you only need one of its kind in the world. I said there will be no competition in this market. And it will be so expensive that maybe we will make it jointly with the Americans, the Europeans, the Asians, the South Americans. And perhaps we even employ World Bank money. Before you go into something like that, you have to explore every option. And putting all this money into the big plane, you do not have too much money left for the rest of the family.'[7]

There is, of course, another more cynical interpretation of Boeing's willingness to sit down with its arch-rival to discuss the building of a plane which, if it materialized, would knock Boeing's 747 off its perch at the top of the aeronautical food chain. In the history of Boeing no aircraft has been more successful and more profitable than the 747: it is generally thought in the industry that Boeing makes a $30 million profit on a list price of around $150 million. The jumbo not only gave Boeing a monopoly on the long-haul, mass-transit sector of the market throughout the 1970s and the 1980s, but the profits it earned enabled Boeing to cross-subsidise and to undercut the price of Airbus's smaller planes. As Bernard Ziegler said, 'Boeing enjoy a monopoly because it has fully amortised its investment, and it can dramatically cut the price of the aircraft if it needs to, so it is very difficult to compete with them head-to-head.'[8] This is a coded reference to the fact that the competition from the stretched versions of the 737 was so fierce that for years Airbus was obliged to sell its A320s at below cost.

Jean Pierson argued that the longer the talks went on, the longer Boeing would continue to enjoy the fruits of its 747 monopoly and the more difficult it would be for Airbus to mount an effective challenge. 'I never discussed the big aircraft with Boeing,' Pierson told me. 'I was thinking if I was in Boeing's position, what would I do? I thought the best thing would be for them to say, "Fuck these Airbus people. We're not going to let them make another 747: that would kill our monopoly. Let's take them and talk and talk and talk. Then one day . . ." And that's what I tried to explain to Schrempp. Jürgen's a good guy but being a German he is unable to do these double games.'[9]

As the months went by, it became increasingly clear that Jean Pierson's scepticism was justified: the talks were getting nowhere. There was disagreement on such technical matters as the design of the cockpit. Airbus wanted the full fly-by-wire system with sidestick controllers, while Boeing insisted on the central control stick. 'It was an image question,' says Thomas. 'Boeing could not bring themselves to accept Airbus technology, even though there were sidesticks on the space shuttle and the design for the American supersonic plane, the SST.'[10] Each side kept its figures to itself; nothing was disclosed. Even so, Boeing was unhappy with the business case. But ultimately the talks collapsed because of the fundamental fault line that had doomed all previous attempts at cooperation. The Europeans failed to see how they could work with Boeing on one programme and not on the others. The scenario was just not credible. It required, as Jürgen Thomas puts it, 'total, absolute peace on one programme and terrible war on all the others. It's a case of *Krieg und Frieden*. Every day you have to make peace, and every day you have to make war.'

The end came in the elegant surroundings of Munich's Vier Jahreszeiten (Four Seasons) hotel where, in April 1995, the two teams held an elaborate farewell dinner to mark the break-up. The final rites were performed at a meeting in Long Island, New York a few weeks later at which it was agreed that they should stop talking and put the studies on ice.

*

Early in 1994, while the talks were still under way, Jean Pierson had signalled that a new and even more aggressive phase in the long battle between Boeing and Airbus was about to begin. He summoned his senior staff to tell them that the old GIE system had, as he put it, 'reached the end of its genetic life' and that he was setting a new target for Airbus. From now on, he declared, the aim was no longer to capture 30 per cent of the world market. 'That strategy has now been largely achieved,' he declared. From now on the objective was to gain nothing less than a 50 per cent market share and in so doing to push Boeing into second place. He issued everybody with a lapel badge with the slogan 'Beat Boeing'. As Airbus had sold just thirty-five aircraft in the previous year against Boeing's 201, this target looked, on the face of it, wildly unrealistic. At that stage, no one knew for sure when the market would turn and how the chips would fall.

When Pierson issued his call to arms, it looked as if the odds were heavily stacked against Airbus. The industry was still in the throes of a four-year recession started in 1991. But the real killer, as far as Airbus was concerned, was not the weakness of the market but the weakness of the dollar against the deutschmark and other European currencies. As Airbus's bills for its raw materials and labour costs were in francs, pounds, marks and pesetas while its income was in dollars, this was a huge disadvantage when set against the Americans who enjoyed a boost to sales from the weak dollar with no corresponding penalty in costs.

'The Big Push made a lot of partners in the GIE very nervous,' says John Leahy, the American-born head of sales. 'They thought that a target of 50 per cent by the end of 2002 was OK. They thought it was sufficiently far out that nobody would have to explain why we hadn't got there.' But if the partners were cautious, the salesmen were bold. 'We were trying to reach the partners and persuade them to go for it and this time it would be different,' says Leahy, whose argument was that if Airbus did not aim higher, the company could end up like McDonnell Douglas. 'The disadvantage was that if we stayed at the 30 per cent level, we would not be able to package the mega-deals nor could we make the production lines more efficient. The best we could do would be to turn out single-aisle planes at 10-a-month, compared with Boeing's 30-a-month.'[11]

By background and inclination, Pierson was a factory manager. So it is not surprising that the main focus of his initiative was on cutting costs and improving efficiency. It was not just a question of making better, more sophisticated airplanes. For quarter of a century Airbus had used the hi-tech card when playing catch-up with Boeing. But if, as it now intended, it was going to compete head-to-head across the entire spectrum of the market on an equal basis with the Americans, it was plain that the prizes would go to those who could produce those planes more quickly and more cheaply than the competition. As Adam Brown said, 'It is clear that we have reached a new objective and the objectives that have driven us will no longer serve. They have to be replaced . . . The implications of things like cost and efficiency are fundamental, right across the board.'[12]

This was not the first time the question of Airbus efficiency had been raised. In the late 1980s a team from BAe led by Bob McKinlay had launched an investigation into Airbus productivity. The first concern was the efficiency of BAe itself, which was going through a torrid time: it was losing money heavily on its civil aircraft division, and under the dismal leadership of Professor Roland Smith it had compounded its problems by taking over what remained of Britain's only major car manufacturer, British Leyland. But the scope of the BAe study was soon widened to include the other Airbus partners. The conclusions were not encouraging. Bob McKinlay explains, 'We were operating in a market in which the prices were constrained by the Americans; the currency was in dollars; and when you put it all together you did not end up with a plus sign. The Europeans in those days were too expensive. It was not just the cost of labour. It was the cost of production and manufacture. Too many man-hours. Too many overheads. We were just not attuned to the business requirements which demand that production costs have to be less than the income you receive.'

As BAe was on good terms with Boeing, the British managed to obtain a great deal of information from Seattle about its production methods and techniques that allowed the team to make direct comparisons between the way Boeing and Airbus made their planes. They were not flattering. 'The conclusion was that Boeing was turning out aircraft more quickly and more cheaply than we were,' says McKinlay. 'We were simply taking too long. The aircraft was built in Toulouse, flown to Hamburg to be furnished, and then flown back to Toulouse for delivery. It probably only added a couple of weeks to the total time, but it made us that bit less flexible. So we looked at that and quite a few other things and deliberately stirred up a rumpus by saying that unless we were more efficient than we are today, we will never be successful.'†[13]

One spur for greater efficiency had been the decision in the late 1980s to split the production of the Airbus family more equally between Toulouse and Hamburg. But it was not until the 1990s that the Airbus partners began to pour money into new equipment for the factories on a large scale. The brand new plant that Aerospatiale opened in Toulouse in 1990 to assemble the A330 and the A340 was the largest in Europe and there was a similarly ambitious expansion programme in Germany. 'It was in the depression of the '90s when we were making 100 aircraft against our normal 300 that the investments were made,' comments Jürgen Thomas. 'It was very expensive what with all the overheads and all the depreciation on the machinery. But if you put more workload in the factory, the result was greater economies of scale.'[14] Airbus people claim that by the middle of the decade the productivity and profitability of Airbus had been transformed.

As work started on the huge hanger at Finkenwerder, in which all the single-aisle planes with the exception of the A320 are made, billions of deutschmarks were invested in two state-of-the-art assembly lines, which can turn out over twelve planes a month. One hundred kilometres away at Nordenham, where the rivers Elbe and Weser flow into the sea, there was an equally large investment in the modernization of the plant that makes the fuselage shells for the entire Airbus range. Machine tools were so automated that today almost nothing is done by hand. The work programme is determined in advance and the parts needed to complete it are selected from the adjoining store and delivered to the work station automatically. Nearly every process, from cutting the metal panels to shaping to machining, is now numerically controlled by banks of computers. The settings for the riveting machines which used to be manually set are now altered automatically. And for the new A318, which made its first flight in January 2002, the riveting machines have been replaced by a new laser-welding technique that does the same job more accurately and forty times faster. The factory doesn't look or feel like an engineering plant. There is little noise, no waste, and what few people there are on the factory floor are working mainly as machine minders and supervisors rather than as operatives. The atmosphere is purposeful yet surprisingly relaxed.

---

†   The investigations into Boeing's efficiency were made in the early 1980s, years before Seattle's production crisis of 1997/98 described in the following chapter. When the study was made, Airbus had not yet been modernized.

Just as significant as the modernization plan was Airbus's fight against the falling dollar, whose collapse threatened to undermine the consortium's finances. As the dollar fell 20 per cent to a low point of DM1.37, the management in Hamburg launched 'Operation Dolores' – an acronym that stood for 'Dollar Low Rescue'. Others called it 'Operation Dolor' – the Spanish for 'pain'. Ten years later managers still wince at the memory. 'We were really pressed to find solutions,' says Manfred Porath, the head of final assembly at Finkenwerder. 'It was clear we had to do the same job with less people. There was no option.'[15] The labour force was cut by a third and lead time between order and delivery was reduced by half from eighteen months to nine. There were similar cutbacks at Nordenham, where the labour force fell from 2,400 to 1,700 and management negotiated deals with the unions which resulted in an extra 3,500 working hours per employee over three years. An elaborate system was worked out whereby if there was short-time working, employees could stay at home for a thirty-five-hour working week without loss of pay, but if the workload then increased, they would have to do an extra 100 hours with no overtime. 'It was a very tough period,' Wolfgang Sommer, the plant manager says. 'We spent a great deal of time in meetings with the unions and the workforce was very demotivated.'[16]

*

The breakdown of the superjumbo talks in the spring of 1995 had signalled the parting of the ways, but the superjumbo was far from dead. However doubtful Boeing might have been about the business case for a 600-seater, Airbus Industrie was determined to press on. 'We were convinced of the necessity of such a programme,' says Jürgen Thomas. 'If we can't do it with Boeing, we have to do it ourselves.' The driving force was an almost messianic belief in the idea of the Airbus family that had been an article of faith in Toulouse since the early days of Franz-Josef Strauss. 'I remember when Boeing was here in '76,' recalls Thomas. 'I had only been here for a short time but I was put in charge of the task force by Roger Béteille. I was thirty-nine. I was asked to present to Boeing our future family. They were very polite; they didn't say anything but I saw some laughing. We had a single product. We had fifty aircraft sold. And I was talking about a family. These guys asked me to talk about a long-range aircraft – a big, wide-bodied twin. Crazy, crazy, I thought. But I thought, I'm paid for this, so let me do it. I did it. But Boeing didn't believe me.'[17]

Twenty years later the vision that Thomas had initially doubted was almost complete: the only item lacking was an Airbus plane that would not only match but supersede the 747. Such a plane, Airbus hoped, would not only complete its family, but would kill off, or at least badly wound, Boeing's long-serving cash cow. By the early 1990s the long-distance A340, which could fly further but carried fewer passengers than the 747, had already begun, in a modest way, to inflict some damage on the so-called 'long/thin' routes. By bringing in a superjumbo carrying up to 600 passengers, the planners in Toulouse hoped to trap Boeing in a classic pincer-movement in much the same way as the German Sixth Army had been surrounded by the Russian forces at Stalingrad in 1942. 'We have already attacked them from below with the A340,' said Bernard Ziegler. 'Now the idea is to come over the shoulder with a high capacity plane.'[18] It was an elegant concept. But before it could be executed, there were a host of practical problems to overcome.

On paper, the case for a new plane was compelling. The 747 was near the end of its natural life: it was based on a design conceived in the 1950s, had been developed in the 1960s and had been in commercial service for over a quarter of century. Some day, sooner rather than later, the 747 would have to be replaced. The more the Airbus analysts studied future trends in the market, the more convinced they became for the need for the Very Large Commercial Transport. By this they meant a plane that could carry anything ranging from 555 to 655 passengers over distances between 7,800 to 8,750 nautical miles. Looking at how the market might grow over the next twenty years or so, the Airbus analysts concluded that by the end of second decade of the twenty-first century, there would be a need for around 1,235 such aircraft. This calculation was based on an industry-wide consensus that the growth in air traffic would continue to grow at five per cent per annum for the foreseeable future. Even Boeing agreed with this growth estimate. Where the American company differed sharply was in the number of VLCTs that would be required.

When I called on Boeing at the height of the controversy in March 2000, Randy Baseler, the company's senior market analyst, told me, 'We think that no more than eighty planes seating over 500 people or more will be sold over the next ten years, and that by 2018 the number will still be no more than 360.'[19] What lay behind Boeing's figures was the belief that there has been a profound change in the pattern of airline travel since President Jimmy Carter's decision to de-regulate the airline business in 1978. 'When the government comes out, airlines compete and airplane sizes come down,' Baseler contended. Where once passengers flew from airport hub to airport hub and then took a connecting or feeder flight to their local destination, Boeing argued that now passengers were preferring to fly directly to their final destination. In other words, the market was 'fragmenting', as the marketing men put it. And what this meant was that there was greater demand for smaller medium to long-distance planes like the Boeing 777 or the Airbus 330/340 and less for the giant people-carriers like the 747 or, by extension, the Airbus superjumbo or the 747 super-stretch. Boeing believed that the only market for ultra-large planes, bigger than the 747, were on a handful of the really heavy routes like London–Singapore. To support its argument, Boeing says that back in 1987, the year before deregulation, the sole link between Chicago and Europe was a single 747 daily flight to London; now there are twenty-one daily flights out of Chicago to destinations all over Europe. Airbus replied that this comparison was misleading, as Boeing had omitted to include non-American airlines.

The Airbus vision of the future was quite different. To those who believe that planes are already too large and airports too full, the Airbus planners offer no comfort at all. They paint a picture of a future in which the skies will dominated by planes as long as a football pitch and as high as a three-storey house. There is, however, a physical limit on how big aircraft can grow. Most experts think that the laws of physics, which state that if an object's volume is cubed, its surface area is only squared, means that a 1000-seater plane is probably beyond the limit of what is practically possible. To carry 1000 people for any distance would need enormous wings to generate the lift, as well as a big increase in take-off and landing speed. A plane of this size would be too heavy and too fuel-hungry to be economic. Even so, the carrying capacity of a superjumbo could soon be close to that of a long-distance train.

The most striking aspect of this research was not so much the estimates of the likely size of the market, but the analysts' conclusions as to its shape. The assumption was that only a comparatively small handful of airlines would buy the VLCT and of those that did, the great majority would depend on the Asia-Pacific region for their business. The forecasters concluded that of the fifty-eight airlines operating the VLCTs by 2019, almost half of the total would be used in the Asia-Pacific, compared with a little over a third in Europe and North America. In twenty years' time, they said, more than half the world's fleet of superjumbos would be used exclusively on flights from the world's top ten airports, of which eight would be serving Asia-Pacific. The conclusion was that although the demand for very large passenger aircraft was likely to be no more than 10 per cent of the total, it was, at the same time, going to be an immensely valuable business: worth nearly $320 billion, so Airbus reckoned. This calculation assumes an off-the-shelf ticket price of $260 million per plane, which seems on the high side, but Airbus thought it was well worth going for, even if it had to share this pot with Boeing.

The prize might be rich, but to build a plane as large and as costly as the superjumbo was an operation fraught with risk. Within Airbus itself, there were many experienced, professional engineers who thought what was now being called the A3XX was as rash a venture as that of Icarus, the son of Daedalus, who fell into the sea after the wax of his wings melted when he ignored his father's warnings and flew too close to the sun. As Hartmut Mehdorn put it to me, 'I think everybody knows that [it] is extremely high risk from every point of view: technically, airframewise, enginewise, moneywise, certificationwise. It is outside the normal Airbus family. With the traditional step-by-step Airbus approach you have a communality of anything between 60 to 80 per cent between one plane and the next. But with the superjumbo you have a communality close to zero. Airbus has to be very careful with what's coming up.'[20]

The British agreed. British Aerospace saw the new plane, so insiders say, as a significant burden and was sceptical, if not openly hostile. If the French were the

torch-bearers of the sacred flame, the British were the unbelievers. At that time
BAe's commercial director rarely visited Toulouse, and although the wing operation
at Broughton was admired in France, it was treated as a self-contained unit and
very much left to its own devices. Following the collapse of the Boeing talks, Airbus
Industrie had pressed on to appoint Jürgen Thomas in the spring of 1996 as head of
what it called the Large Aircraft Division. Before long, Thomas had more than 200
people working for him. But in Filton, just outside Bristol, where most of BAe's
senior management worked, the A3XX remained very much on the back burner. As
it was under the wing of the vague-sounding future programmes office rather than
the more purposeful future projects department, joining the A3XX was not thought
to be a wise career move. When Chris Voysey moved from the military to the civil
side of the business in 1997 to take charge of building the wing, he felt very alone. 'I
was just one person in a small office, waving through the glass panel to the open plan
space beyond,' he says. 'I tried to recruit a number of people but they refused as they
saw it as a personal risk.'[21] But to many at BAe, the A3XX was a challenge they preferred not to accept.

From an engineering point of view there were formidable obstacles almost
everywhere one looked. For example, the super jumbo, with a wingspan of over 260
feet, would need a much larger wing than anyone had ever built before; it would be
bigger and heavier than the largest of the 747s; the landing gear would need up to
twenty wheels if airport runways were not to be crushed under a plane with a landing weight of 383 tonnes; and the sheer capacity of the superjumbo would mean that
devising means of rapid escape for passengers in an emergency would require great
technical skill and ingenuity. For upper deck passengers the drop to the ground
would be at least 27 feet. On top of all that was the question of noise. If the four-
engined superjumbo was noisier than big twins like the A330 or Boeing's 777, then,
quite simply, it would be banned from most of the world's major airports.

But the greatest challenge of all was to build a plane that would carry 35 per cent
more people and more cargo than the biggest 747, yet have significantly lower operating costs than the Boeing plane. If Airbus could not deliver the passenger seat mile
figures the airlines were looking for, Airbus knew that its A3XX would be a no-
hoper, however rosy the long-term market projections might be. By the autumn of
1996 Jürgen Thomas and his team had already set the target for the wing builders
and the engine makers to aim at. They were told, 'Don't come back until you have cut
cash operating costs by 17 per cent.'

'The key element of the plane is the economics,' says Michel Jarry, whose job it
was to sell the idea to the airlines. 'The economic superiority of this airplane is
absolutely gigantic. Previously, when we had battles between the A320 and 737 or the
A340 and 777, the airlines were fighting with us over a two per cent difference in operating cost. But here the figure was 15 to 17 per cent.'[22] As Jarry sat down with the
airlines, this was the message he had to hammer home. 'The key element was to have

the airlines recognize this. If they believed, they would buy. And if they didn't, they wouldn't. The Airbus argument was that there was close to 50 per cent more space in the cabin of the A3XX than there was in that of the 747. The cost to the airline of putting all this space into the air was, because of the extra size and weight of the A3XX, between 12 to 15 per cent *more* than the 747. But because the carrying capacity of the A3XX was so much greater, the cost *per passenger seat mile* was significantly *less*.

In the run-up to the launch the Airbus marketers generated enormous publicity by releasing drawings of the plane which portrayed it as a high-flying pleasure palace. So vast was the plane that there would be, so the chief drummer, John Leahy suggested, enough space for casinos, saunas, gyms and even shops. With sleeping berths, lounges and cocktail bars, the first class section would be more like a cruise ship than a modern jetliner. This impression was reinforced by the mock-up Airbus built at Toulouse where only the first class was furnished and the remainder of the passenger section was left as an intriguingly empty space. Those with long memories recalled that Boeing had done exactly the same thirty years before when drumming up interest for the 747. In fact, when Jarry and his team presented the A3XX to the airlines, all options were deliberately left open. Jarry says that some airlines would pack in the extra people on the grounds that they are getting 50 per cent more space at a cost of an extra 15 per cent. But others might reason that they could use the extra space to offer extra services for passengers like separate lavatories for men and women. 'You have it in restaurants. Why not planes?' he asks. When it comes to casinos and the like, Jarry is more circumspect: 'When you are advertising, you need to exaggerate.'

In designing a modern airliner, there are an almost infinite number of variables that can affect the final result. But the two most critical factors in determining performance are aerodynamic lift and weight. 'The trick is to find the right balance between weight and aerodynamic efficiency,' says Chris Voysey, whose team designed the wing for what was to become the A380. 'The Boeing wings are lighter than ours but less aerodynamically efficient. While in our case the opposite is true.' The object, Voysey explains, was to achieve BAe's level of aerodynamic efficiency at Boeing's weight. In search of this golden mean, BAe tested between 200 and 300 wing configurations. The search was to last two years and there were times when the BAe team was close to despair.

While the design of the wing was a major problem, there has also the hugely important question of the power plant. Airbus knew that if the A3XX was to be credible, it had to offer the airlines a choice of engine. There were only two manufacturers in the world capable of doing the job: America's Engine Alliance, an *ad hoc* marriage between Pratt & Whitney and GE formed especially to build a brand-new engine for the superjumbo, and Britain's Rolls-Royce.

The British company's breach with Airbus some thirty years before had cost it dearly: of the 4,724 engines supplied for Airbus planes between 1969 and 1999, only fifty had been made by Rolls-Royce. As Sir Ralph Robins, the long-serving chairman who stepped down in March 2002 after forty-seven years with the company, told Bill Gunston, 'I regret our misjudgement of the importance of Airbus Industrie. Of course ours was a different company, with different leadership, but we had the whole Airbus programme in our pocket and we did nothing with it – not that we were in a position to do so, as it transpired.'[23]

When Rolls-Royce rejoined the private sector in 1987, there were Rolls-Royce engines on only five different types of aircraft, all American. Sir Ralph decided that this must change: from now on, he said, Rolls should try to have one of its engines on every new aircraft. Gradually, step-by-step, Rolls began to rebuild its relationship with Airbus. But it was not until 1996 that Rolls-Royce erased its past errors by becoming the sole engine supplier for Airbus's ultra long-range A340-500/600. The engine in question was the Trent 500 that Rolls had been developing for the 747-500/600. But with the cancellation of the Boeing plane, the Airbus order became all the more important. Not only was it a big project in itself, but its derivative, the Trent 900, was to be one of the two engines Airbus was to offer on its superjumbo. The rival was the Engine Alliance's GP7000. Designed to produce up 80,000 lbs of thrust, the Trent 900 is a monster, 9ft 6in. (2.89m) across. The specification for the A380 was 68,000 lbs but the engine was made more powerful than needed to cope with the demands of the heavier freighter and later upgrades. In October 1996 Airbus signed a memorandum of understanding with Rolls for the new engine. Five years later, in the autumn of 2001, Brussels approved a British government loan to Rolls-Royce of £250 million to help with the development of the engine, and Rolls itself brought in four of its main suppliers, including Honeywell and Goodrich, to share the risk of a project whose cost is probably close to $1 billion. Just how much the engine makers charge for their products is a closely-guarded secret. But when *Flight* magazine reported that Singapore Airlines had received a 93 per cent discount on the list price of the 100 engines for the ten superjumbos it ordered in the autumn of 2000, Rolls-Royce did not deny it. The money is made, not on the sale of the engines, but on the contract for spares and maintenance that can last for up to twenty years. Engine building, like airframe manufacture, is no business for wimps: it requires a strong cash flow, much patience and steady nerves.

*

To ward off the growing threat to its 747 monopoly, Boeing planners had for some time been examining ways of extracting the last ounce of value from the 747. The company had already produced the Boeing 747-400, which carried over 400 passengers almost twice as far as the original 747. But now Boeing was looking for ways to improve it still further. In the run-up to the 1996 Farnborough Air Show, the industry was awash with rumour that Boeing was about to launch two longer-range versions of the 747 – the 747-500 and the 747-600, the larger of which would be able to carry 550 passengers and thus come within touching distance of the A3XX which, after all, existed only on paper. It was said that Boeing had signed up Singapore, Malaysia and United as the launch airlines, that there were thirty orders and that everything was set to go. To Airbus's huge relief, nothing happened. 'We went to Farnborough with a very young team and we said "we've only just started but maybe the game's already over",' says Michel Jarry, who had just taken over the job of selling the idea of the big plane to the airlines. 'When we learned that there was not going to be an announcement, we were very relieved and said, "well, at least we're not dead – not yet".'

Recapturing the mood at that time Jarry explains:

> If Boeing had gone ahead, it would not necessarily have been the end of the story. We would have had to concede that Boeing had captured the early part of the market and we would have postponed our plans. But there would have been heated debate inside the company because not everybody was convinced that the A3XX (the Airbus code name for the plane) was a good idea. Sometimes there was more support from the market outside than inside. We were all volunteers. We had left other jobs – which were good jobs, you know. Many of our colleagues said, 'You are crazy. It's a joke.' I remember the days when very few airlines were buying 747s and colleagues were saying, 'Look, no one's buying 747s – so there is no market.' I think that was a good thing because it showed that the 747 was at the end of its life, but we constantly had to argue, to discuss and to explain internally.

The first indication that the A3XX might be a winner had come three months earlier when Jarry and his team invited twelve carefully chosen airlines, including several non-Airbus customers like British Airways and Qantas, to come to Carcassone for a major presentation about the A3XX. 'The purpose of the meeting was just to say to the world that we have a plan,' says Jarry. 'We got recognition. There were plenty of airlines that were really happy to see us. They did not like the monopoly situation. So they encouraged us very, very strongly to go ahead.' Among the airlines at Carcassonne were several who had been mentioned as potential 747-600 customers. The Airbus marketeers nervously enquired if they were interested in the A3XX as they seemed so close to buying the 747-600, but were told not to worry as there were some disadvantages to the Boeing plane.

At the second meeting at Carcassonne six months later, the mood was still positive. But this time, the airlines had a shopping list. Some of the items caused a sharp intake of breath among the engineers at Toulouse. Among the things the airlines wanted were: a step up in size, bigger seats, more aisles, an extra 1,000 miles of range, better fuel economy, and a machine that was altogether greener with fewer knocks and less noise. The engineers tried to talk the airlines out of these demands, saying that their specification was unrealistic. But what the airlines were saying gave the A3XX team pause for thought. The conclusion was that, at 540 tonnes, the plane was too heavy and consequently the range was too short: the plane would be able to fly non-stop from Asia to Europe, but crossing the Pacific from Sydney to the US was still out of reach. More work was needed.

Some time before the December meeting at Carcassonne, one of the airlines called Jarry to warn him that Boeing had scheduled a briefing in Seattle on what it called the 747X for the very same day, and forecast that most people would go because there was a new generation 737 roll-out. Should Airbus put its A3XX briefing forward or push it back? Most of Jarry's colleagues advised him to postpone. But Jarry disagreed. His plan was to get in first and prime the airlines with questions to Boeing that Airbus wanted answered. How did the new plane fit into the Boeing family? How many classes would there be in the cabin? What was the fuel burn? And so on and so forth. The only drawback was that as the airline people would have come straight from the A3XX briefing, they would be carrying a great deal of sensitive documentation about Airbus's own plans. So Jarry hatched a cunning plan. The offering of small gifts is very much part of the industry's culture. Visitors to Toulouse or Seattle are usually offered lapel pins, neckties with aeronautical motifs, notepads, or the company history as mementoes. On this occasion, Jarry went one better. He asked his designers to come up with two wine glasses: one for Bordeaux and one for champagne which would be presented in a wooden box. It was a fine gift and extremely fragile. Knowing that most people on the trip would be stopping over in London on the way back from Seattle, Jarry innocently suggested to his guests that, as they would doubtless like to hand-carry the precious wine glasses, it might be convenient if Airbus sent the bulky documentation direct to London by courier. It was an offer that most gratefully accepted.

As Boeing and Airbus salesmen were engaging in these little games, a much bigger game was going on. On Friday 6 December, Boeing's Phil Condit called Harry Stonecipher, his opposite number at the McDonnell Douglas headquarters in St Louis, Missouri, to say that the Boeing board would be meeting on Monday and that 'we're going to have a serious discussion about the possibility of doing something with McDonnell Douglas'. Stonecipher replied that his board was also meeting that day to discuss possible deals. It was agreed that Stonecipher would fly to Seattle to meet Condit the following day.[24]

The two men were very different. The son of a Tennessee coal miner, Stonecipher left school at sixteen and married at eighteen. After graduating from Tennessee Technological University with a degree in physics in 1956, Stonecipher worked for a short period for General Motors as a senior lab technician before joining General Electric's jet engine division where over the next twenty-six years he worked his way up the ranks to become general manager and, ultimately, head of GE's commercial and military transport operations. In 1987 Stonecipher moved to Sundstrand, a troubled defence company, where within a very short time he became president and chief operating officer. It was Stonecipher's success in turning Sundstrand round that caught the eye of John McDonnell, the chairman of McDonnell Douglas. In 1994 Stonecipher joined McDonnell Douglas as chief executive officer, the first man to lead the company whose name was not McDonnell or Douglas.

The St Louis-based company was badly in need of fresh ideas and new orders. It had left its glory days far behind. On the civil side of the business, it was leaking market share to Boeing and Airbus, and on the military front the company which had made billions on its F4 and F15 fighters had suffered the indignity of losing out to Boeing and Lockheed Martin in the race to be finalists for the Defence Department contract to build what was to be the spearhead of the US Air Force's offensive capability in the twenty-first century, the Joint Strike Fighter.

Stonecipher is the epitome of the 'give 'em hell' school of management. He admired President Harry Truman for his decision to sanction the use of nuclear weapons and during his brief time at McDonnell Douglas he succeeded in nearly quadrupling the share price, which rose from $18.48 just before his arrival to $70 on the eve of the merger.

Phil Condit of Boeing is in character and outlook almost the complete opposite of Stonecipher. Where the McDonnell Douglas man was aggressive and overbearing, the man who led Boeing was reflective and outgoing. He, too, had a substantial record of success behind him. A graduate with degrees in mechanical and aeronautical engineering from the University of California and Princeton, he had made his name in Boeing as the man who launched the 777. Gordon Bethune, the COE of Continental Airlines, who worked with Condit in the late 1980s, says of him, 'He glows in the dark, he's got so much brain.'[25] But for all that, his management style is gentle, if not, by the standards of American big business, downright eccentric. According to *Fortune* magazine, in the 1990s he launched management development programmes that included listening to the piano, watching improvisational dance, and having an invited poet read passages aloud from *Beowolf*. *Fortune's* Jerry Useem comments, 'Invited to Condit's house for the evening [ever the engineer, Condit had designed a miniature train that chugged through four rooms and could deliver drinks to the guests], the managers were each to write down an unpleasant memory about Boeing. Then they consigned it to the flames of Condit's fireplace.'[26]

When Stonecipher took Condit's phone call that Friday afternoon in December, he had known for some months that there was no longer any future for McDonnell Douglas in the civil aviation business. The previous October he had gone to the Long Beach plant to discuss the future of McDonnell Douglas's own entry into the great superjumbo race – a four-engined, twin-decked, 600-passenger plane called the MD-12. There had been some talk of the Taiwanese taking a stake in 'the Asian Airbus' and there were even discussions with British Aerospace about building the wing, but the Asians eventually backed off and by the autumn of 1996 the MD-12 was clearly a dead duck. At Long Beach the Douglas president, Michael Sears, told

Stonecipher, 'I would love to do this airplane. Our people would love to do this airplane. But fundamentally it is probably not the best thing for the shareholders of this company.'[27] There was only one possible conclusion: after more than seventy years in the business, the company that Donald Douglas had founded should pull out of civil aviation. And although Stonecipher considered other deals, the one he favoured was a merger with Boeing.

It was in this frame of mind that he arrived in Seattle on Tuesday 10 December. The two men met at Boeing's private suite at the Four Seasons hotel in downtown Seattle.[28] It was Condit who opened with a question:

'Okay, where are you?'

'I have authority from my board to buy TI or bid on Hughes or do this deal. And I want to do this deal,' Stonecipher replied.‡

'I have authority from my board to try and do this deal,' Condit answered.

Within an hour there was an outline agreement. The price that Boeing would pay for McDonnell Douglas would be $13.3 billion in Boeing stock; Condit would be chairman and chief executive officer, and Stonecipher would be his number two as president and chief operating officer. There were many who thought that these were generous terms and that for someone on the losing side, Stonecipher had come out of the deal particularly well.

For Airbus the McDonnell Douglas deal transformed the landscape. In the space of no more than fifteen years, two out of its three American competitors had disappeared. There was now a duopoly. Like two heavyweight boxers in their respective corners, Europe's Airbus Industrie faced North America's Boeing across the Atlantic. But although they were the only two contenders left in the contest, in terms of size and reach they were far from equally matched. The new Boeing was a massive aerospace and defence conglomerate with a total revenue of $56.2 billion. Airbus Industrie was, for all its achievements, still puny by comparison. There was every reason to think, as the next phase of the battle began, that Airbus would be crushed. But events were to prove otherwise. The months immediately preceding the merger had seen the outbreak of a vicious price war as Boeing and Airbus fought each other for sales in a rapidly recovering market. Both companies came under intense pressure to increase production, but it was Boeing, not Airbus, that cracked under the strain.

‡   Stonecipher was referring to the defence divisions of Texas Instruments and General Motors, both of which were up for sale.

CHAPTER TWELVE

WE WILL BURY YOU

THE FIRST INDICATION THAT Boeing was not going to have everything its own way came less than six weeks after the news had broken of the McDonnell Douglas take-over. On 21 January 1997 Boeing announced that it was not going ahead with its 747-600 on the grounds that it believed there was no market for such a large plane. The previous autumn's rumours that Boeing had lined up a string of orders for the stretched 747 turned out to be false. Boeing now admitted that far from there being a queue of customers ready to buy up to thirty planes, the only airlines to have shown any interest were British Airways and Singapore Airlines. 'The airlines didn't jump so we pulled the offering,' said Boeing's senior analyst and marketing vice-president, Randy Baseler.[1]

At the time, the cancellation of a project about which Boeing had always seemed somewhat half-hearted was not of great moment, at least as far as Condit and Stonecipher were concerned. Their main task was to oversee the smooth amalgamation of their two companies into a single entity. They now presided over an aerospace colossus, easily the largest maker of civil and military aircraft in the world. But melding two companies together would not be any easier than it had been thirty years before when McDonnell took over Douglas Aircraft. Aircraft companies the world over tend to bear the imprint of the personalities of their founders or their leaders. And this was as true of Boeing and McDonnell Douglas in the late 1990s as it had been in the era of 'Mr Mac' and Donald Douglas in the late 1960s.

Boeing had been a company that was inordinately proud of its engineering-led culture. There were those who said that in its heroic years Boeing was less of a business than 'an association of engineers who built amazing flying machines'. The story goes that years before, while Stonecipher was still at GE and Condit was a promising young Boeing executive, the two men had dinner with Boeing's legendary 'T' Wilson. During a long discussion about wing design, Stonecipher remarked in passing that he thought Boeing was 'arrogant'. Without a second's pause, Wilson retorted, 'And rightly so.'[2] In the wider business community, Boeing was regarded as a role model. In the year of the merger, *Fortune* hailed Boeing as the eighth most admired company in the country and America's number one aerospace business, a position it had held for the last fifteen years.

Boeing and McDonnell Douglas were very different in culture and outlook. John McDonnell, the son of 'Mr Mac', had worked for his father's company for forty-three years and still regarded it as a family business. But under McDonnell's appointee, Harry Stonecipher, McDonnell Douglas had become a much harder-nosed company where the accent was on cost-cutting. Stonecipher himself had not been at Seattle for many months before repeating his criticism of Boeing's 'arrogance' and describing its past financial performance as 'absolutely dismal'. Boeing's management style, by contrast, was altogether gentler. Historically, Boeing was very tough with its huge battalions of blue-collar workers laid off in droves when the market turned down, only to be rehired in equally large numbers when the market recovered. But senior managers at Boeing were, on the whole, well treated and long-serving. One reason why the massacre of management in the wake of the launch of the 747 had been such a shock was that it was so alien to Boeing tradition. Under Stonecipher, all this was to change.

The other major concern of Boeing's new duo was how to deal with the consequences of a remarkable upturn in demand for its aircraft that had started about nine months before the merger and was now running at full spate. In the depths of the slump the two big plants at Seattle and Long Beach, California, had turning out no more than eighteen planes a month. But by the beginning of 1996 Ron Woodard, the head of Boeing's commercial aircraft division, glimpsed the first sign of a recovery. With a phrase borrowed from Nikita Khrushchev in his famous 'kitchen debate' with vice-president Richard Nixon, Woodard announced that it was his intention 'to bury Airbus'.[3] It was a neat inversion of the Russian position: whereas the Soviet leader was forecasting that socialism would triumph over capitalism, the Boeing line was quite the reverse. Like most people in Seattle, Woodard was convinced that Airbus was a state-sponsored enterprise. On his brief visits to Europe the hard-driving, aggressive Woodard did not bother to conceal his contempt for Europe's plane makers. When it was suggested that BAe's admired wing factory at Chester might a model for Boeing, Woodard shot back, 'The Brits? Come off it.' When asked about the Airbus operation, he said that it should turn itself into a proper company and 'stop seeking state aid for new projects'. On Airbus's superjumbo he was equally forthright: 'Development costs are at least twice what they are talking about and the market is questionable. There is no way anyone in business to make money or keep shareholders interested in them could do that programme. It makes no sense.'[4] In a New Year message to Boeing's in-house newspaper, he predicted that the Airbus challenge would wither away, and boldly declared, 'Our goal is a 67% market share.' He told a colleague, 'My number one priority is to make life for Airbus as miserable as possible.'[5]

Woodard's strategy was plain enough. With demand already rising, he planned to build market share by starting a price war with cuts across the board. With Airbus chipping away at Boeing's market share, Woodard was determined to take the initiative. One Wall Street analyst remarked, 'You don't want to hang about if you're

Boeing and give away market share.' In the words of Boeing's historian Eugene Bauer, 'With Woodard in the driver's seat, and financial discipline all but abandoned . . . an unchecked drive to defeat Airbus Industrie escalated to the point where 737s were being sold at breakeven prices – in some cases even below cost.'[6] At the same time, Boeing moved to shut Airbus out of the huge American domestic market by negotiating special deals with the Big Three, American, Continental and Delta Airlines. The proposal was that in return for fixed prices, the airlines would agree that Boeing should be their exclusive supplier for twenty years.*

There was little that Airbus could do in the short term to ward off the Boeing offensive – except bluff. Which it did. John Leahy comments that '1996 was a time of bluff and counter-bluff.' While Boeing was pulling in the orders, Airbus adopted a strategy of what it delicately calls 'overbooking options'. In other words, Airbus exaggerated the size of the order book by deliberately blurring the line between options and firm orders. Leahy used this tactic so enthusiastically that he was rebuked by the supervisory board, which told him, 'It may be great PR. But what are the real figures?'[7]

For Airbus and for Leahy himself, it was a period that required a cool head and a steady nerve. A New Yorker by education and upbringing, John Leahy was part of the new generation of native-born salesmen brought in by Jean Pierson in the mid-1980s. He had joined Airbus Industrie of North America in 1985 about the time of the famous Pan Am deal. He had made his reputation in the flurry of dealmaking in North America between 1986 and 1988 when Airbus won critical orders from United Airlines, Northwest Airlines, US Airways and Air Canada. By 1993 Leahy, who has same neat, boyish look as Alan Mulally, his counterpart at Boeing, had moved up the ladder to become commercial director. As Airbus's top salesman, Leahy is smooth, quick thinking and aggressive. Once he warms to a theme, he is not easily diverted, and if there is an opportunity to put Boeing down, he is not one to miss it. When, as the A3XX sales campaign was reaching its height in the early spring of 2000, he was asked what he thought of Boeing's efforts to prove there was no market for the superjumbo, he replied, 'Boeing's like a man facing a firing squad and asking for a last cigarette. The company's just playing for time.'[8]

That may have been true then, but in 1996 it was Airbus that had to play for time. Woodard knew – and so did Airbus – that the Europeans were incapable of ramping up production as fast as Boeing. And by the time they had reacted, it would be too late. Woodard was convinced that the Boeing factories would be able to cut the time from order to delivery from the standard eighteen to twenty-four months, to only nine. In so doing he would be able to drive Boeing's annual order book up

---

*   The European Commission later forced Boeing to unscramble this deal on competition grounds but at the time it gave Airbus a nasty fright.

from 150 to 500 or 600 airplanes and thus bury Airbus. Leahy claims that although Boeing's price-cutting tactics worked well, Airbus did not suffer unduly. 'I didn't lose a deal because people had to wait eighteen months or two years for their planes. Nobody switched over because they didn't want to wait. Maybe we lost some options but that was no big deal. Options are icing on the cake and half of them aren't taken up anyway.'[9]

As Airbus saw it, the one snag in the Woodard strategy was that success depended on Boeing's ability to deliver the planes as fast as the airlines were ordering them. But the trouble was that Woodard had failed to check with the production people as to whether his plan was feasible.

In the early autumn of 1996 as slump turned into boom, Boeing started to ramp up. That September, it increased production at the Everett plant of its 747s from two a month to three and a half. By the following June it was up to four. As demand exploded, Boeing's factories production methods began to creak under the strain: incredibly, they had remained largely unaltered since the 1940s when Boeing was going flat out building its B-17 and B-29 bombers for America's war effort. By the early autumn of 1997 the 747 production line was in complete disarray. There was not the same degree of automation in Seattle as at the Airbus plants in Toulouse and Hamburg, and Boeing made its planes by dividing the assembly process into a succession of discrete 'jobs'. Not only was there a shortage of workers, but, more seriously, a shortage of parts meant the individual 'jobs' on the line were being done behind schedule and out of sequence. As a 747 has more than 6 million components, it is easy to imagine the consequences.

The knock-on effect not only hit Boeing, but also threw its large and far-flung family of suppliers into turmoil. 'We have $25,000 engine mounts that can't be finished because we are waiting for $40 nuts and bolts,' complained John Gazecki, the chairman and chief executive of one Boeing sub-contractor in Tacoma, Washington.[10] The late arrival of parts from firms like this had a catastrophic effect on the 747 programme.

These difficulties were compounded by Boeing's traditions and old-fashioned production techniques. For more than half a century it had been an article of faith at Boeing that customers should be allowed to specify exactly what kind of plane they wanted, down to the most minute detail. The planes might look as if they were being mass-produced, but the degree of customization meant that they were virtually tailor-made. Airlines were treated like customers at McDonalds: according to the best traditions of American fast food retailing, they were given an amazing degree of choice. It was not just a question of selecting something important like the engine: airlines could specify which of 109 different shades of white paint they preferred, they could indicate whether the spring on the clipboard in the cockpit should be mounted on the top or the side, or how many holes there should be for the air-conditioning duct at the front end of the rear cargo compartment and whether they should be on the left or the right. However attractive these options might be to the airline, for the production engineers they were a nightmare. Each time a customer chose a bulkhead configuration, the decision affected the placement of no fewer than 2,550 parts.

If the range of choice customers were given was bewildering, the system Boeing used to keep track of all these different preferences was byzantine in its complexity. Every time a customer declared a preference for a certain configuration, the engineering department would use a special numerical code to 'tab' the hundreds of pages of engineering drawings that record every variation of the item ever made. The drawings of bulkheads alone in the 747 ran to just under 1,000. The system was so arcane that it took up to two years for workers to understand it and even when they did, mistakes were frequent. At any one time, up 30 per cent of the drawings were wrongly numbered. When a part went missing, either because it was misnumbered or simply lost, someone called an 'expediter' would be despatched on a bicycle to fetch the correct part so as to keep the assembly line rolling. To ensure that there were sufficient parts on hand to feed the lines, Boeing kept huge stocks of spare parts on the factory floor, which were only replenished when the bottom of the bin hove into view. In the post-mortem that followed the crisis, Boeing came to realize that it was holding what some analysts reckoned was up to $18 billion-worth of inventory and that it was taking two of three times longer than other companies to turn it over. Far from being lean and hungry, as a manufacturer it was fat and inefficient.

For some reason no one can remember, this manually-operated system was known as 'effectivity', even though 'effective' was the last thing it was. If ever there was a case for computerization, this was it. In the early 1990s Boeing replaced its old hand-driven methods with computers, but the manner in which it was done made things worse rather than better. Instead of inputting all the data on a single, centralized system accessible to all departments throughout the company, the engineers devised a scheme in which the information was stored on 450 separate computer databases which, unfortunately, were unable to communicate with each other.

In an attempt to cut through these problems, in 1994 Condit's predecessor, Frank Shrontz, launched a billion-dollar modernization programme known in the company by the unlovely, jaw-breaking acronym DCAC/MRM, which stood for 'Define & Control Airplane Configuration/Manufacturing Resource Management'. Designed to eliminate the glitches between the engineering, marketing and manufacturing divisions of Boeing and thus reduce the cost of making an aeroplane by up 25 per cent, it was a good idea that was introduced at a very bad moment. Woodard had hoped that the benefits of DCAC etc. would have started to have come through when he launched his price-cutting campaign. But the programme was still a couple of years away from being implemented when the crisis broke. The fact that it was incomplete made the situation even more chaotic. The attempt to double production right in the middle of the switch to the new system had been too much. By the end of September 1997 the 747 line was running at more than 14,000 jobs behind schedule. In normal times Boeing would reckon that a deficit of 3,000 jobs was manageable, but anything more than that was a problem.

It was at this point that the production managers told Ron Woodard that the 747 and 737 assembly lines had effectively seized up. The jobs were so out of sync that the only alternative was to stop the lines to give everybody a chance to catch up. The news came as a surprise. 'We had been working our way through these problems and I thought we were getting on well,' says Woodard. 'But then our Everett people came down and told me we were just not getting there. We went through all the data in my office and the data said the same thing. We realized that no number of parts and people was going to get the 747 line back into position. We would have to suspend production.'[11] Four days later Phil Condit announced to an astonished world that Boeing was halting the 747 line for twenty days and that final assembly at Renton, which was building the next generation of 737s, would also be suspended for the same reason.

The irony was that in the initial stages of his sales campaign, Woodard had been brilliantly successful. His forecast at the beginning of 1996 that Boeing would achieve a 67 per cent market share had turned out to be uncannily accurate. With a total of more than 1,000 sales for the entire industry, orders in 1996 were at an all-time high. And the year-end figures showed that with 682 new orders against Airbus's 303, Boeing had outsold its rival by a margin of two to one. What nobody could foresee was that 1997 would be very different: by the autumn of that year Boeing was embroiled in its production problems and in the Far East fears were growing about the stability of Asia's 'tiger' economies. Before the year was out Boeing would announce that its production problems in the third quarter had led it to a $1.6 billion write off and a further $1 billion off profits in 1998. Overall, the company said it would make a net loss for 1997 of $178 million – the first for fifty years. It was a result that would cost Ron Woodard his job and gravely embarrass a proud company.

It was not entirely Boeing's fault. As Gordon Bethune, chairman of Continental Airlines and a former Boeing employee, said at the time, 'This company is trying to do so much at the same time: increase production, make its manufacturing lean, and deal with mergers. It's like a guy who's juggling eggs, and then someone tosses him an orange. It's easy to drop something.'[12]

While Boeing was suffering its long night of the soul, there were significant, although less traumatic, changes at Airbus. In January 1998 Jean Pierson's thirteen-year reign came to an end when it was announced that Noël Forgeard would take over as managing director of Airbus Industrie. Pierson says that there was nothing surprising about his departure. He had decided three years earlier that he would go in 1998. More to the point, perhaps, it was clear both to the politicians and the partners that Airbus was on the verge of an entirely new era which demanded a more or less clean break with the past.

One year earlier, at the beginning of 1997, the partners had began for the first time to discuss in earnest the replacement of the old GIE structure with what they called a 'single corporate entity'. In other words, the partners had agreed that the time had come to transform the curious animal that was Airbus Industrie into something resembling a normal company. The anomaly of having partners who were both shareholders and suppliers would disappear, to be replaced by a company with a far more conventional structure, with ordinary shareholders, a board of management and, most important of all, open and fully transparent accounts. This last point was important for two reasons: firstly, it would give the lie to those, especially the Americans, who argued that Airbus was a hopeless, loss-making concern that only survived because it was propped up by massive government loans. And secondly, proper, audited accounts would enable Airbus's own management, it was argued, to see for the very first time just how profitable (or unprofitable) the various parts of the operation actually were. 'It was crazy,' says Philippe Delmas, the chief adviser to the present managing director. 'Nobody knew what the real costs of making the planes actually were. Nobody knew whether the company was making money or not.'[13] Although the company would still rely on government support when launching new aircraft, the idea behind the concept of the Single Corporate Entity was that the politicians would pull back and allow the industrialists get on with the business of making and selling aircraft.

As we have seen, these thoughts had been around for quite some time. But what gave them much greater urgency was the growing impetus behind the A3XX. The closer the superjumbo came to reality, the more clearly everybody came to realize that the project was too big and too risky for an unreformed GIE to swallow.

The British, in particular, argued that the project was so huge and the costs were so great that to embark on it without a clear idea of what those costs really were would be folly. 'We could no longer have this nonsense of partners as both shareholders and suppliers,' says Mike Turner, BAe's man on the Airbus board. 'We have to put the factories and the engineering under one management on a day-to-day basis. We needed the integrated company and we needed the A3XX. The two went hand-in-glove. You couldn't do one without the other. The A3XX was such a huge risk that you needed to optimize it, otherwise you couldn't do it.'[14]

The British, who were particularly irritated by Spanish threats to use their veto, were not alone in wanting change. The politicians, too, were growing impatient at the delays. The consensus was that the days of the GIE were numbered but the problem was how to bring it about. It was against this background that Noël Forgeard became the new managing director of Airbus Industrie, with a mission to dismantle the organization he had just joined. 'When I joined Airbus at the beginning of '98, it was on the assumption that the consortium would be transformed into a company. Otherwise I would never have done it,' he told me. 'The top priority of the GIE was mainly sales and I am not basically a salesman. I am a manager. I joined

Airbus to turn it into a company. Very simply, you cannot manage enormous programmes between various locations without a central authority. You could say, as my predecessor did, that the GIE had reached its genetic limits and I think that is a good expression.'[15]

This time the succession went a good deal more smoothly than it had thirteen years before when Jean Pierson took over from Bernard Lathière. In appearance, the affable, bespectacled Forgeard looks more like a senior civil servant than a captain of industry. His colleagues say he is extremely clever and very ambitious. And although he is nothing like as large or as colourful a personality as Jean Pierson, the fifty-one-year-old Forgeard had an impeccable political and industrial track record. As a former adviser to the French President Jacques Chirac, he is *de facto* part of the political establishment, while his previous job as chief executive of Matra BAe Dynamics, a joint venture between France's Lagardère, the missiles to magazines conglomerate founded and run by Jean-Luc Lagardère, and British Aerospace, meant that he was well versed in the world of defence, aerospace and Airbus politics. In France, Jean-Luc Lagardère is known as 'The Acrobat' and the Lagardère connection was soon to be an all-important element in the Airbus story.

Within weeks of taking over, Forgeard scored a notable success when he landed a massive £3 billion order from British Airways for fifty-nine A319s and A320s, with options on a further 129. It was the largest single order for new aircraft BA had ever made. And for the first time in Airbus history the consortium had won an order from an airline which under Lord King, the previous chairman, had a relationship with Boeing so close as be almost incestuous. It was, after all, BA's preference for the Americans, coupled with overt hostility to Airbus in the early years, that was one of the main reasons for Britain's withdrawal from the project. Now under a new chairman and new managing director, Robert Ayling, BA was burying the hatchet. Ayling said afterwards that the reason he bought Airbus rather than Boeing was because the A320 was cheaper to operate than Boeing's 737-600s. But that was only part of the story. Equally influential was that Airbus salesmen, sensing that here was an opportunity to put one over on Boeing, were willing to give BA a £1 billion discount in the shape of special terms for maintenance, the purchase of BA's old, unwanted planes, and compensation for BA's decision to scrap its options on more 737s. Ayling acknowledged as much when he said, 'At the end of the day, it all came down to cost.'[16] And although BA sugared the pill by placing an almost equally large order with Boeing for thirty-two 777s, Boeing was furious. 'The unlevel playing field still exists,' a Boeing official told the *Financial Times*. 'Producing at a loss is not an option for us or our shareholders.'[17]

In France and Britain the BA deal was greeted with great acclaim. Tony Blair, the British prime minister, travelled to Toulouse to take part in the celebrations, and France's minister of transport joined in the spirit of things by saying that Air France, too, was modernizing its fleet and would also be buying Airbuses. It had taken a long time – more than thirty years to be exact – but at long last Europe's flag carriers were lining up to support Europe's premier aircraft company just as the politicians always hoped they would. Behind the scenes there was less jubilation. Boeing's suspicion that the planes were being sold at a rock-bottom prices was, for BAe's Mike Turner, uncomfortably close to the mark. 'The marketeers who came to the supervisory board weren't in it for the price,' he says. 'They were in it for the volume. The French were driving this for volume. And probably in the early years of Airbus, we needed this volume. We needed market share. It wasn't a strategy they would admit to, but we tolerated it. After we did the British Airways deal, I said at the supervisory board "that's the last time anybody mentions strategy". We need a pricing grid and minimum prices for every aircraft size.'[18]

The Airbus counter-attack, which began with the BA deal in the spring, was so effective that by the end of the year the Europeans had seized the initiative. For only the second time in its history, Airbus had outsold Boeing. The margin in market share between the two was tiny – no more than one per cent – but the implications were huge.

In making his debut at Farnborough that autumn, Forgeard had hinted at just how difficult the task of persuading the Airbus partners to pool their assets into the common Airbus pot was proving to be. 'To get industrialists to vest a major part of their activity into a new entity demands a very prudent and thorough process,' he remarked diplomatically. 'Our partners had set themselves 1999 as the year of incorporation. Mid-'99 is more likely. The stakes for Europe, financially, industrially, strategically are simply so high that we need to take time to build a structure that will robustly stand the test of time.'[19] This was putting it kindly: the plain fact was that the partners were adamantly refusing to share information about their own Airbus businesses with each other. In reality, the talks were deadlocked. The partners had been told that they must exchange information by 28 July at the latest. But the companies refused and the deadline passed. As long as the deadlock lasted, the chances of Airbus becoming a normal company were zero. Something had to be done.

CHAPTER THIRTEEN

END GAME

ONE SUMMER EVENING IN LATE July 1998 Bernard Taylor of Robert Fleming, one of the City's more blue-blooded but smaller merchant banks, was about to leave for a performance of Handel's *Xerxes* at New College, Oxford, when he received a call from Paris from a very important client. The caller, Philippe Camus, was one of 'the Lagardère boys' – a favoured member of the small group of high-flying executives who surround Jean-Luc Lagardère, the founder of the eponymous conglomerate. At the time Camus, who has a degree in physics, was running Matra, Lagardère's high technology division, and he was calling to tell Taylor that the French government was about to announce that it was to going to privatize the state-owned Aerospatiale by selling a third-share to Lagardère.

At the opera Taylor, whose wife had organized the performance, met Richard Lapthorne, the finance director of BAe. Saying, 'Richard, I have to talk to you', Taylor drew Lapthorne aside and told him the news. 'Richard went as white as a sheet and then spent the rest of the time on the telephone. He missed the opera completely,' Taylor recalls. Among those he talked to was Sir Dick Evans, BAe's chairman, and John Weston, the managing director. He also tried to reach Lord Simpson, the chief executive of GEC, which owned Britain's other major defence business, Marconi, but as Simpson was attending a debate in the House of Lords about lowering the age of consent for homosexual sex, it was left to Taylor to try Simpson after the opera had ended. Taylor says, 'When I did reach him, he said, "I don't know which is worse. What I've just been doing or the effect this news will have on our expansion plans for Europe. A fundamental building block has now shifted."'[1]

This was stunning news. It was hailed as both removing an obstacle to the restructuring of Airbus, and also as opening the door to the creation of a European aerospace-cum-defence grouping with the size and strength to match the new American gorillas. 'It was the transitional step towards the creation of a European aerospace business,' says Philippe Camus. 'This is what we had in mind. But we did not know how it would happen.'[2]

The rationalization of the American defence industry over the past couple of years, culminating with Boeing's take-over of McDonnell Douglas, had caused near panic in Europe. 'We have got to create something in terms of scale that will enable us to be close to the Americans,' BAe's Sir Dick Evans told me.[3] To Evans, Airbus was the key. His concern was not so much the future of Airbus itself but the future of the European defence industry. His argument was that of Europe's big three, France's defence industry was the most fragmented and disorganized; it was also the only one that was still very largely state-owned. But just as internal forces were pushing Airbus towards reorganization, these same pressures, he contended, would create the necessary conditions for a pan-European defence company. 'Airbus is the grenade that will create the bang that forces the restructuring,' he said. He was quite right about the bang. What neither he nor anybody else foresaw was what the consequences would be.

Ever since the governments had starting pushing the industry to sink its differences and work together to create a common European aerospace and defence company, the British and the Germans had been saying that they would refuse to play this game if Aerospatiale remained a nationalized company in whole or part. In March, Manfred Bischoff, DASA's chief executive, had said quite bluntly, 'The concept of government shares in the united aerospace industry must be ruled out.' [4] Dick Evans at BAe agreed. So why had Lionel Jospin's socialist government changed tack and agreed to sell off something it had always regarded as a precious national asset? Part of the answer was that the French had understood the weakness of their position. To strengthen it, the Jospin government had already privatized important parts of France's defence and electronics sector. For example, the previous year Matra, the space satellite-to-missiles group, had been sold to Lagardère, and Thomson-CSF, the defence electronics group, was being hived off to Alcatel. But there was a more immediate explanation for the French government's move.

On Sunday 28 June, Philippe Camus celebrated his fiftieth birthday by having lunch with the minister of defence. Matra/Lagardère was feeling left out of the privatization party, and with the sale of Thomson-CSF to Alcatel, its options were closing. 'Matra was in a difficult position,' said Camus. 'Either we could keep going with satellites and so forth or we could try and do something else.' Camus' first plan had been to persuade the government to sell him Aerospatiale's missile business, but this fell down because the government had already promised it to Thomson-CSF as a sweetener in the privatization deal with Alcatel.

However, there was an alternative. Camus knew that both Aerospatiale's management and its owners, the French government, were worried that the strong pressure to reinvent Airbus as a single corporate entity could mean that the company and the state would lose control of an extremely important asset. If this business was handed over to the new Airbus integrated company, only the rump of Aerospatiale would remain and that would probably be sold off to the highest bidder. That would, in effect, be the end of Aerospatiale, which had designed and built Concorde and which, for more than thirty years, had been the pride of France's aerospace industry. How could Aerospatiale be saved?

This was the question that Camus and the minister discussed over lunch. Camus had already talked to Aerospatiale's management and had informally floated the idea of merging Lagardère's latest acquisition, Matra, and Aerospatiale. At lunch he went a good deal further. Making it plain he was speaking with the knowledge and approval of his master, Jean-Luc Lagardère, he told the minister that the group was ready to enter into a partnership with the government. The plan was that Lagadère would be the largest private shareholder in the new company with a stake of around 30 to 33 per cent; 20 per cent would be floated; with the result that the government holding would fall to just under 50 per cent. The minister was sympathetic. On 23 July, only 25 days, after Camus' birthday lunch, the French government announced the privatization of Aerospatiale and its merger with Matra on terms very similar to the ones Camus had suggested. As the French saw it, this was the first step in the transformation of Airbus into a European aerospace group in which the French would inevitably play an important part. 'We were late and were trying to catch up,' says Marwan Lahoud, who had joined Aerospatiale as senior strategist only a month or so before.[5] But the question was: how would the other players in this game react?

One reason, so Camus says, why the French government acted so quickly was that alarming rumours were already circulating in Paris of a possible link-up between BAe and DASA. To say that the French were aggrieved would be putting it mildly. Firstly, a merger meant that the British and the Germans would acquire a controlling interest in Airbus and that the French would become a minority partner and have less clout in a European defence company. In the second place, it was evidence, so the French believed, that the British and the Germans had double-crossed them.

Earlier that year there had been a meeting of the Airbus supervisory board at which there was a long discussion about the lack of progress on the single corporate entity idea. Although the talks had been going on for over a year, none of the partners were willing to put their cards on the table and disclose exactly how much they had put into Airbus and what they were making out of it. What made matters doubly difficult was that Airbus was much more important to some than to others. To the Spanish it was no more than a profitable sideshow; to the British it was a useful business but one that accounted for no more than 15 per cent of BAe's annual turnover; to the Germans and especially to the French, however, it was a matter of life and death. For DASA and Aerospatiale, Airbus work was around 50 per cent of their total annual business. Under the old GIE arrangement the Airbus business was controlled by the partners; in the 'new' Airbus company, they would only be one of a number of shareholders. It is therefore little wonder that it was difficult for the partners to agree on the valuation of the assets of the Airbus operation and how they should be divided. If they had a hard time agreeing on how the share of the work should be divided on individual projects (which they did), then trying to reach agreement on how the component parts of the entire operation should be apportioned was a task that would test the patience of a saint – and they were no saints.

The chairman, Manfred Bischoff, the head of DASA, said, 'We can't go on like this.' And he suggested that the three main partners, DASA, Aerospatiale and British Aerospace, should work up a proposal that would be acceptable to everybody. The losers here would be the Spanish, but as their stake was very small and as their attempts to punch above their weight by the threatened use of their veto had not endeared them to their Airbus partners, nobody was going to shed tears on their account. Besides, nobody thought of the Spanish as players in what was now being called the European Aerospace Defence Company (EADC). 'We spent three or four months working on an agreement,' says BAe's Mike Turner. 'And we got very close to the basis of a deal amongst the three of us. But while this was going on, we had the DASA British Aerospace negotiations. Yves Michel [the head of Aerospatiale] got upset and that was the end of that. We never exchanged final data.'[6]

As the idea of a three-way Airbus-driven defence link began to fade, the British started to explore a tie-up with DASA. The seeds had been sown earlier in the year, when on a visit to New York, BAe's Richard Lapthorne discussed the problems with Richard Roundell, an old friend and former investment banker turned consultant, who ran a company which analyzed difficult strategic problems with the help of a Cray supercomputer in Stanford, California. Lapthorne asked Roundell if he would simulate the likely outcome of any Anglo/German/French negotiations by feeding in all the different permutations and then asking the computer to predict what the actions of the other parties might be. The results were not encouraging. After producing a million pages of raw data (which worked out at $1 a page in fees), the computer predicted that if BAe went for a three-way merger, there would still be a stalemate after ten rounds of negotiations. 'At that stage the French were still thinking too much about Airbus, and not enough about the European defence company,' says Lapthorne. 'There were simply too many traffic lights at red.'[7]

One reason for the all the chopping and changing at BAe throughout 1998 and 1999 was the very real uncertainty amongst the top people as to what sort of company BAe wanted to be: should it be European, American or something in between? It is a theme that runs through the entire Airbus story like the peppermint stripe in a stick of Blackpool rock. Just as, thirty years before, Rolls-Royce, together with the Wilson government, had agonized about where its best interests lay, so now British Aerospace and the Blair government was facing a new version of the same problem. 'One of the factors that was holding us back from too close a link with the French was the knowledge that it would damage the American side of the business,' Lapthorne says. The other factor was that BAe, which had come close to buying Thomson-CSF, had no great regard for the Europeans' defence business and saw any merged company as primarily a civil aviation, Airbus-orientated operation. Finally, despite the injection of the Lagardère interests into Aerospatiale, both the Germans and the British felt that the French government's influence in Aerospatiale was still too strong. Shortly after the announcement of the Lagardère deal, BAe's

John Weston told *Le Monde* that there should be no government involvement at all in the new company. 'We want a completely diluted shareholder base, like BAe's today,' he said.[8]

While John Weston was arguing that the privatization of Aerospatiale had changed nothing, privately he was engaged in negotiations with Manfred Bischoff, DASA's chief executive, with a view to a full-scale merger between Daimler-Benz Aerospace and BAe. This was in breach of the Airbus agreement under which the partners were obliged to keep each other informed about any developments that affected the consortium. But the British and Germans took the view that as these were talks were between Airbus shareholders, not partners, they were entitled to keep Toulouse in the dark. Throughout that summer there were numerous meetings between BAe and DASA people, sometimes at DASA headquarters in Munich, sometimes, more discreetly, in English country hotels like Chewton Glen on the edge of the New Forest. The restaurant has a Michelin star and there is a helicopter pad in the grounds. It was private and it was comfortable. Only the waiters spoke French.

There was every reason for discretion. If the deal went ahead, it would not only completely alter the balance of power in Airbus itself, but it would also change the face of the European defence industry. The British and the Germans saw the merged company as the nucleus of a new Airbus operation which could then lead on to something even larger – a European defence and aerospace company which others, including the French, could join at a later stage.

BAe had taken the precaution of telling the British government what it was planning and had been given every encouragement: the company was told that a DASA merger would fit in well with Tony Blair's aspirations to build his European policy around a special relationship with Gerhard Schröder, the German chancellor. In Berlin the British ambassador, Paul Lever, and his assistant, Peter Watkins, worked hard to push things along. In Britain, Peter Mandelson's Department of Trade and Industry followed Number 10 in its enthusiasm for the German solution. But though everyone was careful to say nothing in public, the French found out. News of this sensational development first began to leak out in late July, just as France was preparing to shut down for the August summer holidays. For some six weeks there was no official reaction. But in early September, on the eve of the Farnborough Air Show, the French minister of transport, Jean-Claude Gayssot, broke the silence. In an interview with the *Financial Times*, he warned that if the Anglo-German merger went ahead, it would jeopardize the plans to turn Airbus into a single corporate entity. Referring to the principal three Airbus partners as 'a tripod', he said, 'It is clear that if tomorrow this tripod were called into question, the rules of the game would be modified.' When he was asked, point-blank, whether the merger would mean the end of the single company project, he replied enigmatically, 'We look at the problem with a different eye.'[9] The French were so outraged that they were to demand a 50 per cent share of Airbus to counterbalance the Anglo-German alliance, and at a meeting of the supervisory board in Toulouse, Aerospatiale refused to exchange valuations with its Airbus partners. DASA replied by accusing France of taking Airbus 'hostage'. 'They do not want any other European restructuring to take place without them – and they are using this to stop it,' said Bischoff.[10]

On 12 October came the official confirmation that the rumours had been correct and that the two groups were planning a full-scale merger some time 'early next year', but it added that if the French wanted to join later, the door would always be open. On the other hand, the announcement was curiously vague: there were no hard details about price or the value of the assets to be exchanged, and nothing about who was going to run the merged company.

The first indication that things were turning sour came when BAe and DASA began to differ about the management structure of the merged company. Although BAe was a much bigger concern than DASA and would therefore have a majority of the shares, the single biggest individual shareholder would be DASA's parent, the car giant, DaimlerChrysler, which had been put together by Jürgen Schrempp of Daimler-Benz and Robert Eaton of Chrysler. BAe was coming to dislike Schrempp's autocratic style, his habit of delegating dirty work and his short attention span. But one of the main reasons for the breakdown, it says, was that Schrempp was asking for too great a degree of control over a company that was not central to DaimlerChrysler's core business. 'For them DASA was just a sideshow, a subsidiary of the car-making business,' says an insider. 'Yet the Germans were asking for veto rights on something that was not central to them but life blood for us. It just wasn't on.'

BAe's Mike Turner comments, 'DaimlerChrysler put conditions on the table which were completely unacceptable to us.' They insisted, so Turner says, that there should be a sub-committee created to approve what the Germans called 'strategic issues'. And the condition was that all decisions of this committee should be unanimous. 'It's ridiculous,' Turner protests. 'This was the tail wagging the dog. How can you have a plc where you have a sub-committee saying what goes to the board and what doesn't? What they were asking for was a veto over the running of the company. That was the crunch. That was the key issue.'[11]

Whether or not this difference would have been enough to derail the merger is an open question. What is certain is that in the late autumn of 1998 the picture altered completely when BAe realized that George Simpson and John Mayo of GEC were preparing to put its Marconi division up for sale. Marconi was 'the jewel in the crown' of Arnold Weinstock's GEC, which Simpson had inherited when he had taken over from the old maestro in September 1996. Weinstock had acquired Marconi when he bought English Electric in 1968, and over the next thirty years he had built it up to become the heart of GEC's defence operations, which covered radar, communications and avionics. It was GEC's most profitable activity and was responsible for about a third of the group's total turnover and profits. It employed the cream of GEC's scientists and technicians; it was particularly strong in communications and navigational equipment; and its avionics business was respected both in Britain and America. It did not, however, fit in with Simpson's and Mayo's plans for their restyled GEC.

The new team wanted to reposition GEC as an information technology company and were anxious to move out of the defence and heavy electrical contracting business as fast as they could to reinvest the proceeds in broad band internet technology. Overall they spent close to £15 billion. The strategy turned out to be a complete disaster that utterly wrecked the company. In eighteen months, as the internet bubble burst, the value of the company's shares fell 99 per cent – from a high of more than £12 to a low of just over 12p. In selling Marconi, Simpson and Mayo were, in effect, tearing the heart out of the company. It had taken Arnold Weinstock more than thirty years to build GEC; it took Simpson and Mayo less than three years to destroy it. The destruction of GEC was one of the worst acts of vandalism in British industrial history; it was to lead to the departure of Simpson and Mayo, who both collected handsome pay-offs. But this was to come later. At the time, the Marconi deal was hailed for its brilliance and opportunism.

Mayo was by background and outlook an investment banker who prided himself on his skills as a 'deal-maker'. He had little feel for what companies actually did or how to improve their performance. He was driven, above all, by a desire, as he put it later, 'to maximize shareholder value'.[12] Just before Christmas 1998, GEC announced that 'it had decided to separate its civil businesses from its aerospace and defence activities'. In other words, it was putting Marconi up for auction and inviting bids from interested parties. It was the final play in what John Mayo called 'Project Super Bowl'. Named after the American pro-football competition which involves a series of play-offs before reaching a climax at the end of January, Mayo wanted to capitalize on the frenzy of reorganization that was going on in the defence industry on both sides of the Atlantic. If Marconi was to be sold, now seemed to be the time to do it.

GEC's decision to sell Marconi did not come as a complete surprise to BAe. George Simpson had worked for BAe as head of the Rover car division before it was sold off to BMW and had stayed in touch. There had even been discussions about a three-way merger between BAe, DASA and Marconi, but these had broken down at a meeting early in December when Jürgen Schrempp said he wanted to complete the BAe DASA merger first. Simpson, realizing that this would spoil his plans to achieve the best price for Marconi, refused.

BAe was under no illusion about the game Simpson and Mayo were playing. But equally it believed that the price was worth it. With both the Americans and the French ready to produce their chequebooks to snap up Marconi, BAe had to act quickly. 'It became clear to us that George and John Mayo had decided to walk the company,' says Mike Turner. 'And the last thing we could have in our domestic market was Marconi going to a competitor. I think we would have been virtually dead if that had happened. The competition would have divided the domestic market and unless you have a strong domestic base, how can you play in the international game?'

On 19 January 1999 the two companies announced that BAe and GEC's Marconi were to merge to create what it claimed was the world's second largest defence company behind America's Lockheed Martin but ahead of Boeing/McDonnell Douglas. BAe had to defend its own patch at all costs: at £7.5 billion, the price was, so BAe reckoned, about 30 per cent more than it was worth. But there were other costs apart from money. The Marconi deal left DASA stranded at the altar. It was the Germans' turn to be furious. In the immediate aftermath Manfred Bischoff, DASA's wounded chief executive, lashed out. He warned that the creation of a pan-European defence company might have to be postponed indefinitely, accused BAe of undermining the restructuring of Airbus into a single company, and hinted that he might have to seek consolation in the arms of the French. Revealing that DASA had been talking to the French even while negotiating with the British, Bischoff said, 'Now it is clear these talks have received a new momentum.' [13]

It is doubtful if Bischoff would have been so confident if he had known what the French were doing. On Saturday 22 January, four days after the announcement of the Marconi deal, there was a meeting in Camus' office in the Boulevard Montmorency (which has a splendid view of the Auteuil racecourse in the Bois de Boulogne). It was here that 'Operation Pegasus' was launched, the code name for a secret plan, hatched by BAe and Aerospatiale/Matra, to create an Anglo-French Airbus company in which DASA was to play no part. In the company it was referred to as 'the Pegasus parachute'. The calculation was that with BAe now embarked on an independent course as a defence company, the moment was ripe to cut the Airbus knot by joining forces with the British to buy DASA out. It would be a *fait accompli*. As a plan it was every bit as cynical and as opportunistic as the thinking behind the BAe-DASA merger. But it would fail for two reasons. In the first place, news leaked to MI6, the espionage wing of British intelligence, who immediately passed it on to Downing Street who told BAe it should drop all contacts with the French. The second flaw was that the French government was not in on the plot.

The moment had come for the French to implement Plan B. In February, quite unabashed, the French began to make overtures to DASA. And this time it was BAe that was kept in the dark. The talks started quietly and at a low level. 'Initially, we were simply asking how we could help,' says Camus. From the beginning it was understood that this was to be a dialogue between the people who owned Airbus, not the people who ran it. Only a small, select group inside the parent companies of Lagardère and DaimlerChrysler were in the know. The people at Aerospatiale and DASA were left in the dark; even Noël Forgeard was out of the loop, though his old boss, Jean-Luc Lagardère, would phone him from time to time.

The talks went so well that within a couple of months Jürgen Schrempp and Jean-Luc Lagardère became directly involved. The first detailed discussions on the mechanics of a complete merger between Aerospatiale/Matra and Dasa took place in New York at the end of April, when the DaimlerChrysler management was in town for a board meeting. By July, the French and the Germans had reached agreement on the creation of what they called the 'European Aeronautic Defence and Space company' – known as EADS for short. They saw it as Europe's answer to Boeing.

A few days before the official announcement in Paris in mid-October that Aerospatiale and DASA were to merge, a dinner was arranged at Le Train Bleu restaurant at the Gare de Lyon between the senior people and advisers from Lagardère and a team from British Aerospace, including Mike Turner. The British had no idea what was afoot and were, according to one insider, 'shocked and surprised' when they heard the news. Like everybody at BAe, Turner was taken aback at how quickly the French and the Germans had moved to do a deal. 'Some of us believed that it would be possible to get back in with the Germans once we had completed the Marconi deal. That was a belief around here,' he says.[14] The purpose of the dinner was not to embarrass the British but to invite them, late as it was, to join the EADS party. The French and the British had always got on well, and Lagardère's people, whose advisers were themselves British, were anxious to have the British in as a counterweight to the Germans. But when the British asked, 'When do you want an answer?' the reply was, 'You have until tomorrow.'

The French insist that they sincerely wanted the British, but if this was a genuine attempt to include them, it failed. The next day the British said, 'thanks, but no thanks'. 'They tried to get us in,' says Turner. 'But clearly although defence is a huge issue, it is not a big issue for them. Airbus was the huge issue for them. But we do have to keep an eye on the United States. We have a clear choice here. Do we go down the European route, or down the US route, or somewhere down the middle. The last thing we wanted to do was to be locked into a French and German company where defence isn't the main priority bearing in mind what the view of the American defence establishment is, particularly about the French.'

On Thursday 14 October the news broke that DaimlerChrysler Aerospace SA (Dasa) of Germany and Aerospatiale Matra of France were to merge. With a turnover of 22.5 billion euros, and a workforce of 88,900, the new group was to be Europe's largest aerospace and defence company and the world's second biggest after Boeing. But while Boeing is as much a defence company as it is a maker of civil aircraft, the EADS profile is dominated by Airbus, which accounts for at least 60 per cent of its turnover. The military aircraft and defence side of the business accounted for little more than 10 per cent.

The group's management structure was as cumbersome as its name. Reflecting its Franco-German origins, there were to be two chairmen, two managing directors and two headquarters, one in Paris and one in Munich. It was agreed that the top man in Paris would be Lagardère's Philippe Camus, while his counterpart in Munich was Dasa's Rainer Hertrich. Bischoff was the German chairman while Lagardère was his equivalent in France. Camus admits that this division is political. 'The aerospace business is made up of nations and we have to take account of the nations that are behind us. This is why we have this duality at the top.'[15]

With no place in the new structure for the Spanish, it was only a matter of time before either the French or the Germans bought out Spain's state-owned CASA. As Spain's centre-right Aznar government regarded CASA more as an investment than as a strategic stake in the European aerospace industry, there was no real obstacle to a sale. The only question was who would buy it? Aerospatiale or Dasa? The French who thought that the Spanish operation would enhance Aerospatiale's expertise in carbon fibre technology had made some overtures. But, after some high-level political pressure, the issue was to be settled in favour of Dasa. Even so, some important questions remained. What was the precise relationship between the new group and British Aerospace going to be? What was the shape of the new Airbus company? And how would the deal affect the progress of the superjumbo?

*

While the Europeans were wrestling with the problems of reorganization, Boeing, having bounced back after the traumas of 1997 and 1998, had decided to re-enter the fray with yet another stretched version of the 747. With a capacity of up to 660 people, it was known as the 747X, and was intended to challenge the Airbus superjumbo head-on. But because it was a derivative of an existing plane, Boeing reckoned it would be ready before the Airbus offering and would only cost about one-third of the $10 billion Airbus was planning to spend on the A3XX. The 747X had been given the go-ahead in the late spring in the hope that it would be ready for a market launch in about eighteen months. But, as always, everything would depend on the reaction of the airlines.

Although Airbus remained outwardly as confident as ever, the Boeing move caused a flurry of concern in Toulouse. There was still a lot of development work to be done on its own big plane. The wings, in particular, were giving trouble. The target for the BAe designers was to produce a wing that would, through a combination of weight saving and aerodynamic efficiency, cut cash operating costs by at least 17 per cent. It was a hard struggle. By February 1999 they were still miles from the target: the performance of the new wing was well below that of the A330/340 being used as a benchmark. 'In the emotional cycle that was a black day,' says Chris Voysey, the head of BAe's A3XX project. 'At that level of performance, we didn't have an aircraft. We were lower in performance than we would have liked. We put the best minds in the company on the job and tried to find out why the wing was not performing as well as it should be.'[16]

At the same time, there was a serious falling out with the Germans over the construction of the wing. As the wing for the A3XX was too long to be made in a single section, it was decided that the Germans should make the outer wing beyond the engines and the British should do the inner wing, the so-called wing box that contains the fuel tanks. Each wing would then be slotted into the 10-tonne box in the centre of the fuselage being made by Aerospatiale out of the same carbon composite material used in America's 'Stealth' bomber. The centre box was one of Airbus's secret weapons in its war with Boeing's 747X. It was the first time this technique had been used and it offered great advantages in terms of strength and weight.

As the designs of the wing took shape, an argument developed between the British and the Germans about whether the wing itself (not the centre box) should be made of carbon or metal. The German view was that they should make their part of the wing out of carbon, which would then be sent to the UK for finishing. The British protested, arguing that it made the technical task of fitting two sections made of two different materials extremely difficult. Furthermore, they said, although carbon is lighter, it is also more expensive and its use would make the cost of building the A3XX appreciably more expensive. The British were convinced that the Germans were up to their old tricks and trying to filch the wing business from them. At the height of the battle, Anglo-German relations became badly strained. 'We would have drinks and supper together,' says Chris Voysey, 'and then resume the deadly battle the next day.' The atmosphere was not improved by BAe's decision to dump Dasa in favour of Marconi. 'For a time there was real anti-British feeling,' Voysey remarks.

These issues were still unresolved at the end of 1999 when the supervisory board gave John Leahy permission to sound out the airlines. Leahy knew that if the project was to have any chance of getting the go-ahead from the Airbus board, he would need orders from at least two airlines in Asia, one in Europe, one in the Middle East and one in North America. As the plane was still heavy on weight and light on range, he suspected that he might have a hard time persuading the airlines to buy, but even so he was surprised at the reaction. The same airlines that had been so enthusiastic in the discussions at Carcassonne were now much more sceptical. Airbus was no longer talking to the technical people: the target now was the money men whose interest was exclusively in the bottom line. 'When we showed the plans to the commercial directors of some airlines, they said "that's interesting",' Leahy recalls. 'And we said, "It's way past 'interesting'. Are you going to place an order?"'[17] In the States the number one target, United Airlines, told Leahy it wasn't interested. Qantas and Singapore asked for more range and more payload. The airlines also insisted that Airbus meet Heathrow airport's QC/2 standard for noise restrictions. And all the time the weight kept creeping up – from 540 to 548 to 560 metric tonnes.

In Toulouse even the most stout-hearted began to waver. 'Some of our brightest and most intelligent began to argue that we should not try so hard and that if we can give them 85 per cent of what they want, that should be enough,' said Leahy. The commercial launch was put back and the pressure on the designers intensified.

Noël Forgeard admits that the winter of 1999/2000 was crunch time for the A3XX. 'When we came to the end of '99, it became clear that in the technical area we needed a little more time.' The aircraft had a range of 8,000 nautical miles, which was good enough to fly non-stop from Asia to Europe, but not good enough to cross the Pacific from Sydney to North America. There was also a need to cut the noise levels to meet the stringent regulations at Heathrow. 'The decision could have gone either way,' says Forgeard. 'Boeing had begun to wake up. And they were extremely active in the market place.'[18]

By the early spring of 2000 the wing team was within 1.2 per cent of its cost cutting target and within 259 miles of the target operating range. The plane still did not have a name, nor was there a fixed date for its commercial launch. But Leahy was beginning to pick up positive signals from at least three or four important airlines. Predictably, Air France was enthusiastic, Lufthansa was dragging its feet, and British Airways was making sheep's eyes at Boeing. The main focus of the sales battle was on Singapore Airlines, where Boeing was trying very hard to persuade it to buy the 747X. Singapore's examination of the rival planes was exceptionally thorough. 'It was the most demanding exercise that we could have ever expected,' says one Airbus insider. As news began to filter back to Toulouse that the A3XX had passed the test, there was a huge sense of relief. It was at that point that Forgeard began to think the huge gamble might pay off and it would be safe to go for a commercial launch. The contest between Airbus and Boeing over the superjumbo bore an uncanny resemblance to the one they had fought a quarter of century before when Airbus embarked on its 'Silk Road' initiative. Even though not a single airline had yet publicly committed itself, it was beginning to look as if the crisis was over.

On 14 March 2000 the British government announced that it would put up £530 million of launch aid for the A3XX, which the industry secretary, Stephen Byers, described as 'the most advanced civil aircraft development programme ever undertaken in the UK'.[19] The minister claimed that the project would create up to 22,000 jobs in Britain, including 8,000 at BAe, and would safeguard a further 62,000. What he did not say was the reason why the British government had been the first to put up the money was to make absolutely sure that the wing work stayed in Britain. The danger was that as BAe's part in the new integrated company had still not been agreed, the work might go to Germany. BAe's Mike Turner observed, 'The £530 million the government sensibly gave locks the wing into the UK. The government's message was, "If you don't do the wing in the UK, you don't get the money." They sensibly did the deal before the AIC [Airbus Integrated Company] was formed. If they had waited until afterwards, the wing could have gone anywhere.'[20]

Although the British insisted that the government package was in line with the 1992 agreement, the Americans' reaction was immediate and predictable. Boeing protested that the Europeans had failed to demonstrate that the project was being carried out under commercial conditions and that they were acting 'against the spirit' of the 1992 treaty. 'We believe the project is not really commercial,' a spokesman said. From Washington a spokesperson for the US trade representative stated, 'We are very concerned about subsidies to Airbus both with respect to past aircraft programmes and the A3XX.'

From the start there was never any question that the European governments would refuse launch aid for the A380. The governments had already given an informal undertaking that they would provide $2.5 billion of an estimated $10.7 billion total cost. The money would be repaid over the next seventeen years. This pledge was well within the parameters of the 1992 agreement which permitted the granting of launch aid provided it did not exceed one-third of the total cost. The calculation was that $3.1 billion would come from risk-sharing partners and sub-contractors; and Airbus itself would have to find $5.1 billion. Later in the year France's transport minister, Jean-Claude Gayssot, told a press conference at the Farnborough Air Show that France intended to spend Ffr 9.2 million on the A3XX in 2001 and Ffr8 billion between 2001 and 2005. 'As you can see, there is no hesitation at all as far as France is concerned,' he said cheerfully.

That the Americans would protest about government support of the A3XX was no surprise to Mogens Peter Carl, the EC's director general of trade. His prediction that the issue would remain dormant until Airbus decided to launch the superjumbo turned out to be entirely correct. 'As soon as the A3XX started to become more of a concrete project, you saw the apparent pressures mounting on the Clinton administration, with an outright attempt by them to get us to accept a *de facto* negotiation of the terms of the launch of the A3XX,' he says.[21]

When the news reached Brussels that the Boeing board had instructed Phil Condit to go to Washington to ask the formidable Mrs Barshefsky, the US trade representative, to launch a GATT complaint, the EC prepared to counter-attack. 'We had picked this up beforehand and had prepared a counter-complaint based on the countless studies we had made of the American system. Everything was ready,' explains Carl. But the moment passed, the complaint was never made and the troops were stood down. Many months later the EC announced that after an exchange of confidential information, the Americans had accepted that the A3XX financing was within the rules and not in breach of the 1992 agreement.

*

With EADS a done deal, the outstanding business was to negotiate where BAe stood on Airbus. Was it in or out? How much should it put in if it stayed, and, conversely,

what could it take out if it wanted to leave? It took about six months for the negotiators to find the answers. The main sticking point was BAe's insistence that it be
compensated for the fact that the work it was doing on the A3XX wing was, so it
believed, worth more than its 20 per cent share in the new Airbus company. Over
Easter there were several meetings between BAe's Mike Taylor and finance director
George Rose, and Lagadère's chief strategist, Jean-Louis Gergorin, and his number
two, Marwan Lahoud, at Bernard Taylor's holiday home in Provence. When things
got difficult, Philippe Camus would be summoned from Paris. But by the mid-
summer of 2000 they had reached an agreement.

With a sense of theatre so beloved by merchant bankers, the final details were
settled in Robert Fleming's box at Ascot between the second and third races on
Ladies Day. It was agreed that BAe would have 20 per cent of what was called the
'Airbus Integrated Company' of which EADS held the remaining 80 per cent. In this
respect BAe, which had had a 20 per stake in the consortium, was no worse off than
it had been before. But the real issue was not ownership but control. In the GIE,
BAe had had a veto. But as a minority shareholder in the AIC, the British could
always be outvoted. This didn't seem to bother BAe that much. It had negotiated a
get-out clause which allowed it to cash in its 20 per cent if it felt like it any time after
2003. BAe regarded the deal as a kind of put-option: as long as it continued to
make money out of Airbus, it would stay where it was and rake in the profits. But
if the situation looked like changing, it could just as easily pull out and collect its
money.

For Airbus, Friday 23 June was a red-letter day. A press conference was summoned at the Grand Hotel in Paris at the unusually early hour of 8 a.m. to announce
the birth of the new Airbus company. It had been such a rush that the agreement was
not signed until after Jean-Luc Lagardère had started his introduction. Bernard
Taylor, who had acted as midwife, remarked dryly, 'Normally it's nice to complete
the deal before the press conference starts.'[22]

With the 'Ascot agreement', the last remaining obstacle to the creation of the
Airbus company had been removed. It had not taken the form that BAe had wanted,
nor did it please the old-timers at Airbus Industrie in Toulouse. After so many years
in charge, the Aerospatiale people resented playing second fiddle to the 'Lagadère
boys'. 'My personal feeling,' the 'father' of the A3XX, Jürgen Thomas, said to me, 'is
that Airbus should have had full autonomy. It should not be guided by shareholders
who have different interests. We are in the civil business of making commercial aircraft whereas the others are in a diversified business – missiles and space and so
forth. So I think we should concentrate on our business here. Our policy and our
investment decisions should not be guided by the shareholders.'[23]

As managing director of the Airbus company and a member of the board of
EADS, Noël Forgeard understandably demurs. There is a sense that he, too, regrets
the loss of Airbus Industrie's autonomy, and is wary of interference by Paris or

Munich in the day-to-day business – but he is too much of a politician to say so. 'Our shareholders have the control and it is they who provide the necessary funding,' he says. 'In life, everybody depends on somebody else. There is always someone above you. There is nothing abnormal about this. I think it is good for Airbus to belong to a group that has other businesses. The civil aircraft business is a cyclical business. It is not in itself a problem for Airbus to report to EADS. But is EADS the right organization and the most efficient? With all respect, that is another question.'[24]

When I talked to Forgeard in Toulouse in December 2001, the reorganization of Airbus as a jointly-owned EADS/BAe subsidiary was more or less complete. So I asked him about the savings and other benefits. He replied, 'The most obvious saving is in purchasing. Take aluminium. It's enormous. We buy about 12 billion euros a year. We used to buy it separately; the French, German and British companies each had their own contract with the supplier. Now we buy centrally on behalf of everybody and get a 10 per cent discount as a result. That saves us a lot of money.'

The big benefit, Forgeard said, was a significant increase in the speed of decision-making and an end to those time-consuming arguments about work-share that were such a feature when the consortium was in charge. 'In the old days, the only way you could get a decision was by consensus. If one person said, "I don't agree", everything stops. Let me give you an example from the A380. The argument about whether the wing box should be made of metal or carbon fibre went on for months in the GIE without a decision. After the creation of the AIC, it was settled within weeks.'

Mostly importantly, the creation of the AIC cleared the way for the commercial launch of the superjumbo.

A commercial launch is always a key point in the story of any new aircraft. It is the moment when the company says that it is ready to begin the hard bargaining that will hopefully lead to a firm order. The launch should have taken place ten days earlier at the Berlin air show but it was put back because the French and the Germans were still feuding about where the plane should be built.

'The French were determined that the plane should be built in Toulouse and that it should be supplied by air as usual,' says one well-placed source. The Germans were arguing equally strongly that the plane should be assembled in Hamburg. They said it was much simpler and more economical to build such a huge plane in a place that has easy access to the sea, rather than in a land-locked location like Toulouse. For many months the French refused to admit that it was impractical to supply Toulouse by air with sections of the A3XX fuselage and wings. The superjumbo's fuselage and wing sections were simply too long to fit inside the Beluga air trans-porter. One idea that was seriously discussed was that Toulouse should be supplied by airship. And it was only after much debate that it was agreed that Airbus would have to go back to sending parts to and from Toulouse by sea and road as it did, to much protest from the locals, thirty years before. It was, as Yogi Berra said, '*déjà vu* all over again'. Forgeard admits that Toulouse is not the easiest site. But he insists that the decision was not a political one. Toulouse was chosen as the place for the final assembly of the A380 because 'the know-how is in Toulouse'. He adds, 'This was, for me, the basic, major element in the diminution of risk in such a big programme.'

In announcing the commercial launch, Noël Forgeard struck an appropriately upbeat note. 'The market has signalled loud and clear that it wants the A3XX, and this has been recognized by our shareholders who all fully endorse the programme,' he wrote in a special edition of *Airbus News* for the Farnborough Air Show. 'We shall now proceed to firm up the announced expressions of interest and we have every confidence that the industrial launch will be achieved at the turn of the year.'

*

The first breakthrough for the A3XX came at the very end of April 2000 when Emirates, the Dubai-based airline founded by the fabulously wealthy Al Maktoum family, said it was ready to buy up to ten A3XXs even before the plane had been commercially launched. It was a shrewd move calculated to attract publicity for an airline that fifteen years earlier did not even exist. It had been started in 1985 with $10 million that the Maktoums had given to Maurice Flanagan to put Dubai on the airline map. Now seventy-three, Flanagan, a part-time playwright and poet, is one of the great characters in an industry dominated by 'suits'. A long-serving British Airways man, he first went to Dubai in his late fifties to manage the government's air transport business. 'Quite frankly, I went for the money. I thought, this will do nicely for a couple of years. But it was such a nice, exciting place that I stayed on and on and eventually took the Maktoum sixpence.'[25]

Emirates was an Airbus customer from the start. It began with an A300 that Airbus had provided on a so-called 'wet lease', which meant that Airbus provided the pilots and the crew as well as the plane which flew twice a day between Dubai and Pakistan. As business grew, so did the Emirates' Airbus fleet. 'We just got more and more of them: we ended up with sixteen A300/310s,' says Flanagan. 'We established a relationship with Airbus. It is a case of what you see is what you get.'

Over the next fifteen years Dubai, a narrow green strip on the edge of the desert, expanded to the point where it was not only attracting 3 million visitors a year, but had become an important stop-over for flights between Europe and Australia. 'Dubai is ideally placed to be a global hub,' explains Flanagan. 'We fly a lot of passengers from Manchester to Dubai and then put them on another flight to Sydney. Half of Emirate's entire business goes across Dubai. Take the trading world from the west coast of America to China and Japan and down to Australia, flatten it out, balance it on the point of a pin, and there's Dubai.'

By the latter part of the 1990s demand on the London–Saudi Arabia and London–Bombay routes was such that Flanagan felt that before very long, he would be needing a bigger aircraft.

Flanagan says:

> We considered what was available. We looked at the A380 as soon as we heard about it. Boeing had ducked out of the big aircraft market by saying the market wasn't there. We decided fairly quickly that the A380 was the aircraft we wanted. Not because we wanted to put gymnasia or saunas in there. It's not there for that: it's there for people. And the great advantage of it is the economies of scale. It does bring down the seat mile costs compared with the 747. It carries a lot of people so the pressure on slots is less.

Emirates was so keen to establish itself at the head of the queue and claim the 30 per cent discount and the other privileges of being a launch customer that it announced its order at the very end of April, a good seven weeks before the official commercial launch. There was later to be a little spat when Emirates discovered that Singapore had obtained the rights to the inaugural flight.

By the time of the Farnborough Air Show in late July, Airbus had lined up two other customers for what was still being called the A3XX: Air France and the International Lease Finance Corporation (ILFC), which is little known outside the industry but is in fact Airbus's biggest customer. By the end of the year Airbus had added Singapore, Qantas and Virgin Atlantic to the list. The Qantas decision to buy twelve A3XX's was part of a $9 billion package spread over ten years, which also included thirteen A330s and six Boeing 747-400s. Apart from its size, the most significant thing about the Qantas order was that it was the first time in forty-one years the Australian airline had ordered a plane from any manufacturer other than Boeing.

On 15 December, as John Leahy was setting out in a private jet for London, he heard the news over his mobile phone that the plane was to be called the A380. Two hours later he was at a press conference in central London to hear Sir Richard Branson tell the world how 'incredibly excited' he was about 'the opportunities these aircraft will bring'. With an eye to the next morning's headlines, Branson promised that there would be casinos on Virgin Atlantic's planes to Las Vegas and private bedrooms in business class, and that the airline would be taking delivery of the first half dozen A380s in 2006. By mid-afternoon Leahy was on his way back to Toulouse and the next day he was en route to the American Mid-West in pursuit of another customer. Three days later Airbus gave the go-ahead for the industrial launch of the A380. The die had been cast.

CONCLUSION

WHEN NOËL FORGEARD ARRIVED in Toulouse to take over from Jean Pierson, one of the first things he did was to ask for a report on the superjumbo. 'I wanted to reach my own opinion,' he said. 'This initiative was started before I arrived and it couldn't be taken for granted that I would necessarily agree. I wanted to be sure.'[1]

After talking to everybody involved and looking at all the forecasts and figures, Forgeard concluded the project was not only worthwhile, but absolutely essential if Airbus was to establish and maintain parity with Boeing. 'Even if we had 50 per cent of the market, we could not stay there. The value of the big jets is about 25 per cent of the world market in value terms. Without the A380, the most we could have hoped for was some 40 per cent of the world market. When I saw the immense strategic interest, the tremendous work that had been done with the larger families of Airbus, I said to myself, we cannot fail to take advantage of this window of opportunity. We have the technology. We have the guys and we have the dollar to help us.'

It would be another two and a half years before Airbus was ready to start making the A380. But even without it, Airbus was beginning to look as if it was more than a match for Boeing. The American company's last entirely new plane was the 777, which had been in the works since 1988. Since then it had concentrated most of its effort on the longer-range versions of its existing wide-bodied twins and on its abortive attempts to produce and market a stretched 747 as a competitor for the A380. In the meantime, Airbus had conceived and gained approval for the A380, and had brought two other new planes to market to fill out its single-aisle family, the mid-range A319 and the 107-seater A318.

Away from the spotlight shining so fiercely on the battle of the leviathans, there were some sharp contests – the 777 v the A330/340, the A320 family v 737 family – in which the honours were more evenly shared. But the general impression, reinforced by skilful publicity, was that Airbus had seized the initiative, while Boeing was playing catch-up. 'With its product line looking tired, Boeing appeared to have ceded its reputation as an innovator,' wrote Lawrence Zuckerman of the *New York Times*.[2] Both suppliers and customers say they find the Airbus approach much clearer and easier to understand than Boeing's. 'I admire Airbus,' comments one senior Rolls-Royce man. 'They are intensely annoying. They never do what I want. But they are brilliant. They set out a strategy and went and did it. Whereas Boeing? It's not clear where they are going or what their objectives are.'

There was a period in the mid-1990s when it seemed as if the two companies had fallen into a form of lockstep in which Airbus would have 30 per cent of the market and Boeing would have 60 per cent while McDonnell Douglas picked up the scraps. Airbus first overtook Boeing in 1994, but at first this seemed to be just a blip on the radar. However, from 1997 – Boeing's *annus horribilis* – the pattern began to change.*

In 1998, the year in which Boeing finalized the McDonnell Douglas deal, Airbus nudged ahead by a very small margin. In the following year it notched up a great victory when, for the first time in its history, it captured over 50 per cent of the market. With its share up to 55.2 per cent against Boeing's 43.1 per cent, Airbus had pushed their rival decisively into second place. By the end of 2000 the pendulum had swung back in favour of Boeing. In Seattle and Toulouse these figures were the raw material of a hundred victorious press releases. But it was not the dour battle for market share that caught the headlines: few people, apart from those involved, cared whether Boeing or Airbus was in the lead.

The superjumbo was a different matter. All that publicity about casinos and shopping malls in the sky had created a certain horrid fascination. Attitudes had changed in the thirty years since the coming of the 747. In those days flying was still thought to be glamorous. And what the jumbo had promised but never delivered was a degree of space and comfort for everybody that only the rich had enjoyed. What, on the other hand, it did do was to make mass travel available at a price that almost everybody could afford. The public is now far wiser, better travelled and much more experienced. Far from being glamorous, we know that flying is, for the most part, an uncomfortable and stressful business. And even though we know it is unlikely that the superjumbo will bring back the long-vanished golden age of the cruise liner, it is always nice to live in hope. The airlines, however, were more sceptical. They saw all this as marketing fluff and were more interested in the plane's economics. As they looked at the figures, even sceptics like Lufthansa began to come round. Nonetheless, there were sizeable pockets of resistance. By the spring of 2002 not a single American airline had bought the A380, and despite a determined

---

*   Measuring market share is an extremely contentious business. Boeing and Airbus have been quarrelling for years about which measure gives the truest picture of what is actually happening. The choice is between deliveries, gross orders and net orders. The first indicates the level of activity in the year in question, the second shows what would have happened if the airlines had done what they said they were going to do, and the third indicator is orders minus cancellations. The manufacturers invariably choose the one that shows them in the best light. I have used net order figures throughout.

campaign by the Airbus sales team, the Japanese were holding out. Given the importance that Airbus itself attaches to the Far Eastern markets, there are those in the company who are more than a little concerned about the failure so far to break into the important Japanese market. Against that, the decision by Qantas to abandon its longstanding all-Boeing policy is seen as hugely encouraging.

As orders for the A380 passed the fifty mark, and as Boeing seemed to be having no luck at all with its stretched 747X, the noises from Toulouse became ever more optimistic. In March 2001 Lufthansa finally signalled it was ready to come off the fence with an order for fifteen; and although the order was not announced for another seven months, Emirates had already indicated that it was thinking of tripling its A380 order from an initial seven to a quite staggering twenty-two, of which two were freighters and twenty were passenger planes. There was also to be a big freighter order from FedEx, the international haulage company.

It was on 29 March 2001, just a couple of days after Airbus had rolled out its ultra long-range A340-600, which is a few feet longer than the A380, that Boeing finally conceded defeat in its fight against Toulouse's giant people-carrier when it announced it had finally abandoned its attempts to build a superjumbo on the grounds that it could not find a customer. 'We could not find a current market, nor do we believe that there is a long-term market for many aeroplanes bigger than the current 747,' a company spokesman said.[3] As this was the second time in three years that Boeing had offered this excuse, the news was not exactly surprising: everybody in the industry knew that there were no takers for a stretched 747. Equally, Boeing's scepticism about future demand for planes significantly larger than the 747 was very well-known.

What was quite sensational was Boeing had to say next. It revealed that from now on it would be focusing on the production of an entirely new family of medium-sized ultra-fast planes. Dubbed 'the Sonic Cruiser', they would travel some 10,000 miles at around 750mph, just below the speed of sound, which would cut about an hour off a transatlantic flight and some four hours off the twenty-three hour trip between London and Sydney. With a rear-mounted delta wing housing twin engines at the tail and with little stabilizers projecting like ears on either side at the front, the Sonic Cruiser looked more like a fish than an aeroplane. With a rather stubby nose and fins for a tail, it was neither as quick nor as elegant as Concorde. But it looked quite unlike any other commercial airliner. Suddenly, the A380 seemed rather staid and old-fashioned.

The unexpected appearance of the Sonic Cruiser reversed the positions of the two companies. For years Boeing had been saying that there was no need for a superjumbo – that not enough airlines would buy it and, in any case, Airbus would not or could not actually make it. Now it was Airbus's turn to say exactly the same thing about the Sonic Cruiser: there was no market, the economics were all wrong and Boeing would never be able to build such a plane at a cost the airlines would find attractive. Some people even wondered if the Sonic Cruiser was a ploy to distract attention from the A380.

What is certain is that the Sonic Cruiser generated more questions than answers in an industry where tearing apart paper aeroplanes is a favourite activity. Although Alan Mulally, Boeing's perennially optimistic head of the commercial aircraft division, insisted that Boeing was serious and he personally was 'prepared to bet the whole company on the Sonic Cruiser', many felt that Boeing's case was weakened by its admission that the plane's fuel consumption would be 20 per cent higher than a normal plane.

The Boeing team argued that, like Airbus, it was putting its money where its mouth was. While Airbus believes there is a sufficient amount of long distance, high volume hub-to-hub business for it to make money out of the A380, so Boeing maintained there are enough people prepared to pay a premium price for travelling directly from point to point at high speed for the Sonic Cruiser to make economic sense. This argument was put forward before the terrorist attacks on New York's Twin Towers on 11 September 2001. Since then there seems to have been a been a sea-change in the attitudes of the business traveller – the very market Boeing's Sonic Cruiser is aimed at. In the immediate aftermath of the disaster, America's businessmen stayed at home. In Europe company executives either moved to the budget airlines or took local connecting flights as business travel managers hunted for bargains. Much of this was in response to savage price-cutting by the airlines as they fought for business. These developments may be temporary, but even so, they might give Boeing pause for thought before it presses the start button on the Sonic Cruiser.

The immediate effect of 11 September on the air travel business was catastrophic. Two national flag carriers, Swissair and Sabena, whose futures had been in doubt for some time, went bankrupt and tens of thousands of airline employees lost their jobs. Within days, Boeing had said it was lowering its estimates of deliveries for 2002 by nearly 30 per cent and would lay off 30,000 workers – about one third of the work force in the commercial aircraft division. With the market already weakening, deliveries would have been down anyway. But in Boeing's view 11 September had vastly accelerated the downward trend. 'It is global,' said Boeing's chief executive Phil Condit. 'And I believe Airbus will go through the same thing.'[4] In making its own estimates as to the effect of the terrorist attacks on the market, Airbus had come to much the same conclusion. It, too, believed that deliveries in 2002 and 2003 would fall appreciably. But its response was more measured.

The impact on the Airbus labour force was nothing like as drastic as it was at Boeing. By cutting all overtime and encouraging early retirement, Airbus aimed to reduce its workforce by 1,000, to 44,500 by the end of the year: in England 300 people lost their jobs, but even here voluntary redundancies, where people were paid to leave early, took up nearly all the slack. One reason why Airbus employees were not as hard hit as Boeing's workers was that Airbus was a step behind Boeing in the production cycle when the crisis struck. This allowed Airbus to freeze production, whereas Boeing, which was working at full throttle to meet previous delivery deadlines, was forced to cut back when the airlines cancelled or postponed their orders, as many did.

Noël Forgeard says that as soon as the full scale of the disaster that had overtaken the industry became apparent, he took immediate steps to cut costs: the rate at which Airbus was building planes was cut by some 15 per cent, and there was a freeze on all R&D expenditure, with the exception of the A380. At the same time, Forgeard built what he called 'a war chest' by raising $2 billion from the sale of the Airbus-owned, Dublin-based finance company that provided loans and guarantees for customers. With the A380 programme at a stage when it was beginning to consume serious amounts of cash – up to $1.5 billion a year for the next three or four years – Forgeard knew that any drop in income could have drastic consequences.

There is no doubt that Airbus and Boeing were seriously damaged by the crisis that overtook the airline business after 11 September. The collapse of Swissair and Sabena, the Belgian national airline, was the main cause of a 30 per cent drop in the Airbus order book as some 101 orders were cancelled in the last three months of 2001. Boeing was hit even harder: orders fell by some 45 per cent to levels last seen in the recession of the early 1990s. But as the dust began to clear in the spring of 2002, it was clear that neither company had suffered a mortal blow. Airbus say that the future is too uncertain for it to look much beyond 2003, but as far as it can judge, the balance between itself and Boeing will remain very much as it was before. 'This is a cyclical business,' says Noël Forgeard. 'In the downturn, deliveries usually fall by between 8 per cent and 4 per cent of the world fleet. If there are 15,000 aircraft world-wide, 4 per cent of that will be 600 – which means 300 for Boeing and 300 for us.'

The battle has been going on for so long, that few remember just how heavily the odds had been stacked against the Europeans when Roger Béteille and Henri Ziegler were planning their campaign over thirty years before. The most they had hoped for was that Europe would put up a credible challenge – *un defi Européen* – to American domination. If anyone had told them that before the end of the century they would have been instrumental in the retirement from the fray of two out of the three American aircraft manufacturers and that by the new millennium they would be outselling Boeing, they would have thought them mad.

With the creation of EADS and the incorporation of the Airbus company, the organization itself has totally changed. The lines of communication have been simplified and shortened: where once there were four technical directors, now there is only one. At the same time, the personal and professional links between the members of the old GIE are not as strong as they were. The British, in particular, are semi-detached. It is too soon to forecast what BAe will do. But no one at Airbus denies that the new arrangement has loosened the ties that bound the British into the European project. Just outside Toulouse, at the entrance to the airport, there is a large billboard that used to read 'Airbus Industrie'. It now says, 'Airbus – a joint EADS Company with BAE Systems'. It is a clumsy title for an awkward arrangement. The change it signals is as much psychological as it is practical. Previously, BAe was a committed member of a common European project; now it is no more than an investor.

Among the old hands there is much pride and satisfaction about what has been achieved. But there is also a sense of sadness and loss. When I asked Jean Pierson what he thought about the new arrangement with BAe, he replied:

> It is a question of involvement. You need the best engineers to build the wings. But if the engineers are not motivated, you don't have the best engineers. That's what worries me, especially for the superjumbo. Dick Evans and the management is looking for a return on its 20 per cent. But Dick is not losing any sleep because the wing is late. He doesn't care. He'll say, 'That's your problem.' That's not how it used to be. Then he would have said, 'We'll share the problem.' That's the big, big change. The motivation of the British side is disappearing step by step. They are all leaving.[5]

Some see Britain's role in the Airbus story as a metaphor for Britain's entire relationship with Europe since World War II. In the view of one senior civil servant whose job it has been to monitor these events, it embodies Britain's love/hate relationship with the French, her ambiguous feelings about the Germans and, above all, the schizophrenic split in the British mind as to whether Britain is a European country or an American one. This dilemma may have been particularly acute for Rolls-Royce and British Aerospace, but it was also one that the Wilson, Callaghan and Blair governments had to wrestle with. Oddly, Airbus questions were never quite the same problem for the Tories, despite Mrs Thatcher's recurrent fear that she was being presented with, as she used to put it, 'another Concorde'.

But it is not only British attitudes that are revealing. It seems to me that the entire Airbus experience throws a very illuminating light on how the 'new' Europe actually works. On paper the consortium seemed to be the embodiment of everything the founders of what was then called the European Economic Community had hoped for when it was created in 1957. In practice, the day-to-day business of Airbus has been carried out by Frenchmen, Germans and Englishmen who have been determined to defend their own national interests to the last while engaged in what was clearly a pan-European project. The French have never attempted to hide the fact that they think of themselves as the initiators and natural leaders. As the Germans have grown in confidence and strength, they too have asserted themselves. The British, as always, have tended to stand to one side: pragmatic, proud of their technical competence but not always fully engaged.

Airbus was born at a time when the tide of enthusiasm for the European idea was running strongly right across Europe. The Airbus consortium took the form it did because its protagonists persuaded the politicians that cooperation and the pooling of resources was the only way that Europe could hope to mount a successful challenge to American industrial power. Airbus was not the only expression of that idea. The European Coal and Steel Community, and the European space rocket programme (now under the wing of EADS) were other examples. But of all these politically inspired and government-funded initiatives, only Airbus has achieved in full measure what it set out to do. It would never have happened had not the French, German and British governments been willing to provide the billions of francs, deutschmarks and pounds to support the project and, on several occasions, to save it from outright collapse. Furthermore, if the early planes, the A300 and A310, had had to pay their way, Airbus Industrie would have folded within five years at the outside. The Americans wax indignant. But there is nothing exceptional about this, and to expect new planes to show a profit in the first few years is disingenuous, not to say naïve. The entry costs are so great and the payback period so long that there is not a maker of civil aircraft in the world that does not need some form of propping up. Just as the Americans have benefited from the billions of dollars from the Air Force for bombers, fighters and military transports that are closely related to their civilian planes, so the Europeans have relied on direct government subventions in the form of soft loans and launch aid. Airbus has its critics in Europe as well as in America. For the free marketeers and the Euro-sceptics, it is just another example of Europe's irresponsible, free-spending ways with taxpayers' money. But if this money had been given to private industry in tax cuts or investment allowances, who's to say that the result would have been better. Given the performance of firms like America's Enron or Britain's Marconi, the chances are that the outcome would have been much worse. The politicians, conscious that there are not many votes in aerospace and defence, however many jobs they provide, seem reluctant to sing the praises of Airbus. But in Brussels there is unstinting admiration and support. As Mogens Peter Carl, the European Commission's director general of trade, says, 'Airbus has come of age. It is an example of what can be done in terms of European cooperation.'

CHRONOLOGY

1967
25 September   Britain, France and West Germany sign the Lancaster House agreement setting the Airbus project in motion.

1968
11 December   Sud Aviation and Hawker Siddeley announce the cancellation of the A300 and its replacement by the A300B.

1969
17 March   British government withdraws from Airbus programme.
29 May   Ministers sign the Franco-German Airbus agreement at the Paris air show.

1970
1 January   Creation of Aerospatiale with merger of Sud Aviation and Nord Aviation.
18 December   Creation of Airbus Industrie. Franz-Josef Strauss appointed chairman of the supervisory board.

1971
9 November   Air France orders six A300Bs with options on a further ten.

1972
January   Spain's CASA acquires a 4.2 per cent stake in the consortium and signs to buy four A300s.
28 October   First flight of A300B prototype.

1974
23 May   A300B2 goes into service with Air France.

1975
May   Bernard Lathière succeeds Henri Ziegler as president of Airbus Industrie.

1976
November   Merger of British Aircraft Corporation and Hawker Siddeley to form
                  British Aerospace.

1977
May   Eastern Airlines agrees to lease four A300B4s on a six-month trial.

1978
March   Eastern Airlines orders twenty-five Airbuses.
July   Launch of the A310.
31 August   British government announces intention to rejoin Airbus as from
                  1 January 1979.
September   Britain's Sir Freddie Laker says he will buy ten Airbuses.

1981   Airbus outlines plans to enter the single-aisle market with the
                  A320 in response to Boeing's 737-300 and McDonnell Douglas's
                  MD80.

1982
April   First flight of the A310.

1983
October   Britain's British Caledonian signs a memorandum of understanding to
                  buy seven A320s.

1984
12 March   Launch of the A320.
September   Pan Am places a $2 billion order for A300s and A320s.

1985
1 April   Jean Pierson succeeds Bernard Lathière as AI president.
September   Reagan administration sets up a trade strike force in Washington.

1986
January   Airbus develops the A330/340 concept.

1987
22 February   First flight of the A320.
                  US delegation arrives in Europe to air concerns about Airbus pricing
                  and sales tactics.
June   Launch of the A330/340.

1988

March   First delivery of the A320.

3 October   Death of Franz-Josef Strauss. Succeeded as Airbus chairman by Hans Friderichs, former leader of West Germany's Free Democrats.

1989

September   Germany's federal government approves Daimler-Benz take-over of MBB to create DASA (Daimler Aerospace SA).

November   Launch of A321.

1991

October   First flight of A340.

1992

April   Bilateral agreement between the United States and the European Commission on civil aircraft financing.

September   Airbus and Boeing in talks about superjumbo development.

November   First flight of A330.

1993

January   First delivery of the A340.

March   First flight of the A321.

June   Launch of the A319.

December   First delivery of the A330.

1994

January   First delivery of the A321.

1995

April   Collapse of Airbus/Boeing superjumbo talks.

August   First flight of the A319.

1996

December   Boeing buys McDonnell Douglas.

1997

January   Airbus Industrie begins negotiations with its partners on the creation of a 'single corporate entity'.
Boeing announces cancellation of its 747-600 project.

September   Boeing halts production lines of 747s and 737s to clear bottlenecks.

December   French, German and British governments set a 31 March 1998 deadline for the restructuring of European defence industry.
Boeing posts a record $178 million loss.

1998

23 January	Airbus announces Noël Forgeard is to succeed Jean Pierson as Airbus chief executive.
23 July	French government announce merger of Aerospatiale and Matra.
12 October	British Aerospace and DASA reveal merger plans.

1999

20 January	British Aerospace (BAe) drops plan to merge with DASA.
25 January	BAe buys GEC's Marconi division and changes its name to BAe Systems.
February	Aerospatiale/Matra opens informal merger talks with DASA.
April	Boeing reveals plans to build a rival to Airbus's superjumbo, code-named A3XX.
15 October	DASA announces merger with the French to form EADS, the European Aeronautic Defence and Space Company.
2 December	DASA buys CASA.

2000

30 April	Emirates, the Middle Eastern airline, places first order for the A3XX.
23 June	Creation of the Airbus Integrated Company, jointly owned by EADS and BAe Systems.
	Commercial launch of the A3XX.
19 December	Industrial launch of the A3XX, now known as the A380.

NOTES

CHAPTER ONE: THE KOLK MACHINE

1. Airbus archive.
2. *Ibid.*
3. *Ibid.*
4. Interview with author, 14 December 2000.
5. John Newhouse, *The Sporty Game*, New York: Alfred A. Knopf, 1982.
6. Interview with author, 14 December 2000.
7. Airbus archive.
8. *Ibid.*
9. *Ibid.*
10. *Flight*, 16 February 1967.
11. Airbus archive.
12. *Flight*, 2 February 1967.
13. Charles Gardner, *British Aircraft Corporation: A History*, London: Batsford, 1981, p.166.
14. Cabinet papers. PRO CC13(4)67 CAP128 42 Part 1.
15. *Ibid.*
16. *Ibid.*
17. *Ibid.*
18. Interview with author, 14 December 2000.
19. *Flight*, 27 April 1966.
20. House of Lords debate, 1 March 1966.

CHAPTER TWO: POWER GAMES

1. Airbus archive.
2. *Ibid.*
3. *Ibid.*
4. *Flight*, 28 September 1967.
5. Airbus archive.
6. *Ibid.*
7. Plowden report, 1964–5, Cmd. 2853, Vol. 4.

8.   Gardner, p.18.
9.   Quoted by Eugene E. Bauer, *Boeing – the First Century*, Washington: Enumclaw, TABA Publishing, Inc., 2000.
10. C. Martin Sharp, *DH – A History of de Havilland*, Shrewsbury: Airlife Publishing Ltd, 1982.
11. *Ibid.*
12. Plowden report, 1964–5
13. Gardner, p.18.
14. *Ibid.*
15. Jean Jacques Servan-Schreiber, *The American Challenge*, London: Hamish Hamilton, 1968, p.20
16. *Ibid.*
17. Airbus archive.
18. *Ibid.*
19. *Ibid.*
20. Arthur Reed, *Airbus – Europe's High Flyer*, St Gallen: Norden Publishing House Ltd., 1991, p.19.
21. Rolls-Royce Limited. Investigation under Section 165(a) (i) of the Companies Act 1948. Report by R.A. McCrindle QC and P. Godfrey FCA. HMSO London, 1973. See also: Peter Pugh, *The Magic of a Name. The Rolls-Royce story. Part two: the power behind the jets*, Cambridge: Icon Books, 2001.
22. Quoted by Lew Bogdan, *L'épopée du ciel clair*, Paris: Hachette, 1988.
23. *Ibid.*
24. Evidence to the House of Lords Select Committee on the European Communities, 1975/76.
25. Newhouse, *The Sporty Game*.
26. Rolls-Royce Investigation.
27. Quoted by Matthew Lynn, *Birds of Prey – Boeing v Airbus, A Battle for the Skies*, New York: Four Walls, Eight Windows, 1998, p.85.
28. Quoted by Clive Irving, *Widebody, The Making of the 747*, London: Hodder & Stoughton, 1993. p.287.
29. *Ibid.*
30. Rolls-Royce Investigation.
31. Flight, 18 May 1967.
32. Rolls-Royce Investigation.
33. Airbus archive.
34. *Ibid.*

CHAPTER THREE: THINGS FALL APART

1.   Airbus archive.
2.   *Ibid.*
3.   Lew Bogdan, p.195.

4. *Ibid.*
5. quoted by Ian McIntyre, *Dogfight, The Transatlantic Battle over Airbus*, Westport, Connecticut: Praeger, 1992, p.54.
6. Bill Gunston, *Airbus*, London: Osprey Publishing, 1988, p.24.
7. Richard Crossman, *The Diaries of a Cabinet Minister, Vol 3*, London: Hamish Hamilton and Jonathan Cape, 1976.
8. Airbus archive.
9. *Flight*, 19 December 1968.
10. Cabinet papers. PRO 129,44. C(69)28.
11. *Ibid.*
12. *Ibid.*
13. Anthony Sampson, *The New Europeans*, London: Hodder and Stoughton, 1968, p.25.
14. Airbus archive
15. Bill Gunston, p.28.
16. Airbus archive.
17. Bill Gunston, p.39.
18. Airbus archive.
19. *Ibid.*
20. Sir Henry Royce memorial lecture, 22 October 1996.

CHAPTER FOUR: AIRBUS MECCANO

1. Airbus archive
2. Airbus archive
3. Matthew Lynn, pp.76–7.
4. Quoted by Lynn (p.65) from Wayne Biddle, *Barons of the Sky*, Simon and Schuster, 1991.
5. Interview with author, 19 February 2001.
6. Interview with author, 14 December 2000.
7. Sir Henry Royce memorial lecture, 22 October 1996.
8. *Ibid.*
9. Airbus archive.
10. Interview with author, 15 May 2001.
11. *Ibid.*
12. *Ibid.*
13. Keith Hayward, *International Collaboration in Civil Aerospace*, London: Frances Pinter, 1986, p.79.
14. Airbus archive.
15. *Ibid.*
16. *Ibid.*
17. *Ibid.*
18. *Ibid.*
19. *Ibid.*

CHAPTER FIVE: SLEEPLESS IN SEATTLE

1. Interview with author, 14 December 2000.
2. Airbus archive
3. *Ibid*.
4. Eugene E. Bauer, p.204.
5. Anthony Sampson, *Empires of the Sky – The politics, contests and cartels of World Airlines*, London: Hodder and Stoughton, 1984, p.128.
6. Newhouse, *The Sporty Game*.
7. Sampson, *Empires*, p.125.
8. Eugene E. Bauer, p.215.
9. Clive Irving, p.124.
10. Paul Eddy, Bruce Page, Elaine Potter, *Destination Disaster*, London: Hart-Davis, MacGibbon, 1976, p.44.
11. *Ibid*.
12. Paul Eddy *et al*, p.47.
13. *Ibid*., p.82.
14. Matthew Lynn, p.131.
15. Ian McIntyre, p.87.
16. Eugene E. Bauer, p.229.
17. *Ibid*., p.230.
18. Paul Eddy *et al*, p.82.

CHAPTER SIX: THE SILK ROAD

1. Newhouse, *The Sporty Game*.
2. Airbus archive.
3. *Ibid*.
4. *Ibid*.
5. *Ibid*.
6. Interview with author, 19 February 2001.
7. Airbus archive.
8. *Ibid*.
9. *Ibid*.
10. *Ibid*.
11. Steven McGuire, *Airbus Industrie – Conflict and Cooperation in US-EC Trade Relations*, St Antony's College, Oxford, p.46.
12. Airbus archive.
13. Lew Bogdan, p.337.
14. Airbus archive.
15. *Ibid*.
16. Eugene E. Bauer, p.238.
17. *Ibid*., p.239.

18. *Ibid.*, p.239.
19. Airbus archive.
20. Interview with author, 15 May 2001.
21. Bill Gunston, p.85.
22. Airbus archive.
23. *Ibid.*
24. Lew Bogdan.
25. Airbus archive.
26. *Ibid.*
27. *Ibid.*
28. *Ibid.*
29. *Ibid.*
30. *Ibid.*

CHAPTER SEVEN: THE CAMEL'S IN THE TENT

1. Airbus archive.
2. *Ibid.*
3. *Ibid.*
4. *Ibid.*
5. *Ibid.*
6. *Ibid.*
7. Steven McGuire, p.51.
8. *Ibid.* p.55.
9. Eugene.E. Bauer, p.241.
10. Ian McIntyre, p.45.
11. Quoted by Matthew Lynn, p.123.
12. Interview with author, 12 May 2000.
13. Newhouse, *The Sporty Game.*
14. Interview with author, 12 May 2000.
15. *Ibid.*
16. Ian McIntyre, p.50.
17. Interview with author, 12 July 2000.
18. Interview with author.
19. Nicholas Henderson, *Mandarin, the Dairies of Nicholas Henderson,* London: Weidenfeld and Nicolson, 1994.
20. *Ibid.*
21. *Ibid.*
22. Newhouse, *The Sporty Game.*
23. *Ibid.*
24. Airbus archive.
25. Henderson diaries.
26. *Ibid.*

27.   Howard Banks, *The Rise and Fall of Freddie Laker*, London: Faber and Faber Ltd., 1982, p.99. Also: Roger Eglin & Berry Ritchie, *Fly Me – I'm Freddie*, London: Futura Macdonald, 1981.
28.   Airbus archive.
29.   Howard Banks, p.100.
30.   Interview with author, 12 May 2000.
31.   Henderson diaries.

CHAPTER EIGHT: FLYING BY WIRE

1.   Newhouse, *The Sporty Game*.
2.   *Ibid*.
3.   Sampson, *Empires*, p.136.
4.   Arthur Reed, *Airbus – Europe's High Flyer*, St Gallen: Norden Publishing House Ltd., 1991, p.64.
5.   Interview with author, 6 September 2001.
6.   *Ibid*.
7.   *Ibid*.
8.   *Ibid*.
9.   *La Nouvelle Economiste*, 8 June 1981.
10.   Airbus archive.
11.   Interview with author, 15 May 2001.
12.   *International Herald Tribune*, 27 May 1983.
13.   Matthew Lynn, p.162.
14.   Lew Bogdan, p.401.
15.   Interview with author, 5 July 2000.
16.   *Ibid*.
17.   *Ibid*.
18.   Steven McGuire, *International Collaboration*.
19.   Bill Yenne, *McDonnell Douglas – A Tale of Two Giants*, London: Arms and Armour Press, 1985, p.169.
20.   Interview with author, 6 December 2001.
21.   Matthew Lynn, p.163.
22.   Bill Gunston, p.175.
23.   Arthur Reed, p.81.
24.   Gunston, p.175 *et seq*.
25.   Interview with author, 6 December 2001.
26.   Nicholas Faith, *Black Box – why air safety is no accident*, London: Boxtree, 1997, p.91.
27.   Karl Sabbach, *21st Century Jet – The Making of the Boeing 777*, London: Pan Books, 1995, p.159.
28.   *Ibid*., p.158.
29.   Eugene E. Bauer, p.238.

CHAPTER NINE: THE PYRENEES BEAR

1. Airbus archive.
2. *Ibid*.
3. Interview with author, 14 December 2000.
4. *Ibid*.
5. Interview with author, 19 February 2001.
6. Interview with author, 6 September 2001.
7. Interview with author, 19 February 2001.
8. *Ibid*.
9. *Ibid*.
10. *Ibid*.
11. *Ibid*.
12. *Ibid*.
13. Interview with author, 15 December 2000.
14. Interview with author, 19 February 2000.
15. *Ibid*.
16. Matthew Lynn, p.171.
17. Interview with author, 19 February 2001.
18. *Ibid*.
19. Karl Sabbach, p.13.
20. Ian McIntyre, p.140.
21. Interview with author, 6 September 2001.
22. *Ibid*.
23. Interview with author, 19 February 2001.
24. Interview with author, 31 August 2001.
25. Interview with author, 30 August 2001.

CHAPTER TEN: THE AIRBUSTERS

1. Keith Hayward, p.63.
2. Matthew Lynn, p.174.
3. *Flight*, 14 February 1987.
4. Interview with author, 5 December 2001.
5. Lester Thurow, *Head to Head – the coming economic battle among Japan, Europe, and America*, Warner Books, 1993, p.181.
6. Steven McGuire, pp.28–30.
7. Interview with author, 5 December 2001.
8. Quoted by McGuire, p.62 et seq.
9. *Ibid*.
10. *Ibid*.
11. *Ibid*.
12. Lester Thurow, p.29.

13. Matthew Lynn, p.178.
14. Quoted by McIntyre, p.170.
15. Interview with author, 14 November 2001.
16. *La Dépéche du Midi*, 5 February 1987.
17. Interview with author, 5 December 2001.
18. Interview with author, 7 November 2001.
19. Quoted by McIntyre, p.181.
20. Interview with author, 19 February 2001.
21. Interview with author, 5 December 2001.
22. Interview with author, 1 November 2000.
23. A report on the Airbus system by Jacques Benichou, Emilio González Garcia, Peter Pfeiffer, Sir Jeffery Sterling, April 1988.
24. Quoted by Lynn, p.197.
25. Interview with author, 19 February 2001.
26. Karl Sabbach, p.44.
27. Quoted by Lynn, pp.150–1.
28. Interview with author, 5 December 2001.
29. Gellman Research Associates Inc., *Economic and Financial Review of Airbus Industrie*, US Department of Commerce, 4 September 1990.
30. Interview with author, 7 November 2001.
31. Interview with author, 19 February 2001.
32. Laura Tyson, *Who's bashing whom? Trade conflict in high technology industries*, Washington, DC: Institute for International Economics, 1992.
33. Interview with author, 5 December 2001.
34. *Ibid*.

CHAPTER ELEVEN: THINKING BIG

1. Quoted by Lynn, pp.204–5.
2. Interview with author, 19 February 2001.
3. Interview with author, 14 December 2000.
4. Interview with author, 19 February 2001.
5. *Wall Street Journal*, 5 January 1993.
6. Interview with author, 14 December 2000.
7. Interview with author, 6 September 2001.
8. Quoted by Lynn, p.207.
9. Interview with author, 19 February 2001.
10. Interview with author, 14 December 2000.
11. Interview with author, 15 December 2000.
12. Quoted by Lynn, pp.221–2.
13. Interview with author, 15 May 2001.
14. Interview with author, 14 December 2000.
15. Interview with author, 30 August 2001.

16.   Interview with author, 30 August 2001.
17.   Interview with author, 14 December 2000.
18.   Quoted by Lynn, p.208.
19.   Interview with author, 10 March 2000.
20.   Interview with author, 6 September 2001.
21.   Interview with author, 26 September 2000.
22.   Interview with author, 14 December 2000.
23.   Bill Gunston, p.96.
24.   Eugene E. Bauer, p.325.
25.   *Fortune*, 2 October 2000.
26.   *Ibid*.
27.   Bauer, p.324.
28.   *Ibid*.

CHAPTER TWELVE: WE WILL BURY YOU

1.   Interview with author, 10 March 2000.
2.   *Fortune*, 2 October 2000.
3.   *Ibid*.
4.   *Sunday Times Business News*, 15 February 1998.
5.   James Wallace, *Sales & Marketing Management*, February 1998.
6.   Bauer, p.332.
7.   Interview with author, 15 December 2000.
8.   Stephen Aris, *Sunday Times Business News*, 19 March 2000.
9.   *Ibid*.
10.   *Fortune*, 12 January 1998.
11.   *Sales & Marketing Management*, February 1998.
12.   Fortune, 12 January 1998.
13.   Interview with author, 10 December 2001.
14.   Interview with author, 1 November 2000.
15.   Interview with author, 10 December 2001.
16.   *Financial Times*, 26 August 1998.
17.   *Ibid*.
18.   Interview with author, 1 November 2000.
19.   Statement at Farnborough Air Show, 7 September 1998.

CHAPTER THIRTEEN: END GAME

1.   Interview with author, 25 January 2001.
2.   Interview with author, 25 January 2001.
3.   Interview with author,
4.   *Financial Times*, 27 March 1998.

5. Interview with author, 25 January 2001.
6. Interview with author, 1 November 2000.
7. Interview with author, 14 January 2002.
8. Reported in the *Financial Times*, 7 September 1998.
9. *Financial Times*, 7 September 1998.
10. *Financial Times*, 7 December 1998.
11. Interview with author, 1 November 2000.
12. *Financial Times*, 18 January 2002.
13. *Financial Times*, 25 January 1999.
14. Interview with author, 1 November 2000.
15. Interview with author, 25 January 2001.
16. Interview with author, 26 September 2000.
17. Interview with author, 15 December 2000.
18. Interview with author, 10 December 2001.
19. *Financial Times*, 15 March 2000.
20. Interview with author, 1 November 2000.
21. Interview with author, 5 December 2001.
22. *Sunday Times Business News*, 25 June 2000.
23. Interview with author, 14 December 2000
24. Interview with author, 10 December 2001.
25. Interview with author, 24 January 2002.

CONCLUSION

1. Interview with author, 10 December 2001.
2. *New York Times*, 17 June 2001.
3. *Guardian*, 30 March 2001.
4. *Financial Times*, 26 September 2001.
5. Interview with author, 19 February 2001.

INDEX